BLACK KNIGHTS

The Story of the Tuskegee Airmen

BLACK KNIGHTS
The Story of the Tuskegee Airmen

By Lynn M. Homan
and Thomas Reilly

Foreword by
Louis R. Purnell

PELICAN PUBLISHING COMPANY
Gretna 2002

First printing, January 2001
Second printing, February 2001
Third printing, January 2002

Library of Congress Cataloging-in-Publication Data

Homan, Lynn M.
  Black knights : the story of the Tuskegee airmen / by Lynn M.
Homan and Thomas Reilly ; foreword by Louis R. Purnell.
      p. cm.
  Includes bibliographical references and index.
  ISBN 1-56554-828-0
  1. United States. Air Force–Afro-Americans–History–Pictorial
works. 2. Air pilots, Military–United States–History–Pictorial
works. 3. Air pilots, Military–Alabama–Tuskegee–History–Pictorial
works. 4. Tuskegee Army Air Field (Ala.)–Pictorial works. I. Reilly,
Thomas. II. Title.

UG834.A37 H64 2001
940.54'4973–dc21

                                                            00-047850

Printed in the United States of America
Published by Pelican Publishing Company, Inc.
1000 Burmaster Street, Gretna, Louisiana 70053

The men and women of the Tuskegee Experience proved that they had what it takes, not only in war, but in peacetime as well. They had the courage. They persevered. Only in the early 1990s did these brave and dedicated men and women finally receive the attention that they so richly deserved. This book is a memorial to those departed, and at the same time, a celebration of those still living.

Contents

Foreword

What you are about to read is the result of a collaborative effort of two professional aviation historians who, through their research, have been able to present the most comprehensive, accurate, and exhaustive record to date concerning America's first black military pilots.

During World War II these brave pilots fought to defend their country—a country that had initially stated that, due to their racial origin, they possessed neither the brains nor the intelligence to handle such a complicated thing as an aircraft. The Army Air Corps was determined that no black would ever enter its ranks.

When it became apparent during the late 1930s and early 1940s that blacks might seek entry into their sacrosanct bastion of military aviation, they pulled from the military archives the results of a study concerning the Negro during World War I. This study was replete with derogatory findings which they thought would substantiate their decision. However, in spite of this, and with the aid of the benevolent political powers that existed, the 99th Fighter Squadron, and later the 332nd Fighter Group and the 477th Bombardment Group, were formed.

It has been more than half a century since these men fought and died for their country, but a feeling of great pride still lingers in the hearts of those pilots who live today.

I share that pride. I am proud to have been one of them.

Louis R. Purnell
99th Fighter Squadron

Preface

When we began work several years ago on a project dealing with the story of the Tuskegee Airmen, we had little or no idea of the magnitude of the subject or the effect it would have upon our lives. Years later, the things we have learned, and more importantly, the people we have met, have made this the most rewarding project in which we have ever been involved.

As partners in the firm of Homan & Reilly Designs, we curate, design, and produce museum exhibitions, many of which have an aviation theme. We have also authored numerous articles and books on a variety of topics. In 1996, we began to study the history of the Tuskegee Airmen in preparation for the production of a new traveling museum exhibit. As part of the creation of our exhibition, we contacted a number of original Tuskegee Airmen in search of photographs, three-dimensional artifacts, reminiscences, etc. We met with as many airmen and their families as possible, recording their personal stories and experiences.

All gave freely of their time to provide us with a greater understanding of what it was like to participate in the flying program at Tuskegee, in Europe, and elsewhere. They also helped us to better comprehend their lives as African-Americans during the 1940s, facing segregation, Jim Crow laws, racism, and almost daily insults. We are indeed indebted to each of these men and women.

Thousands of hours of research at the Smithsonian Institution's Air and Space Museum in Washington, D.C., the National Archives in College Park, Maryland, and other archival repositories augmented dozens of personal interviews. Various books written on the subject, as well as period newspapers and documents, provided additional information.

While not original Tuskegee Airmen, several other people were also quite helpful. Cora "Tess" Spooner arranged for two days of interviews with some of the earliest graduates of the flying program. Dr. Florence Parrish-St. John shared information and sentiments about the program that her husband, Noel F. Parrish, commander at Tuskegee Army Air Field, had related to her prior to his death. Further insights were provided by William R. Holton of Howard University who has devoted himself to compiling an oral history of the Tuskegee Airmen. Hank Sanford, executive director of Tuskegee Airmen, Inc., has consistently provided contacts and other logistical support. At the Smithsonian Institution's Air and Space Museum, Dan Hagedorn and Brian Nicklas deserve our thanks. At the Air Force Historical Research Agency at Maxwell Air Force Base, we are indebted to Joseph Caver and his most helpful staff.

Our critically acclaimed exhibition, *The Tuskegee Airmen*, premiered in St. Petersburg, Florida, in February 1997. Showing at museums across the United States, it continues to grow in size and depth as we incorporate newly acquired materials. From the wealth of information and images that we have so generously been given came *Black Knights: The Story of the Tuskegee Airmen*.

Throughout this book, as well as in the pictorial that we authored, we refer to the aviation program at Tuskegee Army Air Field as the Tuskegee Experience rather than the Tuskegee Experiment. The former was a program formulated by the United States War Department to prove that black men were unfit to fly airplanes. While the powers-that-be were certain that the flying program would be an abysmal failure, the reality proved to be just the opposite. The term Tuskegee Experiment, on the other hand, has been used in reference to secret medical research by the government in which more than six hundred African-American men were used unknowingly as guinea pigs in an experiment on the treatment of syphilis. To alleviate any possible misunderstanding, the airmen themselves, through their national organization, have requested the use of "Tuskegee Experience" when reference is made to the flying program.

Just as confusion exists regarding the Tuskegee Experience and the Tuskegee Experiment, there exists an equal amount of discussion as to the definition of a Tuskegee Airman. Watching recent movies on the subject, one would find it easy to think that only those who learned to fly and saw combat in Europe were Tuskegee Airmen. It would be easy, but also untrue. The group that took part in the Tuskegee Experience was much more than that. In fact, anyone—man or woman, military or civilian, black or white—who served at Tuskegee Army Air Field or in any of the programs stemming from the Tuskegee Experience between the years 1941 and 1948 is considered to be a Tuskegee Airman.

The roster of graduates of the pilot training program included in this book is based upon a compilation by Harry T. Stewart Jr., a member of class 44-F-SE. Mr. Stewart spent many hours researching orders to document the nearly one thousand pilots who graduated from both the single-engine and twin-engine flying programs at Tuskegee Army Air Field. Theopolis Johnson, a member of class 45-B-TE, has undertaken the enormous task of compiling a cross-referenced list of the participants in all phases of the program. An invaluable aid to anyone researching the Tuskegee Experience, Mr. Johnson's database to date includes more than thirteen thousand records. The willingness of both men to share their information has been extremely helpful to us.

The name of the Army Air Corps was changed to Army Air Forces in 1942. Throughout 1942 and into 1943, official documents indicate that Army Air Corps and Army Air Forces were used interchangeably. Also the African-Americans who became known as the Tuskegee Airmen were not the only blacks in the Army Air Corps. Most of those other men, however, were assigned as support personnel or manual laborers; they served in aviation squadrons, air base defense units, and quartermaster, ordinance, chemical, and transportation companies. Aircraft designation also changed from "P" (Pursuit) to "F" (Fighter) during the late 1940s.

Without the cooperation and support of a great many people involved in the Tuskegee Experience, this book would never have been started, let alone completed. Louis Purnell, a member of the 99th Fighter Squadron and former Smithsonian curator, graciously read our manuscript on three separate occasions, correcting errors both factual and typographical, and providing us with even more research material. His ongoing support has been invaluable. Hiram and Kathadaza Mann, our adoptive parents, have provided not only factual data and images, but also steadfast love and encouragement. While they might ask for us to be better children, we could not ask for better parents.

Through the stories of those who participated in the Tuskegee Experience, we have lived it vicariously. Those shared accounts of tragedy, pain, and accomplishment have made this book what it is. We have been blessed with the opportunity to chronicle their experiences, to keep the stories alive long after we have all faded away. For everything that we have been given by all of these men and women, we are grateful.

Chapter One

Black Men Can't Fly

Two days before Independence Day, members of the 99th Fighter Squadron had little to celebrate. Since their arrival in North Africa on April 24, 1943, the black pilots had done little but stand down while they received an in-country indoctrination. Kept isolated from other troops, they lived in tents and flew from a barren and dusty dirt strip. It was nearly a month before they became part of the aerial wars. Their first real mission was to strafe the Italian island of Pantelleria. It was not the duty that well-trained and aggressive fighter pilots wanted; they wanted action in the air against the Germans.

Three months earlier, as they prepared to embark for Europe, Colonel Noel F. Parrish, commanding officer of Tuskegee Army Air Field, bid the 99th goodbye with these words: "You are fighting men now. You have made the team. Your future is now being handed into your own hands. Your future, good or bad, will depend largely on how determined you are not to give satisfaction to those who would like to see you fail."[1]

It is unfathomable that anyone, except the enemy, of course, would wish to see an element of the United States military fail. But this was different; this was something very new and untried. These men of the 99th Fighter Squadron whom Colonel Parrish cheered on to success were the outcome of what would come to be known as the Tuskegee Experience. They were African-Americans and the first members of an all-black Army Air Corps squadron. From the very beginning, they were expected to fail—not only by bigoted civilians, but also by the War Department, the generals of the Army Air Corps, and by their fellow white pilots. But they didn't fail!

The B-25 bombers lumbered along in an aerial convoy on a flight from Tunisia; their target was Sicily and their load of bombs had been successfully jettisoned. German fighters and dense 88-millimeter antiaircraft fire were a constant threat. Suddenly, a pair of moving specks became visible against the sun. As their rate of closure increased, the silhouettes increased in size. At a speed approaching 400 miles per hour, a pair of German Focke-Wulf Fw-190s headed for the bombers. Lieutenant Charles B. Hall was the first to see the Germans. He pushed the control stick of his P-40 and maneuvered into the tiny aerial corridor between the slow-moving bombers and the attacking Focke-Wulfs. As one of the German pilots maneuvered to the left, Hall fired a burst from his machine guns. The .50-caliber shells ripped through the thin skin of the yellow-nosed Focke-Wulf and the airplane erupted in fire. The German attacker streamed out of control and crashed into the ground. The second attacker fled.

It was a good kill; the Focke-Wulf was as fast as lightning and well-armed. As with most airplanes, several different models had been built. The most common model, the Fw-190 D-9, was powered by a 1,770-horsepower Junkers engine and had a top speed of just over 400 miles per hour. The Focke-Wulf was armed with a pair of 20-millimeter cannons and two 13-millimeter machine guns.

Hall's victory had been a long time coming. If the Army and War Department had had their way, it would never have been realized. Blacks had been part of the American military since the Revolutionary War. However, except in rare and unofficial situations, they were always part of a segregated unit.

Following World War I, several studies were undertaken regarding the role of African-Americans in the military. In reality, the studies were exercises to prove that blacks were inferior to whites and were suited only for menial positions. In 1925, the War Department directed the War College to undertake a study examining the combat records of black servicemen during World War I. The request was strange, since most blacks had been restricted because of segregation policies to service as stevedores, laborers, kitchen help, and doing road construction and the unpleasant duty of grave registration.

Signed by Major General H. E. Ely, commandant of the War College, the results of the study titled "The Use of Negro Manpower in War" were preordained and very negative. It concluded that black men ". . . were cowards and poor technicians and fighters, lacking initiative and resourcefulness." It reported that the brain of the average black man weighed only thirty-five ounces compared to forty-five for an average white man. The report was all the ammunition that most military leaders needed; it "proved" that blacks should be kept segregated from whites and were qualified only for menial, closely supervised jobs. Their mentality, bravery, coordination, and everything else was highly suspect, according to the report, which claimed that African-Americans were ". . . a subspecies of the human population."

In 1931, the head of the National Association for the Advancement of Colored People wrote a letter to the War Department asking that blacks be allowed to join the Army Air Corps. Not surprisingly, the War Department responded negatively. It argued, "The colored man had not been attracted to flying in the same way or to the extent of the white man. . . ."

In 1937, the War College directed that another study of the role of blacks in the military be undertaken.[2] This one was hardly more complimentary. However, with the war heating up in Europe, the study recommended that more blacks be allowed to join the army. Blacks and whites alike were to be called for service in proportion to the civilian population. The numbers would change, the segregation would not. African-Americans would continue to be confined to all-black units and restricted to service in traditional functions; they would still not be eligible for service in the Army Air Corps.

American blacks felt as strong a patriotic need to serve in their country's military services as did whites, and they fought to do so. African-American newspaper editors waged a gallant, vocal, and steady editorial battle to open the military. The *Pittsburgh Courier* was one of the most vociferous in the cry for black equality, and in February 1938 started a weekly series of articles on discrimination. The *Afro-American, Associated Negro Press, Chicago Defender, Cleveland Call and Post, Crisis, Houston Informer, Kansas City Call, Louisiana Weekly, New Jersey Herald-News, Norfolk Journal and Guide, Philadelphia Independent,* and *Philadelphia Tribune,* all African-American newspapers, on an almost weekly basis called for an end to Jim Crow laws and advocated more liberal enlistment policies. The *Pittsburgh Courier* was probably the genesis of an eventual all-black flying group.

Always a strong proponent of the rights and freedoms of blacks, the *Pittsburgh Courier* insisted that blacks have the right to join integrated units of the American armed services. During the war, one of the newspaper's slogans was the "Double V." In white America,

"V" stood for victory against the Italian, German, and Japanese enemies; in the black community, the "Double V" stood for victory
against not only foreign enemies, but the domestic enemy of racism.

When the war broke out in Europe, President Franklin D.
Roosevelt, like most Americans, wanted the United States to remain
neutral. As hostilities escalated, Roosevelt began to prepare for
America's eventual involvement. On September 17, 1938, the president approved an expenditure of a hundred thousand dollars of
National Youth Administration funds to begin a Civilian Pilot
Training Program at thirteen colleges. Training included seventy-two
hours of ground instruction given on the college campus, followed
by a program of flight instruction at nearby civilian airports. The
ground instruction covered everything from navigation to use of
radios and Morse code, parachutes, instruments, and the general
history of aviation. Flight training was comprised of dual instruction which included the basics of flying such as takeoffs, landings,
and routine aerial maneuvers, followed by three hours of solo with
a one-hour dual check ride. Final phase of the flight training was several hours of advanced solo work. The cost of the college program
was a forty-dollar laboratory fee. During this trial program, 330
trainees entered the program; 317 eventually received their licenses.
All were white.

In April 1939, Congress passed Public Law 18 that authorized the
private training of military pilots by civilian schools. On June 27, 1939,
the Civilian Pilot Training Act (H.R. 5619) was signed, authorizing
funding of $7 million per year to train civilian pilots until July 1, 1944.

By this time it was almost certain that America would not be able
to remain neutral in the war in Europe. It was also obvious that
America's Air Corps was not on a par with that of the European bel-
ligerents. The military training schools could not train enough
pilots; civilian schools made great sense. The law, however, would
not apply to blacks or black schools. At the last moment, Senator
Harry Schwartz of Wyoming added an amendment that allowed
African-Americans to be part of the Civilian Pilot Training Program.
Under the amendment, the War Department would lend aviation
equipment to at least two black schools approved by the Civil
Aeronautics Authority.

The Air Corps rejected the idea and publicly issued a statement
rejecting the idea of black pilot training. However, in June 1939,
Congress authorized the Civil Aeronautics Authority to sanction

the Civilian Pilot Training Program in which twenty thousand flying students per year would eventually receive pilot training. Black colleges and two privately owned black flying schools were to be part of the program. The black colleges included Hampton Institute, Howard University, Lincoln University, Agricultural and Technical College of North Carolina, Delaware State College for Colored Students, Tuskegee Institute, and West Virginia State College (the first black college to receive CAA approval).

The Civilian Pilot Training Program was of utmost importance to the history of African-Americans in aviation. Dominick A. Pisano, in his *To Fill the Skies With Pilots, the Civilian Pilot Training Program, 1939-46*, wrote, ". . . the CPTP had been instrumental in allowing blacks, who had faced the same kinds of restrictive Jim Crow practices in aviation as in other areas of their lives, to fly in greater numbers than ever before."

Initially, the flying program at Tuskegee was a combined effort of Tuskegee Institute and the Alabama Air Service, a commercial flying operation at Montgomery's municipal airport. The program first received certification by the Civil Aeronautics Authority as a primary flying school on October 15, 1939. Ground training was conducted at Tuskegee Institute and the flight training took place in Montgomery.

The first elementary ground school course began at Tuskegee Institute in early December 1939. Twenty students, including two women, had enrolled in the program. Requirements included American citizenship, full-time enrollment at Tuskegee, and a student pilot's certificate. Students had to be between eighteen and twenty-five years of age, pass the Civil Aeronautics Authority physical, and have the consent of their parents. The curriculum offered ninety hours of ground instruction and thirty-five to fifty hours of dual and solo flight training.

Tuskegee Institute opened its own flying field, Kennedy Field, known as Airport "Number One," in the spring of 1940. This meant it was no longer necessary for students to make the eighty-mile round-trip to Montgomery. By February of 1941, Tuskegee Institute had received certification in its own right to provide advanced flying courses.

At the close of 1939, there were only 125 licensed black aviators. Eighty-two of those fliers held only student licenses. Following the Civilian Pilot Training Program, the number of licensed black pilots increased substantially. By year-end 1940, the Department of Commerce reported 231 licensed black fliers.

Their hopes buoyed by the success of the Civilian Pilot Training Program, young black men attempted to join the Army Air Corps. In letters to the National Association for the Advancement of Colored People, the Air Corps, the War Department, and the president, thousands of men asked only for an opportunity to serve their country. The general requirements for appointment as flying cadets in the United States Army Air Corps stated that at the time of application, candidates must be "unmarried male citizens of the United States, between the ages of twenty and twenty-six, inclusive; individuals who have satisfactorily completed at least one-half the credits required for a degree at a recognized college or university, or who can pass an examination covering such work; of excellent character; and of sound physique and in excellent health." There was no mention of color.

Reynold D. Pruitt of the Tuskegee Institute Aeronautical Corps wrote, "I would like very much to fly in the Air Corps of the United States army if given an opportunity. I also believe that the Tuskegee student flier will still maintain an average above the seven southern states of the south including white and colored in army or C.A.A. programmes if given near equal opportunities."[3]

On September 16, 1940, Howard Williams of Brooklyn, New York, sent a letter to President Franklin D. Roosevelt. He wrote, "I have applied at several recruiting stations at various times within the past three years for enlistment in the Army Air Corps, only to have been refused participation in the armed forces of the United States solely on the ground that I am a Negro. . . . As President of the United States and Commander-in-Chief of the armed forces of this country, I appeal to you for aid in securing the right to serve in the Army Air Corps without discrimination because of my color, which right was recently given me and others like me by the amendment to the Burke-Wadsworth Bill."[4]

S. Elmo Johnson, a candidate for a masters degree at Fisk University in Nashville, Tennessee, was prepared to put his education on hold for the good of his country. In a letter to the general office of the NAACP in New York, Johnson stated, "I am a candidate for the Master of Arts degree in Sociology here at Fisk. Yet the inevitability of a second World War makes the defense of my country of more importance. I have exhausted every available recruiting agency in this area in an effort to get in the Air Corps to no avail. You may quote me in any respect that will in any way break down the barriers of prejudice and injustice in the National Defense."[5]

Dudley M. Archer mailed a letter to the NAACP after his son was refused entrance to the Air Corps because of his color. After receiving an application for the Air Corps, Graham Archer, a graduate of the Manhattan High School of Aviation Trades in Brooklyn, New York, went to the Naval Aviation Center in New York City for a physical examination. The elder Archer recalled, "The first examiner took the communication from him, marked it colored and sent him to a second who informed him that they are not allowed to recruit colored men."[6]

Invariably, the answer each of these and thousands of other black men received was not the one that they wanted to hear. Lieutenant Colonel V. L. Burge, Acting Corps Area Air Officer, advised Zannie T. Overstreet Jr. that ". . . it is regretted that the Air Corps does not have a colored unit, only white troops being authorized."[7] Burge suggested that Overstreet should consider joining the 9th and 10th Cavalry or the 24th and 25th Infantry which were "colored" regiments.

Major General E. S. Adams, the adjutant general of the War Department, responded to Howard Williams' request for admission by answering, "The primary purpose of the Army Flying School is to secure sufficient pilots trained in military aviation to meet the present and prospective needs of the Army. Since there are no colored Air Corps units in the Army to which colored graduates could be assigned, applications from colored persons, for flying cadet appointment or for enlistment in the Air Corps are not being accepted."[8]

Politics makes strange bedfellows. The presidential election of 1940 definitely opened the door to the Army Air Corps for black airmen. Republican presidential candidate Wendell Willkie in his campaign against the incumbent Franklin Roosevelt promised that, if elected, he would end segregation in the military. Roosevelt's reaction was to meet with three black leaders in September 1940. The African-Americans presented three points of discussion. They sought equal opportunity in the defense industry, an impartial administration of the new draft law, and an opportunity for qualified blacks to learn to fly in desegregated units.

During the meeting held on September 27, 1940, President Roosevelt; Secretary of the Navy Frank Knox; Assistant Secretary

Robert P. Patterson; A. Philip Randolph, president of the Brotherhood of Sleeping Car Porters; T. Arnold Hill of the National Youth Administration; and Walter White, secretary of the NAACP, attempted to deal with the problem of discrimination against blacks in the military. Randolph, Hill, and White presented a memorandum at the conference outlining steps leading to the integration of African-Americans into all phases of the armed forces.

In response, the War Department issued a policy stating that black men generally would be admitted to the military in numbers equivalent to their percentage in the civilian population and the military would allow blacks to join the Army Air Corps. However, segregation would not fall; they would be part of an all-black flying unit.

In an attempt to further reinforce his position, President Roosevelt made three political moves. Colonel Benjamin O. Davis Sr. received a well-deserved promotion to the rank of brigadier general in the U.S. Army and Colonel Campbell C. Johnson, also an African-American, was appointed as an advisor to the director of selective service. Roosevelt also suggested that Secretary of War Henry Lewis Stimson should appoint a black civilian advisor. Stimson grudgingly appointed William H. Hastie, dean of the Howard University Law School and a graduate of Harvard Law School. William Hastie would serve as an advisor to Stimson until January 5, 1943, when he submitted his resignation because of what he considered to be "reactionary policies and discriminatory practices of the Army Air Forces in matters affecting Negroes."

The NAACP constantly prodded the government for an end to segregation in the military. In early August 1940, they had urged a complete removal of all discrimination against blacks in the armed services. In letters to Henry Stimson and Frank Knox, the newly appointed Secretary of Navy, they argued that blacks had been allowed to join the navy only as kitchen staff in the mess corps. Attempts to enlist in the army had not yielded hoped-for results either—blacks had been restricted to segregated units. As reported by the *Chicago Defender*, the NAACP made a cogent argument that the success of the military and the defense of the nation needed to be based upon ". . . the establishment of unity among the American citizens of this country."[9] Walter White, as well as most black newspaper editors, believed that there was no way to achieve that unity as long as America's largest minority group was forced to serve in segregated outfits performing menial tasks.

The outcome of the conference was not necessarily what the black leaders had desired. On October 5, 1940, the NAACP's press release on the conference revealed, "As to the Navy, Col. Knox stated that while he was sympathetic, he felt that the problem there was almost insoluble since men have to live together on ships. Col. Knox stated that 'Southern' and 'Northern' ships are impossible."

Responding to a letter from the Federated Hotel Waiters Union Local 356, Henry Stimson outlined the policy of the War Department regarding segregation. He stated that segregation of military personnel was a battle-tested, tried-and-true policy of the War Department. Based on historical precedent, black and white men would not be permitted to serve in the same outfits. There would be no integration. It was Stimson's belief that what had worked well in the past would continue to work well in the present and the future. Any changes made to the system would undoubtedly produce undesirable results such as a decline in the morale of whites forced to serve with black counterparts. In effect, integration of the American military could seriously jeopardize the country's military preparedness and system of national defense.

Stimson argued that since blacks in the army had served only in segregated units, they had become accustomed to operating under that system. He believed that the system had produced strong rates of reenlistment, high levels of morale, and finely trained black troops. Therefore, there should be no large-scale changes to the system of segregation that had proven so successful in the past. Stimson informed the union that the War Department was ". . . convinced that no experiments should be tried with the organizational set-up of the colored units of the army at this critical time."[10]

Spann Watson tried on several occasions to join the Army Air Corps, only to receive one of the various versions of the pro forma rejection letters sent to black applicants. Unwilling to give up, Watson sent yet another letter on November 14, 1940, to the Assistant Adjutant General, Headquarters Second Corps Area:

> I am writing with reference to my application for flying cadet appointment which was returned by you "without action" on August 30, 1940, on the basis that there were at that time "no units composed of colored men" and "no provision made for such training under existing War Department regulations."
>
> Pursuant to my recent conversation with Warrant Officer Solomon, the Second Corps Area Recruiting Officer at 30 Whitehall Street, New

York City, in which conversation he told me that it was reported that the War Department policy with reference to the enlistment of Negroes in the Air Corps had been changed but that the official order had not then come through, and pursuant to press accounts of the changed policy of the War Department with reference to Negroes in the Air Corps, I am inquiring as to the proper procedure for re-submitting my application.

Why would young, proud, and very capable men put themselves through the process of applying for admittance to the segregated Army Air Corps time after time, only to be repeatedly rejected? Obviously the reasons were numerous and varied from man to man. At the officer's club at Bolling Air Force Base in January 1997, Colonel Spann Watson, United States Air Force, Retired, explained that in his case, the reason had been anger.

Spann Watson and his family left their home in South Carolina when Watson was ten years old. Airplanes had been a rare sight in Watson's rural South Carolina before the family moved to Lodi, New Jersey. They lived two or three miles from Teterboro Airport in New Jersey, only a few miles west of New York City. The Fokker Aircraft plant was located at Teterboro, as was a Curtiss-Wright hangar. Gates Flying Circus provided aerial entertainment on almost every weekend of the year. Planes flew every day; when not in school, Watson and his two brothers could be found at Teterboro Airport watching them. Almost every famous American aviator was there at one time or another. Amelia Earhart, Jimmy Doolittle, Jimmy Waddell, Matty Laird, Wiley Post, and Clyde Pangborn all ended up at the Wright hangar. It was at Teterboro that Watson experienced his first real introduction to aviation and an episode that probably provided motivation for the rest of his life. He vividly remembered:

"One special thing happened. My mother sent me to the post office one day to buy a stamp . . . a two-cent stamp to send a letter to South Carolina. On that stamp was an embossed picture of the *Spirit of St. Louis*. I looked at that thing, I had a photographic mind and I remembered every detail of that stamp. On one of our tours to Teterboro, people were getting rides over New York City for five dollars, or two-fifty, or one dollar to ride around the pattern in a Jenny. There would be absolutely crowds and crowds of people. Sometimes as many as ten thousand people.

"One holiday, the Fourth of July, on that day, some ten, twelve, fifteen thousand people were out there looking at the Gates Flying

Circus. During the afternoon, a plane came circling over the field and it went around a couple of times but still did not land. The man who was doing the sales for the rides to New York City had his megaphone and he said that 'this airplane doesn't know how to land at our airport and we're going to have to send another airplane up there to lead him in.' I said, 'That's the *Spirit of St. Louis.*' He didn't hear me. I said, 'That's the *Spirit of St. Louis.*' He got on his megaphone and this is why I'm in aviation today. He got on his megaphone and said that 'the little colored boy over here said that's the *Spirit of St. Louis,* ha, ha, ha, ha.' That infuriated me and I'm still showing it. The airplane lands and it was Lindbergh in the *Spirit of St. Louis.* The people went absolutely wild. The people would've destroyed the *Spirit of St. Louis* taking souvenirs. Quickly some men circled the airplane to protect it. One of them was my dad. He made sure I got to see it. That man laughed at me—that's why I'm in aviation."

Watson was not called for duty until November 1941, more than a year after his application. All cadets went to Maxwell Army Air Field for physical and psychological testing and an interview for acceptability. There Watson was asked by a white lieutenant colonel, "Boy, what do you think of niggers marrying white women?" Watson wisely measured his response and replied, "Well, if those people want to get married, that's their business." Had he shown his anger at the stinging question that was intended to hurt and elicit a hostile outburst, Watson would have failed the interview and been booted out of the program.

Chapter Two

The Opening of the Door

The Army Air Corps submitted its plan for an "experiment" in December 1940. As mandated by the War Department, an all-black fighter squadron would be established. The 99th Pursuit Squadron (later redesignated as the 99th Fighter Squadron) at full complement would consist of 33 to 35 pilots and 278 ground crew members. The first officers would be white; as black officers were trained, they would take command of the squadron.

African-Americans were not happy with the plan. While opening the door to the Army Air Corps, the plan continued the policy of strict segregation. General George C. Marshall, Army Chief of Staff, wrote, "Segregation is an established American custom. The educational level of Negroes is below that of whites; the Army must utilize its personnel according to their capabilities; and experiments within the Army in the evolution of social problems are fraught with danger to efficiency, discipline, and morale."

William H. Hastie, the administration's civilian advisor, did not for a minute buy into the "segregation for the good of the country" rhetoric of the War Department. While he praised the plan for allowing blacks to join the Air Corps, he soundly rejected the idea of continued segregation. Believing in integrated training at all bases, Hastie wrote, "Acquaintance, understanding, and mutual respect established between blacks and whites at the regular Air Corps training centers can be the most important single factor in bringing about harmonious racial attitudes leading to high morale."

In January 1941, the War Department announced that African-Americans would be allowed to become pilots in the Air Corps. An all-black squadron, the 99th Pursuit Squadron, would be activated.

The January 16 press conference announcing the formation of the 99th stated that thirty-five black candidates would be chosen under the Civil Aeronautics Authority from the Civilian Pilot Training Program. Service personnel such as mechanics, armorers, etc., were to be trained at Chanute Field, Illinois. Black cadets for pilot training would be trained at Tuskegee Institute, Alabama. Fifteen weeks of primary training that included ground instruction, meteorology, and principles of flight would take place at Tuskegee Institute. Secondary training would take place at Tuskegee Army Air Field, which was yet to be constructed.

The press conference announced, "Concurrently, 35 black candidates would be chosen under the Civil Aeronautics Authority (CAA) from the Civilian Pilot Training Program (CPTP) established by Congress in 1939 to train civilians while they were going to college, and given 30 weeks of flight training under white instructors." The funding was approved for a twenty-two-week program to train 460 enlisted support personnel at the Air Corps Technical School at Chanute Field, Illinois.

General Henry H. Arnold, Chief of Air Corps, sent an advance telegram to Tuskegee's president, Dr. Frederick Douglas Patterson, advising him of the details of the program:

> Under Secretary of War will announce substantially as follows at press conference at three P.M. "The War Department will establish a Negro pursuit squadron. The plan will begin by the enlistment of approximately four hundred thirty Negro high school graduates to undertake technical training and other specialized instruction at Chanute Field, Rantoul, Illinois, in courses varying from twelve to thirty weeks. Approximately six months after training is begun at Chanute Field a nucleus of trained technicians will be available for transfer to Tuskegee, Alabama, to start organization of squadron. A site for installations at Tuskegee already has been selected. Pilot trainees will be obtained from those completing civil pilot training program secondary course and will be enlisted as flying cadets subject to present standards. They will be sent to Tuskegee for basic and advanced flying training and unit training in pursuit types of aircraft. The squadron will be organized at Tuskegee as soon as fully trained pilots become available. Instruction will proceed as soon as funds are made available for this purpose by the Congress."

Walter White, secretary of the NAACP, fired out a telegram to William Hastie at the War Department. It stated, "Please advise if *New*

York Times report is correct that a segregated aircorps squadron is to be established by the War Department at Tuskegee Institute. If true, National Association for the Advancement of Colored People vigorously protests surrender of War Department to segregation pattern."

In late 1940, the National Association for the Advancement of Colored People had prepared a lengthy working paper outlining a possible legal action against the War Department. It was their intention to force the government to allow African-Americans to join the Air Corps. Several legal cases for and against the admission of blacks were analyzed. The author stated that the best argument could be found in Section II, Paragraph 2 of Army Regulations No. 615-160: "Any person fulfilling the general requirements prescribed in paragraph 2 may apply for appointment as a flying cadet. The necessary blank forms may be obtained from any Air Corps station or from the Adjutant General."

Perhaps it was sheer coincidence, but only days before the War Department announced the formation of an all-black Air Corps unit, Yancey Williams, a Howard University student, filed a lawsuit with the United States District Court for the District of Columbia over the rejection of his application as a flying cadet. The holder of a private pilot's license and a graduate of Howard University's primary and secondary aviation training courses, Williams brought the suit against Secretary of War Henry Stimson, Army Chief of Staff Major General George C. Marshall, Adjutant General E. S. Adams, Chief of the Air Corps Major General Henry H. Arnold, and Major General Walter S. Grant, commanding general of the Army's Third Corps.

The NAACP had been the impetus behind Williams' lawsuit. In November 1940, the NAACP advised that the organization would be willing to provide legal assistance to any black who had been barred from entrance into the military because of color. Thurgood Marshall, who eventually went on to become Chief Justice of the United States Supreme Court, was at the time a lawyer on the staff of the NAACP. Along with Robert Ming Jr. and Leon A. Ransom, both members of the National Legal Committee, Marshall drafted the suit against the government with Williams as the plaintiff. Wendell L. McConnell of Washington, D.C., served as Williams' attorney.

Williams had passed a physical examination by Army doctors at Bolling Field in July 1940. His application had been submitted to General Grant on November 20. Grant refused to consider the application because Williams was black. An appeal filed with the adjutant general and the secretary of war was refused on December 13 because of Williams' color. The suit charged, "That such conduct on the part of these defendants, who, in their official capacity as officers of the Government and of the Army of the United States and charged with the duty of preparation for national defense in a period when the nation, according to its Chief Executive, the President of the United States, faces the gravest emergency in its history, is a violation of the duty and obligation of these defendants to the citizens and government of the United States and contravenes the fundamental principles of the American democracy." Williams sought a declaratory judgment that would establish the rights of himself and other blacks similarly affected. Yancey Williams' suit was dropped following public notice on January 16, 1941, that the Air Corps would be open to blacks. He eventually graduated in Tuskegee Army Air Field class 44-K.

Once word was out that blacks were eligible to join the Air Corps, requests for applications flooded the office of the War Department, the Army, and the NAACP. Qualified young men from every black college—single, of age, and many with some civilian aviation experience—were anxious to fly.

With the backing of the NAACP, Yancey Williams (back row, fourth from left) filed a lawsuit against the War Department, following the repeated rejection of his application for admittance to the Air Corps. (Private Collection.)

Chapter Three

Tuskegee

The 1942 Military Establishment Appropriation Bill set aside $1,663,057 for construction of Tuskegee Army Air Field. An abandoned graveyard was included in the land either leased or purchased outright from people in the area. When owners didn't readily fall into line and sell, the United States took care of the problem with condemnation proceedings.[1] In an unusual action, the Army awarded the construction contract to the black-owned Nashville, Tennessee, firm of McKissack and McKissack, Inc. McKissack crews and Army workers were augmented by men from the Alabama State WPA project. WPA workers cleared and grubbed land, erected tent frames, and dug drainage ditches. More than two thousand laborers, almost exclusively black, converted the former graveyard, plus corn and cotton farmland, into an airfield. Working in two shifts, they built the facility in just six months. Had black pilots been allowed to train at preexisting army airfields, the expenditure could have been avoided.

African-American leaders had favored Chicago as a site for the training of black pilots. It made sense. From the days of Bessie Coleman, America's first licensed African-American pilot, Chicago had been a hub of aviation training for America's black men and women.

The War Department settled on Tuskegee, Alabama, a stronghold of racial segregation, intolerance, and unbridled lawlessness against blacks. The selection of Tuskegee was viewed by many as just another ploy on the part of the War Department to make the trial fail.

Others believed that the selection of Tuskegee as a training site made sense. Alabama's weather would certainly be better than that of Chicago, and Tuskegee Institute was already part of the Civilian

When the War Department chose Tuskegee, Alabama, as the site at which to train black fliers, an entire air base needed to be constructed. Within months, hundreds of acres of farmland not far from Tuskegee Institute had been turned into a military base complete with two runways. (Private Collection.)

The United States War Department took an almost unprecedented action when the primary contract for construction of Tuskegee Army Air Field was awarded to the black-owned Nashville, Tennessee, firm of McKissack and McKissack. (USAF Collection, AFHRA, Maxwell AFB, AL.)

Pilot Training Program. Both Dr. Frederick Douglas Patterson, president of Tuskegee, and G. L. Washington, director of pilot training, were strongly in favor of the program, possibly paving the way for the selection of Tuskegee. In fact, Dr. Patterson wired Walter White and Judge William Hastie requesting each man to endorse Tuskegee to General Henry Arnold as an "ideal base for army pursuit squadron. True because of year round training possibilities and cooperation possible between training program and facilities of the institute."

From the standpoint of the local black population, Tuskegee Institute made great sense, if only in a symbolic sense. Founded by Booker T. Washington, the black college had been in existence since 1881 and was unarguably the best-known black college in the United States. Tuskegee also had other immediate advantages while a permanent field was being constructed. Patterson was able to promise dormitories, separate mess facilities, hospital space, and ample classrooms for ground schools.

Walter White refused to do as Patterson requested. In fact, when young black men hoping to become part of the program wrote to White for assistance, he suggested that they not apply for training at Tuskegee. The program at Tuskegee was simply another means of segregation and White wanted full integration.

Arguments could be made that administrators of Tuskegee Institute wanted only to further their own interests—the training of black men, whether in academia or aviation. Since the Civilian Pilot Training Program had opened to blacks, the school had been an active participant, receiving much needed revenue. If Tuskegee were selected as a training program for black Army Air Corps aviation cadets, the school would furnish ground school training under a contract with the Air Corps, thus giving it an advantage over the other black institutions providing aviation training. Without a doubt, Tuskegee Institute stood to benefit financially. Tuskegee also aggressively marketed its own civilian aviation training course and enrolled many candidates. The fact that there were eventually two training programs ongoing at Tuskegee caused frequent misunderstandings. Many airmen in Tuskegee's college training program were disappointed to find out that they were not automatically going to be Air Corps pilots.

Tuskegee Institute administrators, while hopefully not protagonists of segregation, knew that segregation was an important part of their success. If white civilian colleges and aviation training facilities were opened to blacks, Tuskegee's student enrollment would likely plummet, threatening its viability. While Tuskegee Institute was being considered for the Air Corps program, one trustee went so far as to endorse segregation. His paternalistic argument stated:

> When Negroes are not segregated they are subject to humiliation and discrimination from a large fraction of the white men with whom they have to work. To be specific, if Negroes were admitted to an army training camp devoted to flying in which the great majority of the inducted men were white, coming from all classes of society and all sections of the country, it is clear that there would be no power on earth which could prevent a certain number of the inducted white men from displaying racial discrimination in their attitude toward the Negroes. If any one thing is needed in flying, it is complete self-possession and absence from extraneous nervous strain. When Negroes do not have to be continuously on their guard against such unnecessary strains during the period of their flying training they will do better as flyers. The percentage of failures will be less. While the situation is not ideal, it is very difficult to find any ideal situation of any kind in this country or elsewhere on earth whether related to the Negro or to any other class or individual. I have come to the conclusion that the plan sponsored by Tuskegee gives the best chance to the Negro at this time for participation in the Air Forces.

Few blacks in the 1940s would have argued for yet another Jim Crow institution, as did this Tuskegee Institute trustee. Yet, the language needs to be looked at from the perspective of the writer with his concerns for the success of what was certainly a revolutionary program. However, most black leaders did not share the beliefs of the anonymous Tuskegee trustee.

One of the most compelling arguments in favor of Tuskegee Institute's selection as a training facility lies at the feet of one individual, Charles Alfred Anderson. Affectionately known as "Chief," Anderson was responsible for the primary training of students and was of the utmost importance in teaching hundreds, if not thousands, of black college students to fly. Anderson owned his own Piper Cub and frequently gave flying lessons to Tuskegee Institute students.

Lieutenant Colonel Hiram E. Mann, United States Air Force, Retired, certainly believed that Anderson had a pivotal role in the development and success of the black flying program at Tuskegee. In the spring of 1941, Anderson took the First Lady of the United States, Eleanor Roosevelt, for a flight above the hills and valleys of Alabama. Mann believed that ". . . him taking her up for a ride was his crowning achievement." For Franklin Roosevelt, the admission of

African-American men into the Army Air Corps was probably simply a matter of expediency. The president was undoubtedly concerned with his reelection. However, Eleanor Roosevelt truly believed in the cause and served as her husband's conscience. In October 1942, Anderson and several other civilian flight instructors were transferred from Tuskegee Institute's CAA program to the United States Air Corps Detachment for the purpose of providing elementary training.

Few people associated with the success of the Tuskegee Experience are more revered than C. Alfred Anderson. Many young American boys in the 1930s spent much of their hard-earned money, their nickels and dimes, on aviation magazines such as *Wings, Daredevil Aces, Flying Aces, G-8 and His Battle Aces,* and *Satan's Wing.* Most young black men had never seen a black flier and were looking for a hero. For many of the young men who eventually went into the aviation programs at Howard University and Tuskegee Institute, C. Alfred Anderson was that black hero.

On October 4, 1974, at the dedication of Moton Field at the new Tuskegee Airport, Anderson was awarded a life membership in the

Director of Training Lewis Jackson, First Lady Eleanor Roosevelt, and C. Alfred Anderson all played a pivotal role in the success of the Tuskegee Experience. Mrs. Roosevelt's flight with "Chief" Anderson undoubtedly helped to promote the cause of the African-American fliers. (Tuskegee University Archives.)

Tuskegee Airmen, Inc. organization. A citation signed by Spann Watson, TAI's national president, read:

> Our memories are wrapped in deep respect, admiration and affection as we salute you as the man who has always reflected the image and indomitable spirit of the pioneering American aviator. You established within Black Air Cadets a sense of pride, the importance of exactness, the significance of excellence, and you set an example for respect. But most of all, you have always been an Aviator's Aviator and we can say a thousand things more but it will suffice to say, only, that you have always been one of us.

Chief Anderson deserves a great deal of credit not only for his contributions to the program at Tuskegee, but also for his part in the development of the Civilian Pilot Training Program at Howard University. In November 1939, Howard's student newspaper, *The Hill Top*, reported on the formation of an aviation program at the school. Professor Addison E. Richmond from the School of Engineering and Architecture would teach students the fundamentals of ground school. After completion of courses in meteorology, navigation, flight theory, and radio communications, the students would then receive flight training at Hybla Valley, Virginia, from Flight Instructor C. Alfred Anderson.

Fliers at Howard couldn't find a place to fly. National Airport was under construction; Hoover Airport, site of the present Pentagon, wouldn't allow them to use its facilities. They found Hybla Valley, a small Virginia airport that was going broke. The Hybla Valley managers finally agreed to let Howard CPTP students use their marginal, decrepit facility, although Howard's fliers had to stay on the opposite side of the field from white pilots. The operations or ready room was a dilapidated shack, but they were happy to have it. There was only one airplane; it was flown again and again. The engine was rated at fifty horsepower but had been flown so much it undoubtedly produced little more than thirty-five horsepower.

Henry C. L. Bohler, a classmate of Yancey Williams, didn't give much credit to the lawsuit brought by Williams and the NAACP as the responsible force behind the opening of the Air Corps. Bohler believed that C. Alfred Anderson's flight with Eleanor Roosevelt at Tuskegee was "more or less what really inspired it, not that lawsuit. However, the lawsuit would have gone to court and it may have been waiting on an answer today."

Black church leaders, newspaper editors, and black flying groups

Henry C. L. Bohler, a graduate of class 44-J-SE, was almost refused admission to the flying program when he did not meet the minimum weight requirement. A high-calorie diet over the next several days contributed the few extra pounds. (Private Collection.)

immediately set up a storm of protest against the idea of a segregated unit. On January 25, 1941, the bold headline of the *Chicago Defender* screamed, "78 Organizations Blast Jim Crow Air Unit." The black National Airmen's Association, headed by Cornelius Coffey and Willa Brown, voted to repudiate the establishment of a "Jim Crow pursuit squadron." Chicago's Council of Negro Organizations, consisting of seventy-eight independent social, civic, religious, and business organizations, strongly opposed the plan.

Cornelius Coffey, president of the NAA, spoke of the determined and seemingly interminable fight African-Americans had waged to gain admittance to the Army Air Corps. While both the Army and Navy cited a historical precedent for segregation, the Air Corps, as a relatively new organization, had no such tradition. Coffey said, "We'd rather be excluded, than be segregated. There's no constitutional support for segregated units and the only traditions existing in aviation as I know it are ones which would make complete integration sane and logical."[2]

The first group of black cadets entered the Army Air Corps flight training program in June 1941. The initial class, 42-C-SE, was made

The first class of pilots at Tuskegee Army Air Field, class 42-C-SE, started with thirteen men. By graduation day nearly a year later, only five, pictured here with an instructor, remained. (USAF Neg. #21001AC, HQ AETC/HO, Randolph AFB, TX.)

up of only thirteen men—Captain Benjamin O. Davis Jr., John C. Anderson Jr., Charles Brown, Theodore Brown, Marion Carter, Lemuel R. Custis, Charles DeBow, Frederick H. Moore, Ulysses S. Pannell, George S. Roberts, William Slade, Mac Ross, and Roderick Williams. Captain Davis, with more than five years in the military, was appointed commandant of cadets. Originally, there was to have been a complement of thirty-three pilot trainees, but the Air Corps failed to select a sufficient number of suitable candidates. When finally at full strength, the squadron would be much more than just 33 pilots; there were to be 64 commissioned officers and 474 enlisted men. There would be crew chiefs, flight chiefs, radiomen, technical inspectors, armorers, and shop men such as welders, machinists, propeller experts, painters, electricians, dispatchers, and parachute repairmen. Clerks and typists were necessary to assure the smooth flow of paperwork.

Major James A. "Straight Arrow" Ellison was the first commanding

officer of Tuskegee. Although a white man, he was a strong supporter of black military aviation. Ellison, a pudgy veteran of World
War I, was seemingly well-qualified for the command. He had been
involved with pursuit aviation for twelve years and had been flight
sector chief at Kelly Field, Texas, and base group commander at an
Alabama airfield. While commander of the 19th Pursuit Squadron
in Hawaii, Ellison was honored in 1937 with the Commander's
Award for best air unit. At Tuskegee, however, Ellison never had the
backing of his bosses.

On April 24, 1941, Brigadier General W. R. Weaver advised
General George Brett regarding a commander of Tuskegee ". . . we
should select a pretty smart officer to eventually head up this activity.
Luke Smith has suggested Lieutenant Colonel Frederick von H.
Kimble as being cagey and smart and smooth enough to handle the
situation. I am bringing this to your attention because it is a matter
which affects the entire Air Corps in a way, and it just seemed to me
that you should have this situation presented to you, especially in
connection with its political significance. I do not believe we have
in the Training Center at the present time the right individual to
take this job on. Ellison is O.K. and will make a fine Director of
Training there; but I am not so sure whether he has the background
to handle the political aspects that exist in this particular picture."[3]

Ellison did not remain as commander at Tuskegee for very long.
Lieutenant Colonel Frederick von H. Kimble assumed command on
January 12, 1942. Major James A. Ellison left a few days later.

Brigadier General W. R. Weaver had earlier inquired of Major
General George H. Brett about the possibility of Lieutenant Colonel
Frederick von H. Kimble becoming the commander of Tuskegee
Army Air Field. On April 26, Brett responded to Weaver and wrote,
"With reference to the detail of Lieut. Col. Frederick von H. Kimble
as a commander for this school, I must inform you that his duties in
this office at the present time cannot be spared. I agree with you,
however, that a smart officer should be selected to eventually head
up this Negro school activity."[4] Unfortunately for the school and
the training program, von Kimble did become available. He was,
however, not as Brett thought, a "smart officer." He was certainly
not the right commander for the school.

Life at Tuskegee was hard. Military policies of segregation necessitated construction of a separate base that was not yet completed
when the first personnel arrived. The men were forced to live in

Before Tuskegee Army Air Field was completed, personnel were housed in "Tent City." Conditions were primitive; water was trucked in, and meals were prepared under field conditions. (USAF Collection, AFHRA, Maxwell AFB, AL.)

Following completion of Tuskegee Army Air Field, aviation cadets lived in wooden barracks. By the fall of 1943, the base included six barracks, a mess hall, supply rooms, day rooms, and a headquarters building, with additional structures still to be constructed. (USAF Collection, AFHRA, Maxwell AFB, AL.)

tents until the barracks were finished. Although the Army Air Corps had attempted to establish a training facility at Tuskegee Army Air Field that was a "separate-but-equal" facility, there was nothing equal about it. Because there was only one base available to train black airmen, overcrowding was a frequent problem. To compound the problem, once pilots were trained, they were forced to remain at Tuskegee for an extended period of time.

Contrary to popular belief, the aviation cadets encountered little personal racism from the civilian or military trainers on base. The civilian instructors at Tuskegee, black or white, pushed the cadets hard. It was common for instructors in the back seat to shake the control stick around resulting in many bruised knees for the cadets in front, but that was done to white pilots as well.

Louis R. Purnell, a member of the original 99th Fighter Squadron, pursued several different fields of endeavor after leaving the Air Force to eventually end his civilian career as a curator at the Smithsonian Institution's National Air and Space Museum. Purnell did what only a few other black aviators did during World War II. After a tour of duty in Europe, he returned to Tuskegee as a flight instructor. There he found combat to be safer than instructing, volunteered to return to Europe, and flew another thirty-eight missions. Purnell remembered a typical day of training, recalling, "A perfect example of a cadet who was scheduled to fly . . . we'd all go down to the flying line in formation and stand before our instructors. The instructors would come out and tell you, 'Aviation Cadet Louis Purnell, we're going up to ten thousand feet, and we'll perform loops, slow rolls, etc.' You'd wait your turn, you'd go up. My instructors would say very little during instruction, but they were strict. When you came down there was no exchange of words. He had a little slip and so many errors would amount to a pink slip and so many pink slips and you're out." Three pink slips and a cadet was gone from the program.

A certain amount of forgiveness also existed, since most instructors wanted the program to succeed. Few aviation cadets made it through the program without some type of mishap. Even Captain Davis experienced a training accident. Attributed to pilot error, Davis' accident required total overhaul of the aircraft.

Lee Archer, another excellent flier, soloed at four hours, instead of the normal seven. Ironically, his biggest scare while he was at Tuskegee came on the day he soloed. Archer recalled, "My instructor gave me hell from the time we took off until the time we landed, and finally said, 'Take me down, Mr. Archer. I will not fly with you again.' I thought I was washed out. But he climbed out of the airplane and said, 'See if you can get back yourself.' And that's when I soloed. I think that's the only kind of thing that bothered me . . . that I never thought I pleased them, but apparently I pleased them quite a bit. They were my idols."

Harry A. Sheppard, a graduate of class 43-E-SE and a member of the 301st Fighter Squadron, recounted, "I found that the attitude of my instructors and their competence was superb. I have absolutely nothing but admiration for the quality of the instruction that I got. Bigotry, hatred, and racism at the instructor level, that just did not happen. That was in the hierarchies of the War Department, the legislature, and the Congress. But those instructors were dedicated people, competent, and patient. My instructors gave me the best that they had."

Cadets selected for training at Tuskegee were the elite. But like it or not, everyone was not born to fly and there were bound to be tough times and men who would be eliminated from the program. John J. Suggs, a veteran of World War II, Korea, and Vietnam, believed that at Tuskegee, "The instructors impressed me that they were generally trying to get you through the program and for those of us who washed out, they took it personally and I think it was a handicap they carried with them for the rest of their lives."

African-American civilian flight instructors at Tuskegee Institute's Moton Field included: C. Alfred "Chief" Anderson, Charles R. Foxx, Milton P. Crenshaw, Gilbert A. Cargill, James O. Plinton, James E. "Muscles" Wright, Edward Gibbs, Jack Johnson, Charles H. "Tiger" Flowers, Cecil Ryan, Charles S. Johnson, James J. Hyett, Wendell R. Lipscomb, James Wood, Adolph J. Moret, Sherman T. Rose, Abe Jackson, George W. Allen, Linkwood Williams, James A. Hill, John H. Young, Charles W. Stephens, Roscoe D. Draper, Perry H. Young, Ernest Henderson, Claude R. Platt, Fred Witherspoon, John Pinkett, Nathan A. Sams, Robert Terry, Calvin R. Harris, Hector Strong, Robert Gray, Joseph Ramos, Archie Smith, Matthew W. Plummer, Philip Lee, Charles Foreman, James E. Taylor, Robert Gordon, and Daniel "Chappie" James Jr. Lewis A. Jackson was director of training, while Lawrence E. Anderson served as ground school instructor and George L. Washington as general manager.

The crew of civilian instructors came from all over the United

Civilian flight instructors, most of whom were African-Americans, provided cadets with their first instruction during the primary phase of the flight training program. (Private Collection.)

States; many had already logged thousands of hours of flight time. C. Alfred "Chief" Anderson claimed approximately five thousand flying hours. Lewis A. Jackson, the director of training, logged thirty-five hundred hours of flying, while Crenshaw and Foxx each had nearly two thousand hours in the air.

The black civilian flight instructors were obviously the lifeblood of the program. Most wanted to become members of the Air Corps but were too valuable as instructors. Exempted from the draft, they were vital where they were—at Tuskegee. They were needed to teach the young cadets to fly. Maury Reid, a graduate of class 44-G-SE, recalled, "I didn't fly with an Army officer until about twenty-five hours into the program. I rode with one on a check ride and they passed me on to another civilian pilot. These were the people that sacrificed. I remember one of the saddest things. I had graduated and was going out on a practice flight and a couple of these flight instructors came down to the flight line and they watched me climb into that P-40 and take off. They wanted to be there so badly. They made a great contribution to the program. Without them, the program would probably never have succeeded and they get very little credit.

"We had a cadre of ground school instructors. These people are barely mentioned. We had a cadre of technicians that were trained in all aspects of aviation as a support group. Mechanics. We had meteorologists. We had navigational instructors. They were all black. And most of them wanted to fly but they were disqualified for various reasons. Maybe eyesight or some other physical reason. And they just threw themselves into the program and made a very valuable contribution to the overall structure and they were tough.

"I remember failing a navigational problem, getting a failure on a test. I had all of the parts of the problem correct but they failed me because my pencil wasn't sharp enough and as you go out on the line, I was about two degrees off course by the time I got to the end of the line. And my instructor explained to me, 'You got to do this thing right. There's nothing wrong with your methodology but you've got to do this right. It could be the difference between your getting to the target and back.' I never forgot that because he allowed me to take it over. That was the type of dedication that these people had to make sure we were successful. They worked us. They pushed us. They made me do things I had no idea I could do."

Morale was always low. The number of black pilots eliminated from the flying program was proportionately higher than that of their white counterparts. When black men were eliminated from the flying program, they became privates; many remained at Tuskegee, often engaged in menial service work.

Arque Dickerson, a member of class 43-K-SE, recalled, "For a young man just out of high school, I was in awe. A lot of my heroes were there. People like Sidat-Singh, who was an all-American football player. Bernie Jefferson. It was awe-inspiring. People who were gentlemen and beautiful people to be with. When I think back, I don't think we could have had a better group of people in one place, pointed in one direction to do what we did, and in spite of many of the obstacles that were put in front of us, they managed to do it."

Donald Williams entered the military as a draftee and took his basic training at Biloxi where he also took examinations to become a cadet at Tuskegee. Eliminated in the testing process, he was transferred to Tuskegee in early 1943 in a support capacity. As a statistical draftsman, he prepared charts and graphs on the progress of the cadets in the flying program. Later transferred to Malden Army Air Field in southeastern Missouri, he was the only black to hold such a "white collar" position; the few other blacks at the base held jobs as mess attendants and laborers.

Separately quartered in the southeastern end of the field, they had a bus ride of about ten minutes to the main part of the base whenever they wanted anything. In his job at the main base, Williams used several drafting tools that required frequent washing. On a daily basis, he used the enlisted men's latrine to perform this task. He had been there about three weeks and everything seemed to be going well. Then he was told by his superior officer, a lieutenant, that he could no longer use the latrine. He explained that he was using it only to wash his drafting instruments. The purpose didn't matter. The latrine was reserved for whites and therefore off-limits. In Williams' own words:

"I said, 'Very well.' So then I began a little program of my own. I would get to work at eight o'clock in the morning. At about nine-thirty, quarter to ten, I would have to go to the bathroom. I would go outside base headquarters and I would catch the bus. I may have to wait for the bus for five or six minutes and take a ten-minute ride down to our area and go to the latrine in our area. And then, I would have to wait for the bus to come back and then come back to the base and I would work about ten or fifteen minutes and by that time it's close to eleven, eleven-fifteen, and it's time for lunch so I'd get

A statistical draftsman at Tuskegee and Malden Army Air Fields, as well as in the Philippines, Donald A. Williams demonstrated the adverse effects of segregation upon productivity as he battled against discriminatory policies. (Private Collection.)

back on the bus and go back to my area to eat in our mess hall. My whole day was like that for two week:. That's the way I was getting back, making sure that my productivity was lowered considerably. And it was noticeable."

White citizens of Tuskegee had not warmly embraced the selection of their town as a training site for young black men. It was a typical Southern town controlled by whites; the policy of strict segregation brought about by Jim Crow laws was practiced. Most black military personnel chose to use social facilities at Tuskegee Army Air Field instead of those in town.

On April 23, 1941, one hundred people gathered at a city council meeting in Tuskegee. The major topic was the new airfield, or more accurately, the fact that it was a field for blacks. Ninety-five good citizens of Tuskegee signed a petition to Alabama senators John H. Bankhead and Lister Hill. The petition claimed, "The location of this colored airport would destroy the usefulness of this part of Tuskegee, as well as the east end of Tuskegee, for a white residence section. At this time the east end of Tuskegee offers the only outlet of expansion for white citizens of Tuskegee."[5] Apparently an advance deal had been worked out with the town's leaders regarding location of the field, but the citizens later complained.

Six days later, Major General George H. Brett, the Acting Chief of Air Corps, discussed the issue with a secretary in Senator Hill's office. An excerpt follows:

General Brett: "Why you tell the Senator that as near as I know I don't know what the complaint is about because our—the dope I have on it is-wait a minute-let me look at my map-that the first location surveyed was a location down just north of Armstrong which I would say is about 10 miles south of Tuskegee-now the second location they found soil conditions down there unfavorable—the second location is up at-just north of Cheehaw—which is probably 6 miles north of Tuskegee—now I don't quite understand what the complaint might be-"

Hill's secretary: "I don't know—what that was all about."

General Brett: "Well, Senator Hill called me up personally and said that he had received a long petition that the Flight Field established for this colored training unit was too close to the white population of Tuskegee."

Hill's secretary: "Well, I wouldn't think that was too close—would you?"

General Brett: "Why now—of course, we—they may have surveyed other localities around Tuskegee but the number 2 location, the number 1 having been washed out is up north of Cheehaw—"

Hill's secretary: "Yes I know where that is. That sounds all right to me General—but I'll tell the Senator about it—"

General Brett: "All right—now you might tell the Senator that I just read a long letter from our Special Assistant Secretary of War Mr. Hastie who is intensely interested in the colored people, who claims that he notes that they are building separate barracks for white and separate barracks for colored people and separate barracks for white officers and he objects most strenuously—says that the whites must live with the blacks—"

General Brett: "Now you might tell Senator Hill on that this little thing he is talking about is only just one small phase of the whole problem. Oh yes, they are demanding that—they are demanding non-segregation."

Hill's secretary: "Well, I don't think that is going to work in the South."

General Brett: "Well, all right—I don't know why it should work in the North—I happen to be from Cleveland and I'm sure I don't want to live with a nigger—I don't know why there is any difference."[6]

Such was the situation at Tuskegee.

On March 15, 1941, the office of the adjutant general activated the 99th Pursuit Squadron at Chanute Field, Illinois. Several dozen black men arrived at Chanute Field, located outside of Rantoul, Illinois, on March 21, 1941. They were destined to be the ground and support crews that would provide support for the black pilots of the 99th Pursuit Squadron. By early May, approximately 250 black men were training at Chanute. A month later, 261 enlisted men were in various training programs—162 mechanics, 15 armorers, 46 technical and administrative clerks, 29 radio operators and mechanics, 5 weather observers, and 4 teletype operators.

The men were from all over the United States, but most came from the South and East. Seven members of the national championship Morris Brown College football team, of Atlanta, Georgia, had enlisted as a group. Many were college graduates. Henry Scott, the squadron's first sergeant, proudly said, "I have under my command over 200 of the finest young men in America. The manner that these men go about their respective duties and the effort that they put into

While the first class of African-American pilots was undergoing flight training at Tuskegee, the remaining officers and enlisted men of the 99th Pursuit Squadron were training at Chanute Field, located near Rantoul, Illinois. (USAF Collection, SDAN: 713965, Octave Chanute Museum Foundation.)

The on-base living conditions at Chanute were much better than those at Tuskegee. By June 1941, nearly three hundred African-American men were training to fill such vital support positions as mechanics, armorers, clerks, cooks, and radio operators. (USAF Collection, Octave Chanute Museum Foundation.)

their work show that these fellows really mean business, that they realize what the future holds in store for them."

The officers at Chanute, including Captain H. R. Maddux, squadron commander; Lieutenant Howell G. Craan; Lieutenant Robert C. Smith; and Lieutenant William F. Klum, were all white. With the exception of Klum, all were Southerners.

Chapter Four

Send Us Your Best Men

On July 19, 1941, Major General Walter R. Weaver, the commander of the Army's Southeastern Air Corps Training Command, addressed the black aviation cadets. He told them, "The eyes of your country and the eyes of your people are upon you. The success of the venture depends upon you." Weeks earlier, in an interview with a *Pittsburgh Courier* reporter, General Weaver spoke of the qualifications that would be required of the black officers for the proposed 99th Pursuit Squadron forming at Tuskegee Institute. Weaver went on to urge the black community to ignore any political, social, or economic considerations that might interfere in the choice of men to be commissioned as officers in the new organization. Promising that the military would provide the men with the best possible training and opportunities, he urged the enrollment of those with superior aptitudes and abilities, saying, "For God's sake, send us your best men. . . . For their sake and for our sake, give us your best."

By mid-August, the non-flying officer cadre of the 99th was close to being formed. Upon being commissioned, William D. Townes and William R. Thompson, attending the armament course at Chanute, would be the armament officers for the 99th. Nelson Brooks and Wardell W. Stevenson were being trained as communications officers. Elmer D. Jones and James L. Johnson, both from Howard University in Washington, D.C., would be commissioned as engineering officers after completion of an aircraft mechanics course. In addition to their advanced technical training, the six received training in military courtesy, drill practice, and military law. Four days each week, it was their responsibility to drill enlisted members of the 99th Pursuit Squadron. In early September, First

Lieutenant George W. Webb reported for duty at Chanute to serve as the squadron's adjutant.

After months of training at Chanute, it was time for the black enlisted men who would support the pilots of the 99th to head to Tuskegee. On October 9, 1941, orders were requested transferring the Air Base Group Detachment from Chanute Field to the Air Corps Advanced Flying School at Tuskegee. Thirteen non-commissioned officers and sixty-two privates were asked to arrive at Tuskegee no later than October 28. That action was superseded and it was not for another two weeks that orders would be issued. Special Order Number 263, dated November 7, 1941, directed "P-29 pursuant to authority contained in immediate action letter W. D. the Adjutant General's Office—Subject troops of the 99th Pursuit Squadron and its supporting Air Base Detachment dated November 3, 1941, the 99th Pursuit Squadron A. C. Colored unit and its support air base detachment of approximately 400 enlisted men is transferred from Chanute Field to Maxwell Field at the earliest practical date, for temporary change of station pending completion of facilities at Tuskegee, Alabama this unit will be moved to that place for permanent change of station."

In mid-September the squadron's medical officers reported for duty at Tuskegee. Six medical officers headed by Major DeHaven Hinkson were to be supported by a team of nurses, technicians, and aides staffing a twenty-five-bed hospital complete with operating room. It would be nearly six months before female nurses joined the medical team. In April 1942, five black nurses arrived in Tuskegee. First Lieutenant Della H. Raney served as the chief nurse; Second Lieutenants Mary Petty, Ruth Speight, Kathryn Bough, and Gertrude L. Scott arrived from Ft. Bragg. First Lieutenant Raney was as much a pioneer as the airmen to whom she would minister. The first African-American nurse to report for duty in World War II, she was also the first black to be appointed as a chief nurse and the first to be promoted to the rank of first lieutenant.

On September 2, Captain Benjamin O. Davis Jr. became the first member of class 42-C to solo. Shortly after, Marion Carter, George Spencer Roberts, Charles H. DeBow, Frederick H. Moore, Roderick C. Williams, Mac Ross, William H. Slade, Ulysses S. Pannell, and Lemuel R. Custis had their opportunity. John Anderson, Charles Brown, and Theodore Brown had already been eliminated from

First Lieutenant Della H. Raney was the first chief nurse at Tuskegee and one of the original group of five nurses to report for duty at the base. After serving with Tuskegee Army Air Field's medical detachment until June 1944, she was transferred to Fort Huachuca, Arizona. (USAF Collection, AFHRA, Maxwell AFB, AL.)

By January 1942, the original group of thirteen prospective pilots had been winnowed down— only six had completed the primary training. An additional aviation cadet would be eliminated during advanced training. Captain Benjamin O. Davis Jr., along with four others, made the final grade. (National Archives and Records Administration, #208-FS-872-3.)

the program; Carter, Moore, Williams, Slade, and Pannell eventually washed out as well. No explanations were given. The academic reports from Tuskegee listed the number of students reporting, number graduated, and the number eliminated. The stated reason for elimination was short—"failed in flying."[1] The total number of men who were eliminated from the flying program is uncertain. However, George L. Washington in his *The History of Military and Civilian Pilot Training of Negroes at Tuskegee, Alabama 1939-1945*, has estimated, "About 2,400 cadets entered Primary during the program." This would indicate that the rate of elimination was at least sixty percent. Research at the National Archives shows that the percentage varied widely by class; elimination was as low as ten percent and as high as sixty percent.

Harry Sheppard offered another reason for the high rate of elimination. He said, "We realized what the restrictions were and early on before the other outfits were formed, there was only one squadron to which graduates could go, which was the 99th, so the washout restrictions were very high and stringent at the time. I must say that the instructors didn't have much to do about that. It was strictly a numbers game. They were given the numbers and the check rides that were given the night before graduation were horrendous. People had already ordered their uniforms and had passed everything by way of training requirements and some were washed out."

Whatever the reasons, the rate of elimination of black flight cadets was inordinately higher—probably double—that of their white counterparts. This, of course, was not a surprise to those in the War Department. The Army had planned for a high elimination rate. In fact, a Schedule of Instruction, dated June 18, 1941, called for ten students to enter preflight training each five weeks. By the end of their four-phase training program nine months later, it was predicted that there would be only five graduates.

On January 5, 1942, C. Alfred Anderson wrote to Major General Henry H. Arnold. Anderson argued, "It is also a fact that about eighty percent of the cadets sent here to date have had no previous experience or interest in aviation and inasmuch as the first group will be put into responsible positions and will be representative, I believe that preference should be given to those with previous experience and interest, rather than 'first come, first served.'"[2]

General Arnold did not agree with Anderson's proposal. Ironically, Arnold's primary concern was one of "granting preferential treatment to graduates of the Civil Pilot Training Program." He wrote, "To grant priority to graduates of the Civil Pilot Training course at the expense of other persons who have not had the privilege of such previous training would work an undue hardship and penalize those individuals who were not fortunate enough to have

obtained previous flying training. As you will realize, such discrimination would violate the principle of fairness."³

How very odd that General Arnold would be so concerned about
discrimination and fairness when he had done everything in his
power to keep one segment of American citizens out of "his" Air
Corps. Equally ironic is the fact that only a month earlier, Captain
Noel F. Parrish had written a long letter to the commanding general at Maxwell Field with suggestions for changes in the manner of
selection of aviation cadets. He wrote:

> Suggesting improvement in selection of Negro aviation cadets.
> Problem of developing a Negro flying unit is unusual in many ways
> and differs in one important respect from problem of training and
> organization any other type of unit. Senior pilots of any other unit
> would be men of superior ability and experience. For a Negro unit
> such men are not available. Senior pilots will have very little advantage
> in experience. Great responsibilities will devolve upon them as a
> result of their having been trained a few months earlier than the
> majority of the pilots in the unit. It is obvious that these men should
> be of superior abilities and potentialities.
>
> Recommended that during initial period of Negro pilot training,
> selection of candidates be based upon some indication or demon-
> stration of superior ability rather than upon priority of application.
> Two methods by which this could be accomplished: (1) priority of
> assignment could be based upon comparative scores in adaptability
> rating for military aviation. (2) Such priority could be established by
> the selection of graduates from secondary phase of CPT program.
>
> Although this would be great improvement, believed that selection of
> next few classes from CPT secondary graduates would be simplest and
> most effective method of insuring that ranking pilots of forthcoming
> Negro unit will be men of superior ability. It has been learned by expe-
> rience that CPT training is not always very great benefit to students con-
> cerned. In each class, so far graduated from the Negro primary school,
> there has been one advanced CPT grad. In neither case has this indi-
> vidual been superior in ability or performance to certain other students
> in same class who have had no previous flying experience. Believed that
> using CPT advanced grads. for next few classes, standard of proficiency
> could be raised considerably and percentage of grads. greatly increased.
>
> Of last class of 10 to report to this flying school, 5 have never been in
> an airplane in their lives. Of 5 who have flown, 3 had their first flight
> as students in CPT course. Opportunities for Negroes to fly and
> become familiar with aviation in general are somewhat restricted.
> Although some men who have never seen an airplane may become

The first class of black pilots to graduate from the United States Army Air Corps advanced flying school posed for posterity with one of their training aircraft. Pictured left to right are: Charles DeBow Jr., Lemuel R. Custis, Mac Ross, Captain Benjamin O. Davis Jr., George S. "Spanky" Roberts, and Lieutenant R .M. Long, an instructor pilot. (Air University/HO, Maxwell AFB, AL.)

very good pilots, it is obvious that such a total lack of familiarity with aviation will result in a certain feeling of strangeness, fear, and lack of confidence, which in many borderline cases will prove decisive in the direction of failure. Also, many who are hopelessly unsuited for flying will make applications which they would not have made if they had taken a few flights or had become more familiar with the requirements of flying. These factors may result in a somewhat higher percentage of eliminations among Negro students. If next few classes could be selected from CPT Advanced grads. who have good records, it can be predicted with certainty that the Negro flying unit now in training will function in a manner superior to that which will be possible under any system which would postpone training of these to some indefinite future date and cause them to be so inferior in rank that it would be impossible to place them in positions of greatest responsibility. Furthermore, it is believed that classes of Negro students are small enough to permit more careful selection than is the present practice.[4]

By the end of the five-week primary training, only five cadets remained. Eight had washed out of the first class. Entering the final training phase were Lemuel R. Custis, a Howard University graduate; Charles DeBow, a Civilian Pilot Training Program pilot and graduate of Hampton Institute; Mac Ross, a West Virginia State College and CPTP graduate; George Spencer Roberts, another West Virginia State College graduate; and Captain Benjamin O. Davis Jr., who was almost thirty years old.

During the last week of July, the second class, 42-D, reported to Captain Davis at Tuskegee and immediately began the Army's five-week processing course. Members of class 42-D were William C. Boyd, Sidney P. Brooks, Benjamin A. Brown Jr., Earl L. Bundara, Charles W. Dryden, Clarence C. Jamison, Hercules L. Joyner, Emile J. Lewis, Harold E. McClure, Charles H. Moore, and James R. Smith. During training, all but Brooks, Dryden, and Jamison washed out.

Almost without exception, most of the men in the early classes of the flying training program possessed college degrees; many had even completed graduate school. As time passed and the war continued to demand ever increasing manpower, the men accepted into the flying training program were younger and had less extensive academic backgrounds. Those men lacking the necessary educational experience were placed into a special program. The 320th College Training Detachment, commanded by Captain Theodore H. Randall, was activated in early 1943. A self-contained unit headquartered at Tuskegee Institute, the 320th provided flight students with an intensive program of educational training, military discipline, and physical fitness. Civilian instructors from Tuskegee Institute taught cadets physical and military training, physics, history, English, geography, and mathematics. Operating from four brick buildings called the Emerys, more than a dozen officers and enlisted men handled all of the military roles.

The male students at Tuskegee Institute had little use for the military personnel assigned to the campus. Coeds found the men in uniform to be attractive. From time to time, groups of male students gathered to jeer the airmen. Although relations were frequently strained, the situation was controlled.

CTD students took their meals in the college cafeteria. The cadets published a four-page newspaper named the *CEE TEE DEE* and participated in extracurricular activities such as glee clubs and intramural sports. A ten-hour flight orientation course run by the general

Aviation cadets assigned to the College Training Detachment at Tuskegee Institute lived in one of four two-story brick buildings known as the Emery Dormitories. The buildings had been built in 1902 with funding provided by Julia Emery of London, England. (USAF Collection, AFHRA, Maxwell AFB, AL.)

Somehow, between academic studies, military training, and flight indoctrination, cadets in the College Training Detachment program found time to publish the four-page newspaper named the Cee Tee Dee. (USAF Collection, AFHRA, Maxwell AFB, AL.)

manager of Tuskegee Institute's department of aeronautics and a Civil Aeronautics Authority supervisor was held at Tuskegee Institute's Field Number One.

The actual flying training program was in four phases—preflight, primary, basic, and advanced flying. Primary training included classroom ground school and flying lessons at nearby Moton Field; advanced training concentrated on military flight, including forced landings, loops, rolls, night flying, and gunnery training.

At first, the training was dual; the instructor flew in the back seat. After approximately eight hours of dual instruction, a cadet was expected to solo. If an instructor lacked confidence in a student, he would set up a check ride to ascertain proficiency. Students could be washed out of the program for any infraction with no appeals process. It seemed as if the white flight instructors at Tuskegee Army Air Field used the wash-out process at will. One white trainer was known not very affectionately as "the washing machine," since he washed out so many black hopefuls.

The first airplanes used in the training program were Stearman PT-17 Kaydets, antiquated biplanes. Cadets then moved to BT-13 Valiants manufactured by Vultee, followed by North American AT-6s, complete with flaps, retractable landing gear, and a 650-horsepower engine. Following graduation, the final aircraft was the sleek P-40. It had a bad reputation for being a man-killer. The P-40 was a good but unforgiving airplane; pilots had to give it their undivided attention. A heavy airplane with sluggish controls, it was not an aircraft conducive to easy and clean maneuvers.

While the black cadets learned to fly in airplanes manufactured in American factories, defense contractors such as Boeing, Vultee, and Martin were desperately short of trained and skilled workers. When African-Americans applied for jobs, however, they were refused. To add insult to injury, the secretary of the Nashville branch of the NAACP, Mrs. E. W. Grant, was told to hold out ". . . only the slightest hope of employing them in menial capacities such as porters and cleaners." Giving in to pressure from several groups, including the National Negro Congress, the Glenn L. Martin Aircraft Company, the largest aircraft factory in the East, hired one hundred blacks.

The 99th flew frequent advanced training gunnery and bombing missions to Dale Mabry Field, Tallahassee, Florida. At Dale Mabry, the men had to sleep outdoors in pup tents. They were not allowed in the barracks.

Many different types of aircraft were used in flight training at Tuskegee Army Air Field, including BT-13s, PT-17s, AT-6s, and P-40s. (HQ AETC/HO, Randolph AFB, TX.)

Days at Tuskegee were long, starting at 6:00 A.M. with the call of reveille and ending late at night with the sound of taps being played on the bugle. The cadets were subjected to a system of hazing by upper classmen and forced to recite "dodo" verses or nonsensical poems such as: "Sir: The cow, she walks, she talks, she's full of chalk. A female version of the bovine species is highly prolific to the enth degree. . . ." The response to whether the cadet had had enough to eat was as follows: "Sir: My dietetic integrity admonishes me that I have reached that state of degradation which is consistent with my dietetic integrity. In other words, I've had enough to eat."

In the end, however, most cadets came to realize that the hazing was for their own good. Hazing and bracing were designed to instill

Undoubtedly, many aviation cadets considered the hazing and bracing they were forced to endure to be a form of sadistic torture. For the most part, however, hazing and bracing were used not as punishment but as a method to instill discipline. (Private Collection.)

discipline. Each cadet in the lower preflight stage of training was assigned to a cadet in upper preflight. The lower cadet slept on the upper bunk. If the advanced cadet wanted a glass of water at three o'clock in the morning, he would just reach up and ram the upper bed springs. The lower cadet would jump to do as he was told.

Recalling his first night as a preflight cadet, Maury Reid remembered, "At two-thirty in the morning the lights came on and in came a guy in all his flight gear. He was an advanced cadet. We were all called dummies and he said, 'What are you guys doing in here sleeping? I'm up there lost and I can't find my way home and you guys are down here sleeping with no consideration!' I looked at the guy and thought he was nuts. He said, 'All right, every dummy hit the floor,' meaning everybody get up. I thought this guy had lost his mind. I didn't move, so he reached up there and pulled me, mattress, the whole bed, down.

"And they would put you through a ritual. 'Get over there, dummy, and sit on a little red stool.' You'd prop yourself up against a pole in a sitting position, only there's no red stool there. And you're rigidly at attention. And he would say, 'Sit there.' Some other guy would come along, an upperclassman, and he would say, 'Mister, what are you doing sitting there in that position? Are you comfortable?' And the answer is yes sir, no sir, or no excuse sir. If you say no, you're in trouble. If you say yes, you're in trouble. If you say yes sir, he'd say, 'Okay, then stay there.' If you'd say no, he'd say, 'Okay, then cross your legs and get comfortable.' Now you're sitting on one leg trying to support yourself. The whole idea was your attitude. If you acted like you couldn't do it or you thought that they were nuts, then they would ride you to death.

"They had all kinds of things like that. Like making you get up in the middle of the night and putting on a raincoat next to your skin and taking a cold shower, just to see what your attitude was like. Some people washed out because they couldn't take it. And later on as you got into the heavy part of the training, you realized that discipline was critical."

The entrance into the flying program of James Hurd, a graduate of class 44-H-TE, was somewhat circuitous. Already a married first lieutenant, Hurd escaped from the normal hazing that flight cadets received. However, he was not totally immune. Commissioned as a member of a cavalry unit at Ft. Riley, Hurd wore high boots, britches, and a Sam Browne belt. He was frequently reminded, "We don't ride them here. We fly them here!"

Hurd remembered that it had taken him a long time to get into the program. "When I was an enlisted man in the 10th Cavalry, I had a couple of friends of mine at Tuskegee and one of them used to write and tell me everything that he did, when he first got in the airplane, when he first flew, when he first soloed. I was very eager to go. There were six of us enlisted men at the regimental headquarters of the U.S. 10th Cavalry, and we put in applications to go and the commander of the regiment said that he had insufficient personnel and that scrubbed the chance of my going, I thought. But I never gave up."

From his position as a supply sergeant in the headquarters and service troop, Hurd applied to and successfully graduated from officer candidate school. He recalled, "I was the only one of two hundred in my class that was black. Many times I was deaf to the magic word. I never let anything phase me while I went through. After I went to the 93rd Division, three months after I was there, I had impressed the commanding officer and I was promoted to a first lieutenant. He was called up on the carpet for doing this because there were three white second lieutenants that outranked me by maybe a month or two.

"There was a captain there who was his executive officer and just couldn't get ahead. People were red-lined on the payroll because they couldn't get the records straight. He happened to look on my record and see that I'd been a troop clerk. He asked me, 'Do you know anything about the Army regulations on payroll?' I said, 'Yes sir.' He said, 'I want you to take over here and work these things out.' In the first month, out of two hundred men, I had all of them paid, except three. . . . I really impressed him.

"Again, I put in for going to the Air Corps. The officer of the troop carrier called me and told me he couldn't approve my application because we were getting ready to go overseas and needed everybody. I said, 'Why are these people going?' He said, 'I don't know.' I said, 'This isn't fair; they want people at Tuskegee.' He said, 'If you can get away, all right with me.' He went on leave and since I was the executive officer and the ranking lieutenant in the outfit, they would not make me the acting commander while he was gone. They sent down an officer from division headquarters. He was there about three or four days and I went to him and told him I have a letter from the War Department to report to the nearest flight surgeon for a physical examination to go to the Air Corps. He said, 'I can't do without you. I just got down here.' I said, 'Listen, no one man is indispensable.' Eventually he said, 'Go ahead,' and I went in and took the examination. When my commander came back, he raised hell. I said, 'You told me that if I could go without your having to endorse this, then it was all right with you.' The orders came down and that's how I got into the Air Corps."

Chapter Five

Segregation Goes On . . .
Separate But Not Equal

While the training at Tuskegee was being conducted, black civilian leaders pushed for an integrated military. Walter White, the secretary of the NAACP, forwarded a letter to General George C. Marshall, chief of staff of the War Department, on September 22, 1941, suggesting that the War Department "organize a Volunteer Division open to all irrespective of race, creed, color or national origin." White informed Marshall that "such belief is based upon correspondence in this office and contacts which various members of our staff have had with student bodies ranging from the University of California to Compobelle Island, New Brunswick. A gratifying high number of young white Americans have expressed themselves as believing that racial segregation in the Army is undemocratic and dangerous to our national morale."

Walter White shared his letter to Marshall with P. L. Prattis, executive editor of the *Pittsburgh Courier*. Prattis sent his own letter to General Marshall, reinforcing the need for an integrated service. On December 29, he wrote:

> I think the War Department can and should activate this volunteer division as a first step in removing the barriers which divide Americans in the United States. The creation of such a division could be effected without friction and it would remove some of the sting from the affront to Negro citizens inherent in the present segregated set-up of the Army. . . . But more important at this time is the necessity for positive and dramatic action to demonstrate that America can rise above racial prejudice. There are millions of white Americans who deplore this prejudice. There are millions who would rejoice at the sight of evidence which showed the United States was busy removing this obstacle to complete unity and one hundred percent use of all our

resources, human and material, in the prosecution of the war. . . . What I wish to emphasize is that the creation of a volunteer division, open to all, would be as inspiring to white Americans as to black Americans.

Carl Murphy, president of the African American Newspapers, saw the situation more clearly and undoubtedly realized the administration would not change its position. Murphy wrote to White on December 26, 1941. He argued, "Without being unduly pessimistic, I do not believe General Marshall is going to do anything, nor the Government, until they are in due need and distress. You remember that the opposition to employment of troops in the Civil War did not fade away until the Union Troops had lost 23,000 dead and wounded at Gettysburg. When the dead and wounded begin to pile up in our hospitals, America will be glad to train her colored men for armed services."

Murphy had cause to be pessimistic. On January 8, 1942, Major General E. S. Adams of the adjutant general's office advised Walter White, "The Chief of Staff has requested that I acknowledge receipt of your letter relative to the organization of a volunteer division of the Army open to all without respect to race or color, and requesting a conference with regards to the matter. The War Department does not contemplate the organization of a division such as suggested, and consequently a conference on the subject is not deemed necessary."

On October 4, 1941, the third class of flying cadets reported for training at Tuskegee Institute. The ten new cadets brought the total number of aviation students to thirty. To say the least, these men represented the elite. Each man in class 42-E was either a college graduate or had been attending college when accepted for Air Corps duty. During October, the all-black 3rd Aviation Squadron trained at Savannah Army Air Field in Savannah, Georgia. Following basic training, they would be transferred to Tuskegee to provide ground support for the 99th.

Class 42-C graduated on March 7, 1942. On graduation day, Major General George Stratemeyer, Army Chief of Staff, reminded the men, "The vast unseen audience of your well-wishers senses that this graduation is an historic moment. . . . Future graduates of this school will look up to you as Old Pilots. They will be influenced profoundly by the examples you set." Colonel Frederick von H. Kimble, the commanding officer of the Air Corps Advanced Flying School, pinned silver wings on the chests of the five men as Stratemeyer presented diplomas. The ceremony was sedate, with little pomp and circumstance. On the podium with Stratemeyer and von Kimble were Major Noel Parrish, the director of flight training; Captain Roy E. Morse, director of the ground school; Lieutenant Robert Lowenburg, commandant of cadets; Lieutenant H. Hollis Hooks, the field's chaplain; and the Reverend Harry V. Richardson, chaplain of Tuskegee Institute.

Upon graduation, the five pilots were officially transferred to the 99th Fighter Squadron. The Army Air Corps found itself with a problem. An Air Corps group was normally comprised of three squadrons. What to do with the 99th became the overriding question. Because of segregation, the squadron couldn't be part of an already existing white group. With Captain Benjamin O. Davis Jr. as commander, the 99th Fighter Squadron stood alone. They might have been alone, but they were not without hope. Their fight song was full of spirit, a spirit soon to be sorely tested.

Fight! Fight! Fight! Fight!

Fight! Fight!
The fighting Ninety-Ninth!
We are the heroes of the night
To hell with Axis might

Rat tat! Rat-tat-tat
Round in planes we go
When we fly, Ninety-Ninth
This is how we go!

The same month as General Stratemeyer's speech, a new program was developed as a result of an influx of men from states north of the Mason-Dixon Line. What were referred to as "common sense" lectures became a requirement. Designed to orient the newcomers to the South, the lectures tutored the men in the local customs and Alabama laws in which Jim Crowism and segregation played a major role.

Two months later, in May 1942, another class graduated, and the 100th Fighter Squadron was activated with Lieutenant Mac Ross in command. At the time, the field consisted of 40 officers and 1,124 enlisted men. The garrison was made up of the 99th Fighter Squadron, 100th Fighter Squadron, 318th Air Base Squadron, 366th Materiel Squadron, 367th Materiel Squadron, 96th Maintenance Group, 83rd Interceptor Control Squadron, 907th Quartermaster Company, and the weather, communications, cadet, medical, signal corps, ordnance, and chemical warfare detachments.

That same month, Captain Benjamin O. Davis Jr. received a long overdue promotion. On May 13, he was promoted to the rank of major. Much to his and everyone else's surprise, only ten days later, he was further advanced to the rank of lieutenant colonel.

On April 18-21, 1942, Brigadier General Benjamin O. Davis Sr. had inspected the field. He concluded that ". . . the Air Corps Advanced Flying School, Tuskegee, Alabama, is being satisfactorily administered. . . .That although the morale of the troops at this station is satisfactory at present, it is believed that completion of the housing which has already been authorized, together with construction of the service club and guest house requested by the Commanding Officer, would make their morale superior."[1] General Davis could not have been more wrong in his assessment. Within a month after his inspection, approval for construction of a service club and guest house was denied.

By mid-1942, Tuskegee Army Air Field was home to approximately 217 officers and 3,000 enlisted men. Neither the 99th nor the 100th had received orders and were still undergoing daily training. Few Air Corps flying squadrons could claim that they were better trained than the 99th and 100th. On a weekly basis, new aviation cadets reported for instruction. The fourth class at Tuskegee graduated on July 3, 1942. Willie Ashley, George R. Bolling, William A. Campbell, Herbert E. Carter, Herbert V. Clark, Charles B. Hall, Allen G. Lane, Erwin B. Lawrence, Faythe A. McGinnis, Paul G. Mitchell, Louis R. Purnell, Graham Smith, Spann Watson, and James T. Wiley were assigned to the 99th, which now was at full strength with twenty-six pilots.

Demand for pilot training at Tuskegee was great. Because there was only one facility to train African-American pilots, a quota had to be established; no more than two hundred black men could go through the training program each year. Hundreds applied for the rare berths at Tuskegee; just as many men ended up on a long waiting list. Because of the draft, many were inducted into the army and never received their chance to fly. At the same time, the War Department desperately needed pilots and advertised through newspapers, posters, and rallies. The demand, of course, was for white pilots, not black, and the young African-Americans waited, many in vain.

In August 1942, leaders of the NAACP wrote to Secretary of War Henry Stimson with several complaints about the treatment of black men who were attempting to serve their country in time of war.

Walter White reasoned that the Army Air Corps' quota system in use at Tuskegee Army Air Field was highly unfair and unproductive when the country needed fighting men so badly. Many black men who applied for the few slots available to them found themselves on a long waiting list with no hope of call-up for more than a year. White asked that the quota system be abolished and that the waiting list for air cadet slots be kept to a maximum of ninety days.

Part of the problem was that Tuskegee could accommodate only so many cadets. In addition, only fighter pilots were being trained. White pilots were being trained at several facilities across the United States. Moreover, white cadets had several alternatives available to them. Since they could also be trained as bomber or transport pilots, there was a need for bombardiers, navigators, gunners, and other positions. None of these options were as yet available to young black men hoping to become part of the Army Air Corps. Walter White urged Stimson to open the ranks of bomber pilots to black men.

By mid-August the 99th Fighter Squadron was put on alert for shipping out. Following an inspection of both the base and the 99th, Colonel P. L. Sadler wrote to von Kimble, "I talked to Washington this morning and while they did not tell officially definitely, I believe there will be a slight delay in movement; just how long I do not know."[2] It would be a long wait.

As additional black pilots continued to be trained, the 301st and 302nd Fighter Squadrons were formed. Together with the 99th and 100th, these four fighter squadrons would eventually comprise the 332nd Fighter Group. Activated at Tuskegee on October 13, 1942, the group's motto was "Spitfire"; its call sign was "Percy." Lieutenant Colonel Samuel Westbrook, a white officer, took command. When the 332nd Fighter Group was transferred to Selfridge Field, Michigan, on March 27, 1943, Westbrook went with them. He remained as commander until Colonel Robert R. Selway replaced him as commander of the group in June 1943. Another change of command took place on October 7, 1943, when Lieutenant Colonel Benjamin O. Davis Jr. took over.

During the early part of September 1942, the War Department authorized the decoration of airplanes and tanks with individual designs in an effort to increase the morale of fighting units. Designs had to be submitted to the office of the quartermaster general for approval. The insignia of the 332nd Fighter Group featured a panther on a shield and was approved on January 15, 1943. The 99th did

While waiting to be shipped overseas, pilots flew their P-40s in the skies over Selfridge Field, Michigan, honing bombing and gunnery techniques that would soon be used against the enemy in Europe. (USAF Collection, AFHRA, Maxwell AFB, AL.)

not receive approval for a unit insignia until June 24, 1944. The design featured a golden-orange winged panther superimposed over a medium blue disc.

Secretary of War Stimson conducted a lengthy interview with the press in November 1942, in which he claimed that blacks would be allowed to fill ten percent of available slots in the military. When asked if this would filter down to the Air Corps, he responded, "No."[3]

The year 1942 was drawing to a close; the trained and ready-for-combat 99th still awaited orders. The pilots and support personnel were all aware that their success or failure as a unit would be a critical factor in the future of black Americans in highly skilled positions in the Army Air Corps as well as civil aviation. At a field day held at Tuskegee in December, Lieutenant Colonel Davis told the audience that thus far the program at Tuskegee was a success and that cadets at the segregated Tuskegee Army Air Field flying school were performing on a par with white cadets at other flying schools. According to the *Chicago Defender*, Davis closed by telling the group, "My greatest desire is to lead this squadron to victory against the enemy."

As 1943 opened, Tuskegee Army Air Field was described as a "Hell

Hole" of prejudice. Black leaders and newspapermen charged that discrimination and oppression were all-pervasive. This was common knowledge among the War Department, the army, and certainly the white officers in command of the base. However, because they were largely responsible for the Jim Crow practices and wanted the segregation to continue, they refused to do anything to correct the situation. Meanwhile, black pilots felt the frustration and inwardly railed against it, but bit their tongues and suffered the humiliation because of the overriding importance of the success of the program.

The man responsible for the "Hell Hole" of prejudice was undoubtedly Colonel Frederick von Kimble, who did everything in his power not only to enforce, but to develop a policy of segregation. There was no socializing between whites and blacks. On von Kimble's order, no black officers were allowed to join or visit the officer's club. Promotions of blacks were nonexistent; it was obvious when young whites were promoted over blacks with years of exemplary military service.

When the black officers protested the segregated "colored" and "white" toilets, von Kimble responded that they were "going to take these signs and like them." Lieutenant Colonel John T. Hazard, executive officer at Tuskegee, was described as von Kimble's hatchet man assigned to carry out the ulcerous rules of von Kimble's personal punitive policy of racism. He was characterized as an "impoverished, not-well-trained former Civilian Conservation Corps officer . . . given to explosive cursing tantrums of temper."[4]

While von Kimble was viewed as the focal point, it was charged that the racism came from the top of the military hierarchy. The problem was laid directly at the feet of General Henry H. "Hap" Arnold, commanding officer of the Army Air Forces. The argument can be made that General Arnold believed that while segregation was evil, it was necessary for the good of the service. However, there was more to his beliefs than the good of the service; Arnold believed blacks to be inferior. In a memo to the War Department dated May 31, 1940, Arnold wrote that "Negro pilots cannot be used in our present Air Corps units since this would result in having Negro officers serving over white enlisted men creating an impossible social problem."

On January 14, 1943, after commanding Tuskegee almost from its inception, Colonel von Kimble was relieved of duty as the commanding officer. He was not punished for his ill-conceived policy of segregation. Instead, he was transferred to another post and promoted to the rank of brigadier general. Morale at Tuskegee seemed to improve almost overnight when word got out that von Kimble was leaving. It would be nearly a year before John Hazard was transferred.

While not excusing the behavior of men such as von Kimble and Hazard, the reality of the racial situation in 1943 in America needs to be kept in mind. White Alabama residents were unhappy with the airfield at Tuskegee and the influx of several hundred young black men, many from the North, with access to guns. The white commanders undoubtedly bent over backwards to placate the white civilians, and in their zeal, may have come to enjoy their power a little too much.

White men in the government and higher military positions were not necessarily mean-spirited. Rather, since segregation was a fact of civilian life, it was believed that segregation of the military was the most efficient means to manage the military. However, there were some individuals who went far beyond this policy. They were racists, pure and simple, and would do whatever was in their power to keep blacks out of the United States Army Air Corps.

Colonel Noel F. Parrish, the former training officer, replaced Colonel von Kimble as base commander in February 1943. He was a godsend. A flier's flier, Parrish had entered the Army as a private in Troop F of the 11th Cavalry on July 30, 1930. A year later, he was appointed as a flying cadet at March Field, California. After finishing advanced training at Kelly Field in July 1932, Parrish served one year of active duty with the 13th Attack Squadron at Fort Crockett, Galveston, Texas. He later served at Chanute Field and Barksdale Field and eventually became a primary flying instructor at Randolph Field, Texas. When the Civilian Pilot Training Program was inaugurated, Parrish was assigned to duty at the Chicago School of Aeronautics until his transfer to the Primary Flying School at Tuskegee Institute.

His first action as commander was to have the "colored" and "white" signs removed from Tuskegee Army Air Field. He brought black celebrities and entertainment to the field in an effort to improve sagging morale. Ella Fitzgerald, Cab Calloway, Joe Louis, and Lena Horne were frequent visitors to Tuskegee.

The score on Colonel Noel Parrish seems to be evenly divided. Many consider him to be almost as important as Colonel Benjamin O. Davis Jr. in the success of the flight training program at Tuskegee Army Air Field. Others claim that he was little more than a smooth-talking politician who through syrupy words was able to get the black

Originally assigned as commanding officer of the 66th Army Air Force Training Detachment at Tuskegee Institute in 1941, Colonel Noel F. Parrish, third commander of Tuskegee Army Air Field, was a keen student of the human mind. (USAF Collection, AFHRA, Maxwell AFB, AL.)

Lieutenant Fred Minnis, special services officer, arranged social activities, including dinners, dances, and celebrity visits, at Tuskegee Army Air Field in an attempt to boost morale. Most famous African American entertainers of the day visited the base to perform for the men. (Private Collection.)

airmen to do his bidding—the quintessential paternalistic master or benevolent father figure taking care of his ignorant and incompetent children.

On September 30, 1944, the *Pittsburgh Courier* said, "Foppish, polished, affable Colonel Noel F. Parrish, Commanding Officer of Tuskegee Army Air Force, has shaken more hands and flashed more smiles than a Republican Presidential candidate in the early days of the New Deal." The newspaper scathingly went on to describe Parrish as a clever, well-spoken man who had fooled many African-Americans into believing that he had their interests at heart, while in fact working against them. The article described Parrish as the consummate politician and as unctuous as a snake oil salesman.

Jack Day, a special correspondent to the *Pittsburgh Courier,* claimed that blacks at Tuskegee Army Air Field made similar comparisons between Colonel Parrish and Colonel von Kimble who had preceded him as commanding officer at the base. Day argued that while von Kimble made his dislike for blacks apparent, Parrish was more covert, insidiously hiding his prejudices. In a series of special articles for the newspaper, Day wrote that Tuskegee Army Air Field was being run by a group of white officers who sought only their own advancement, caring nothing for the men under their command. He charged that not one black officer could live off post, and conversely, not one white officer including the commander lived on post. Day also wrote about one black officer who made an analogy to white lords arriving at the plantation each morning and departing each evening.

A newspaper is in business to sell papers. The articles about Parrish were little more than a cheap attempt to boost circulation and toe the line with the NAACP. The *Pittsburgh Courier* was a united force with the NAACP, and the NAACP was, while one hundred percent behind the black fliers, also one hundred percent against segregation. Among the fliers who went through the aviation program at Tuskegee, Parrish is as beloved a figure as any.

Parrish was indeed a unique man. Knowing that as a staunch advocate of the program at Tuskegee and a strong supporter of the black airmen, he was almost certainly doing irreparable harm to his military career, what motivated him? Parrish was a member of the first class of aviators to graduate from Randolph Field in Texas in 1932. A high school graduate at fourteen and a graduate of Rice University at eighteen, Parrish nearly flunked out of flying school because of a personality conflict with his first instructor. Contrary to military procedure, Parrish managed to be assigned to a different instructor and things went well thereafter. Never forgetting his own experience, he wanted to satisfy himself that every aviation cadet at Tuskegee Army Air Field got a fair break.

Much of Parrish's early support of the flying program and his agitation for equality and integration were probably based on pure pragmatism. Dr. Florence Parrish-St. John, Noel Parrish's widow, elaborated by saying, "He realized that the U.S. military forces were supporting two air forces. There was a black one and a white one. He was forever contacting people in Washington, people all over the country. He was contacting the black newspapers for support, the politicians, the people in positions of influence everywhere because he wanted to know what they were thinking. He wanted to influence them to tell them what was happening there and to share what he had found out. So he was in touch all over the country with this variety of groups and he realized that there were these two air forces and he thought, 'What a waste.' So he said that he knew he could never sell the merging of these entities on the basis of what it should be merged under, which is simply the use of your resources. He had to put it strictly on the basis of a dollar. Nobody in the War Department wanted to get to this point. So he flew up there in his airplane, to Washington, and he proposed that this be done and of course it eventually was. He'd have gotten fired from today's Air Force for some of the things that he did."

A rational thinker, Parrish tried to view things as analytically and impartially as possible. Dr. Parrish-St. John explained that her husband's "assessment was that von Kimble had no understanding whatsoever of black people, he had no comprehension of how to even be comfortable with them. Consequently, he [Parrish] went in with as blank a piece of paper toward Kimble as could be expected because he wanted to give the man, if there was an advantage to give him, he was certainly willing to do it. From my conversations with him, I recall Noel saying that von Kimble saw his role as what he had always done, which was to be an officer, and to, my words now, to order people around, and to be the top commander and he wanted to continue that and that didn't leave room for dealing with a new situation, a different goal, a different organization in a sense of organizing to achieve this goal.

"Von Kimble also had partialities that Noel felt were inappropriate for this environment. In my opinion, von Kimble was very likely what we would call a racist. I never heard Noel use that term when he was describing him. I said to him one time, 'What did you do when you first took over as commander?' He had been the director of training. I said, 'What did you do? It was a different job? What did you do different as a commander?' He said, 'Well, what I did was to find the lowest ranking person that had committed an infraction and zap him. You just have to do something to establish the fact that you're the commander.' He didn't really want to hurt anybody, but he just felt that he needed something on the book. He needed an example.

"Also Noel either rescinded or just ignored some of the rules that von Kimble had established on base and Noel went where the men went. He ate all of his meals with the guys and when people came in for entertainment he was there. Somebody told me he went to all of the ball games and he was very proud of all the activities. Noel was very comfortable with who was on the base. That never bothered him at all. He was interested in flying and this is what you shared. They were all interested in flying; this is what they wanted to do. His idea was, 'Let's get this show on the road.' I said, 'Well, did you ever think that you didn't want that assignment?' He said, 'No, it never did occur to me. That was my job.' And that was the attitude that he took in with him."

Of Parrish, James Hurd, a member of the 617th Squadron of the 477th Bombardment Group, said:

"I thought the world of him. I liked Parrish a whole lot better after. We became very close friends. His wife is the one that designated me to write up the program for the Noel F. Parrish Award and design it and so forth. . . . Parrish, I recall what impressed me a lot is the fact that they put out this order down while I was in school there in 1943 and 1944, that there was to be no discrimination in the dining halls and food service, and there was at the time. Of course, he even went to the Pentagon to talk about it because of the outfit that he had. None liked it, so to speak. And they told him 'You're going to carry out the regulations and that's it.' So when he came back, he had a meeting with the officers and he said, 'Now in the South, we have' . . . he was from Texas . . . 'we have a policy that if you eat with somebody, then you're their very good friends, and I know that a number of you' . . . he was talking to the white officers . . . 'some of you follow that policy very closely there and you don't want the dining together and this kind of thing but you will be dining together and we will no longer have the little dining facility in the post exchange.' In there, the white officers had a little dining room and they preferred that, rather than eat in the big dining room with all of the rest of the officers. And he just laid it on the line for them and he said, 'We will comply with that regulation and I want all of you to know now that if there are any officers here who feel that they cannot because of the policy that they are bringing up, and want to get out of the service, I will do my best to help you get out.' Of course, no one wanted to get out at that time. But he laid it on the line."

Fortunately for history, often by coincidence, certain people are in a certain place and time. Parrish's entrance as commander of Tuskegee was a turning point for the program. Things had been going from bad to worse. Morale among the troops was at an all-time low. It was unarguably a pivotal point. Did Parrish, in fact, save the program? Probably not, but if Parrish had been like von Kimble, the program at Tuskegee might never have continued. He gave the black men hope and inspiration. Other commanders didn't want them. Parrish embraced them and prepared them for duty outside Tuskegee Army Air Field.

In Colonel John Suggs' opinion, "If Parrish hadn't arrived at that particular time, the outcome may have been totally different."

On April 8, 1943, largely in response to the January resignation of William Hastie, Under Secretary of War Patterson put out an in-depth defense of the Army Air Forces' policy regarding race. Although long, it serves to fully bring to light the policies of the War Department.

In answer to questions from Wilbur La Roe Jr., chairman of the committee on civic affairs of the Washington Federation of Churches, Patterson declared that the number of blacks in the military would be in direct proportion to their percentage of the population. He went on to elaborate:

> Negro organizations are being established in each major branch of the service, combatant, as well as non-combatant. Assignment to the air and ground forces must be in the same proportion as stated above. The same modern facilities have been provided at the Tuskegee Air Force Flying School for the training of Negro pilots as are provided at the schools which train white pilots. At the Officer Candidate school and the technical schools Negroes attend the same schools as white candidates.

> The army follows the general principle that it can attain its maximum strength only if its personnel is properly placed in accordance with the capabilities of individuals. All enlisted men on their entry

into the service are graded by the army general classification test and the mechanical aptitude test. Because of the proportionately larger number of highly technical duties required of men in the Air Force, War Department policy provides that 55 percent of them qualify by passing the G. C. test with a grade of 100 or better. The remaining 45 percent assigned to the Air Forces who do not meet this qualification are assigned to comparatively unskilled jobs. Experience to date has shown that while 47 percent of all white enlisted men meet this qualification, the same minimum standard is met by less than 10 percent of the Negroes inducted. As a consequence, in order to absorb the same proportion of Negroes as exists in the total population, a small percentage of them who enter the Air Corps are qualified for entrance into the technical school, the large majority must be assigned to unskilled tasks.

It is true that Negroes are so far being given the opportunity for training on single engine pursuit ships. It was believed wise to start by training a fighter group, where only one airman per plane is involved, namely the pilot. To train a heavy bomber group it is necessary to train in addition to the pilot, a navigator, a bombardier, an aerial gunner, a radio operator, an additional mechanic and several other technicians. Because of the technical and other features present in flying, it was decided to proceed toward the formation of the more complicated units after having gained experience with the simpler units. While white officers have charge of training at Tuskegee, Negroes will be given command duties as soon as they qualify for them. There is one officers' mess at Tuskegee, to which all officers are eligible. However, it is customary for the white officers when they do not eat at home, to use the facilities of the Post Exchange. These facilities are available to all military personnel on the post.

The reason for establishment of Aviation Squadrons (Separate) is given above. They provide a place for men in the Air Forces who do not have the qualifications for more technical work. The duties they perform are to a large extent labor and housekeeping jobs that have to be done at every Air Force base. While there are no white units actually named "Aviation Squadrons (Separate)," there are many white headquarters squadrons which perform the same type of duties at Air Force installations. A sufficient number of qualified Negro applicants have been secured and are in training to support the Negro flight group now in training. When new Negro units are organized, there will be opportunity for additional weather officers. No Negroes qualified to be service pilots have yet been used by the Air Forces. To date there have been few applicants for this duty, but this number will increase as individuals now attending school become qualified. The use of qualified Negro service pilots is now under study. Until February 1, Negro medical officers at Tuskegee were not in residence at the School of Aviation Medicine at Randolph Field, but since that date Negro medical officers have been assigned to residence study there. The schooling was originally covered by extension courses and commutation to Maxwell Field. When this situation was called to the attention of Air Force headquarters, the change was made in order that Negro medical officers might have the same opportunity as white medical officers. The Air Forces are now bringing the Negro fighter squadron to strength, including ground crew personnel, and will train them to carry out their combat mission. The question of training additional units, including a bomber group is now under study. The Air Force will continue to use Aviation Squadrons (Separate). The squadrons will be constantly screened to secure personnel for technical training.[5]

Squadron members, black newspaper editors, unions, and civic leaders openly questioned why a highly trained aviation unit remained grounded when it was so badly needed in Europe. An April 25, 1943, edition of the *Chicago Sunday Tribune* echoed those sentiments when it ran a photograph of the recently graduated pilots of the 99th Fighter Squadron and issued an editorial detailing the extensive training the African-Americans had received. The newspaper bemoaned the laggardly pace of training and utilization of the men, saying, "A source of strength to the nation is being neglected, and there will be no patience with that."

A top-ranking general of the Army Air Forces speaking anonymously to a reporter from the *Pittsburgh Courier* said, "We have trained these boys all right. They are the best trained flyers in America today. They are really ready for combat but the trouble is that those guys up at Washington can't make up their minds what to do with them."

No one verbally supported the black pilots of the Tuskegee Experience more than Eddie Rickenbacker, ace of the World War I 94th Aero Squadron. In a March 1943 speech, Rickenbacker, president of Eastern Air Lines, said, "The 99th must make good! They have to make good, because they are conscious of the seriousness of our struggles and of the opportunities involved if they are successful. I have much hope for the 99th Pursuit Squadron." In this same speech, Rickenbacker stated that "there always are places for Americans who work hard."[6] But that was just so much rhetoric. After the war, when black pilots applied for flying jobs at Eastern, as with other airlines, they got nowhere.

A flight of P-40 fighter aircraft practiced combat maneuvers at Selfridge Field, Michigan, in 1943. The pilots of the 99th Fighter Squadron would be equipped with the P-40 Warhawks following their arrival in North Africa. (National Archives and Records Administration, #208-VM-1-5-69G.)

Chapter Six

To War,
to War . . . Finally

After spending the winter of 1942 and most of the spring of 1943 awaiting orders, the 99th Fighter Squadron finally received word that it would be moving out. Dated April 1, 1943, orders directed that "the 99th Fighter Sq with assigned Units (Personnel listed) are trfd for this sta TAFS Tuskegee Ala to Camp Shanks NY and WP thereto o/a April 3, 1943 reporting on arrival to the co threat for dy, change of sta is permanent."

On April 2, 1943, after several false alarms, the pilots and crews of the 99th left Tuskegee Army Air Field by train headed to New York. The squadron boarded the S.S. *Mariposa*, a retrofitted cruise ship, for the Atlantic crossing on April 15. Four hundred members of the 99th, along with thirty-five hundred white troops, steamed out of a Brooklyn, New York, port destined for North Africa. Lieutenant Colonel Benjamin O. Davis Jr. was in command of all troops—white and black—on board the ship. Sidney P. Brooks, James L. McCullin, Erwin B. Lawrence, Paul Mitchell, and Sherman White, all fighter pilots in that first group to travel to Europe, would never return, casualties of the war.

By the time the *Mariposa* docked at Casablanca, Morocco, on April 24, the battle for North Africa was almost over. The men of the 99th recalled the weather upon their arrival as warm and beautiful. While they awaited the arrival of the pilot boat to take them ashore, they watched local men in small boats diving for coins tossed in the water. Once ashore, they marched some three miles to the camp area, where they enjoyed their first meal on African soil—canned C-rations warmed over a small fire or by wrapping a can with wire and lowering it into a fifty-gallon drum of hot water. That night, the men slept on raised platforms, fearing the companionship of snakes.

From Casablanca, the 99th traveled to Oued N'ja, near Fez, arriving on April 29. Their camp was segregated from white troops by government policy as well as distance. Tents were their homes; the mess was out of doors—living conditions at Oued N'ja were horrible. Each day Colonel Benjamin O. Davis Jr. kept his men busy. Enlisted men worked on readying aircraft and building a base. Pilots took off from a crude dirt strip, putting their old Curtiss-Wright-manufactured P-40 Warhawks through their paces.

Of Oued N'ja, Davis said: "Our stay there was probably our most pleasant stay overseas. Most cordial relations existed between the members of the squadron and the members of the fighter-bomber group nearby. The pilots of the two organizations engaged in impromptu dogfights to determine the relative superiority of the P-40 and the A-36. Enlisted men of the two groups got along together very well in all types of athletic contest and other means of recreation.

"The town of Fez was found to be one of the most delightful spots that any of us had ever visited. One unusual feature of our stay there was that members of my organization and members of their organizations visited the town of Fez every single night for over a period of a month, and not one unpleasant incident arose.

"The officers of the squadron were made socially secure in the town by the visit of Josephine Baker. Miss Baker insisted on presenting several different groups of our officers to the prominent French and Arab families in the town. All in all, Miss Baker was very largely responsible for our most pleasant social relations in the town of Fez.

"It was during our stay here that four P-39 pilots, whom we had met on the boat on the way over, came to visit us. They were ferrying some P-39[s] from Oran to Casablanca and en route they, of their own volition, simply stopped over to pay us a visit. I mention this simply to indicate that a considerable bond existed among those who fly regardless of color or race.

"Our equipment was of the best. We ferried in twenty-seven brand new P-40s and all of us experienced for the first time the thrill of flying a brand new airplane. Lieutenant Colonel [Philip] Cochran—the Flip Corkin of *Terry and the Pirates*—was our most capable instructor. He imbued all of us with some of his own very remarkable fighting spirit, and in addition to that he taught us what to do and what not to do in aerial combat.

Marking their arrival in North Africa, Lieutenant Colonel Benjamin O. Davis Jr. and the staff officers of the 99th Fighter Squadron were photographed at Fez, Morocco. (National Archives and Records Administration, #111-SC-184968.)

"We had two other instructors who were with us until we left for Tunisia, Major Keyes and a Captain Fechler. Both of these officers had extensive combat training, one in England and one in the African campaign, and both had just been returned to the training command for instructional purposes. These officers worked unceasingly to make us ready for the real test and all of us felt very grateful for their efforts."

The P-40s flown by the 99th were not top-of-the-line equipment. Severely criticized by the Truman Report, the low-altitude fighter had limited firepower and poor protective armor. Produced at a cost of slightly over fifty thousand dollars per copy, the P-40s were powered by a 1,200-horsepower Allison engine. It had a cruising speed of approximately three hundred miles per hour with a ceiling of thirty-two thousand feet. While not the perfect airplane, it was attractive because it was available; nearly fourteen thousand P-40s with varying modifications were produced. Many of these had been given to Allied countries. Britain was the recipient of nearly one hundred P-40L models called the Kittyhawk; many of these had been returned to the United States and ended up in North Africa with the 99th. The armament consisted of four to six .50-caliber machine guns and one five-hundred-pound bomb. The P-40s were not the best aircraft, but the 99th made the best of a bad situation, as they had from the beginning.

After the arrival of the 99th in North Africa, there was still doubt in the minds of the higher-ups that the squadron was capable of combat flying. According to Louis Purnell, "They sent a man up to test us by the name of Philip Cochran, who in the Milt Caniff comic strip *Terry and the Pirates* is Flip Corkin. So he came over to our air base and he cruised up in a jeep in a mixed uniform. He had on a poplin shirt and winter trousers, and a garrison cap. He asked for Davis. He said 'Where's Davis?' We looked at him, and he was a major at that time, Philip Cochran was. Davis was a lieutenant colonel. And he said, 'Go and get Davis.' And he said, 'What are you guys doing? We didn't send you over here to police up North Africa.' We were actually picking up trash. He said, 'Go in there and get Davis and tell him to get out here.' None of us were going to do that. So he got out of his jeep and went into the orderly room and finally found Davis. He chose four of us to go up with him and he gave us our baptism in what he thought was combat flight activity. We followed him through. It was a rat race and he came back down. And one of the things he did to start us off on a wayward journey was to mark us as natural-born dive-bombers. He himself was the commander of a dive-bombing outfit and that's where they kept us, down in the ditches, doing the dirty work, the short calls. That's when we moved from the staging area where Philip Cochran was, up to the combat area of Fardjouna.

"The people we flew with were reluctant to fly with us. Spann Watson was off on the first flight of four to go with the white fellows who flew with the 33rd Fighter Group and they briefed them almost separately. They looked at the black pilots and said, 'You boys keep up.' And that was our briefing. Otherwise we didn't come in contact with them, other than to join them in the mornings and attend briefings and critiques after the flights. We weren't going in town so we wouldn't meet them in there, but the hostility was there—it was just latent. We got along as best we could. But little things would flash out every once in a while.

"After my fiftieth mission with the 99th, I came back and I went back to Europe and went over to the 332nd. On the day before Christmas, the bombers were forced to land at the fighter base. They were snowed out down in southern Italy. Up around where we were, the field was open. At that time we had a stand-down. All the enlisted men on those bomber crews, they found shelter somehow or other with our men, and at that time I was the censor officer, the mail censoring officer for enlisted men's mail.

"I picked up this letter; it was from one of the bomber crews, a gunner. And it said, 'This is the time, just before Christmas, when we all should be together. I'm not even at my own airfield. I'm at a nigger airfield, sleeping in nigger beds, and eating nigger food.' So he signs it Sergeant Schwartz. I picked up the thing and gave it to the adjutant and he gave it a cursory look. I looked at that thing and I said, 'If I were to take this outside and show it to somebody, there would be a riot here tomorrow.'

"Two mornings after, when the weather cleared up, I commandeered a jeep, and meanwhile I found out the tent where this guy slept. I met him on the line getting into his plane where he was a crew member. I talked to him. 'Did you forget anything, Sergeant?' 'No.' I asked him several other questions and he responded with noes and yeahs. So I said, 'Sergeant, if you see the bars on my shoulders and the stripes on your sleeves, you're to answer me yes sir, no sir. Do you understand?' So he looked at me, and I said, 'By the way, Sergeant, it wasn't so bad after all, sleeping in nigger beds, staying

During his two tours of duty in North Africa and Europe, Captain Louis Purnell encountered numerous instances of racial prejudice. Despite the heroic accomplishments of the black airmen, examples of bigotry and hatred were never far away. (Private Collection.)

at a nigger field, and eating nigger food.' And I said, 'I'll see you up there.' I turned away and I didn't even see the expression on his face. The prejudices were still there. But you had to come in contact with those individuals. There was a lot we didn't know about, but it was always there."

After a month at Oued N'ja, the 99th moved from Morocco to Fardjouna, on the Cape Bon Peninsula near Tunis. Fardjouna was a former German airdrome littered with crashed aircraft left behind by the fleeing enemy. In June 1943, members of the 99th got their wish—they were finally going into combat. Benjamin Davis' pilots spent much of the month bombing gun positions on Pantelleria Island. Armed with five-hundred-pound bombs with instantaneous fuses, the pilots in the P-40s would fly over at an altitude of ten thousand feet, dive to three thousand feet, and release their bombs. Their squadron call sign was "Beauty"; their biggest concerns were flak and mechanical problems. There were occasional unidentified planes, but little or no enemy aircraft.

The 99th was now attached to the 33rd Fighter Group, commanded by Colonel William "Spike" Momyer. Their first real combat assignment was to fly escort for B-17 and B-24 bombers that were bombing the Italian island of Pantelleria. The four-engine B-17 Flying Fortress, built by Boeing, was literally a flying fortress. Capable of carrying almost nine tons of bombs, the B-17 was armed with twelve .50-caliber machine guns. Consolidated Aircraft Corporation's B-24, nicknamed the Liberator, carried similar armament. Economists have estimated that the United States spent $45 billion for the production of airplanes during World War II. Construction of the heavy bombers was part of that package.

On the morning of June 9, 1943, the 99th was escorting twelve Douglas A-20 Havoc attack bombers on a mission to Pantelleria. As the bombardiers screamed out "bombs away," they jettisoned their bombs at an altitude of three thousand feet and were rallying for their return to base. A group of German fighters pounced on them from out of nowhere. Eight American fighters stayed with the bombers while five P-40s of the 99th went in pursuit of the four German Messerschmitt Me-109s. Lieutenants Charles Dryden, Leon Roberts, Lee Rayford, Spann Watson, and Willie Ashley committed the unpardonable—they broke from formation. It was an action that would come back to haunt them.

The five P-40 pilots had exceeded their mission of escorting and

While pilots in sleek fighter aircraft provided coverage for the bombers from onslaughts by waves of German aerial attackers, they could do nothing to prevent damage by the heavy and deadly German antiaircraft fire. (Private Collection.)

protecting the bombers. In response to the enemy action, the Americans had pursued the attacking Messerschmitts, seeking to engage them in further combat. In the *Pittsburgh Courier* of July 3, 1943, Dryden recalled, "They broke off and climbed above us and stayed there waiting for another chance to dive on us. We stayed around until the controller ordered us home."

The Messerschmitt Me-109 has been claimed by some aviation historians to be one of the greatest single-seat fighter planes ever to be produced by any country. Approximately thirty-five thousand Me-109s were built by Willy Messerschmitt's company during World War II. Bayerische Flugzeugwerke AG's E-series 109, widely used against the Americans, was powered by a Daimler Benz 1,100-horsepower DB 601A inverted V-12-cylinder engine, producing a top speed of 354 miles per hour. The armament included a pair of synchronized machine guns with a thousand rounds of ammunition each and two 20-millimeter Oerhkon cannons, each carrying sixty rounds, mounted in the wings.

The Me-109 was one of the premier German fighters; black airmen would see plenty of them firsthand before the end of the war. Other Tuskegee pilots taking part in the history-making first combat mission that day included First Lieutenants Lemuel R. Custis, Clarence C. Jamison, Sherman W. White, and Second Lieutenants Charles B. Hall, George R. Bolling, William A. Campbell, Herbert V. G. Clark, Willie H. Fuller, James B. Knighten, Allen G. Lane, Erwin B. Lawrence, Paul G. Mitchell, John W. Rogers, Graham Smith, and James Wiley.

On June 10, two P-40s of the 99th and a pair of P-40s of the 59th Fighter Squadron were escorting a flight of twelve B-25s to Pantelleria. Following a rendezvous in the area of Korba, the bombers and escort aircraft headed to Pantelleria. The visibility over the water was fair; over the island, it was hazy. Suddenly at eight thousand feet, approximately ten Messerschmitt Me-109s and Focke-Wulf Fw-190s appeared. The Messerschmitts attempted to attack the formation but were quickly chased off by a flight of ten British Supermarine Spitfires.

The Spitfire was a fighter with which to be reckoned. Armed with eight .303-inch wing-mounted Browning machine guns, the single-engine Spitfire was one of the few Allied fighter planes capable of outmaneuvering the Me-109.

The B-25s crossed over Pantelleria and released their load. As they turned for home over the northern part of Pantelleria, approximately four to five miles south of Pantelleria Airport, the Me-109s tried to mount another attack. Rayford and Dryden of the 99th stayed with the bombers as did the two pilots from the 59th, while the Spitfires chased the German attackers.

After weeks of aerial bombardment, Pantelleria surrendered on June 11, 1943.

For the next few days, the 99th flew several missions a day; there were bomber escorts, umbrella patrols, and air-sea searches. The flights usually lasted no more than one to two hours and were without incident. Each day the pilots would go through much the same routine. They would gear up, dressing in flying suits complete with helmet, oxygen mask, wool-lined boots, woolen socks, their yellow "Mae West" life jacket, and an uncomfortable parachute harness. Oxygen masks required careful adjustment. Hypoxia was a problem about which fighter pilots always needed to be concerned. Blackouts often resulted from leaks in oxygen systems or ill-fitting oxygen masks.

The first mission of the day on June 18 was routine. Six P-40Ls took off at 8:45 A.M. for umbrella patrol over Pantelleria. Custis, Clark, Bruce, Hall, Campbell, and Bolling returned at 10:15. The morning was quiet; they had observed six boats near the Port of Pantelleria, but little else.

Six P-40s piloted by Charles Dryden, Lee Rayford, Willie Ashley, Spann Watson, Sidney Brooks, and Leon Roberts took off at 3:55 P.M. headed for a thirty-five-minute patrol over Pantelleria. The weather was perfect for flying; ceiling and visibility were unlimited. At 4:25 P.M. eight Me-109s were spotted at an altitude of eighteen thousand feet coming from the northeast, approximately five miles off the coast of Pantelleria. First Lieutenant Sidney P. Brooks of Cleveland, Ohio, was the first to spot the Germans and warned the flight just as the Messerschmitts dived. The Me-109s were accompanying approximately twelve bombers, probably well-armed twin-engine medium-range Heinkel He-111s. An additional flight of ten German fighters kept altitude, providing top cover for the attacking Luftwaffe pilots. The P-40s were at an altitude of eleven thousand feet when they were attacked by four Me-109s flying in a slight echelon. As the pilots of the 99th turned into the Messerschmitts, the firing began. One of the P-40s was hit in the right wing and tail by cannon and .30-caliber machine gun fire. The P-40 pilots steered their planes into a circling maneuver known as a partial Lufbery.

The Messerschmitts continued the attack, dived at the P-40s, and then broke away in a climb. The second group of Messerschmitts got into the fight. At least one of the Germans was hit. The mission report stated, "One enemy aircraft was last seen at 1800 ft. excessively smoking, it was not seen to crash and burn. Two probable damages claimed on two other ME-109s." The enemy airplanes broke from the dogfight and headed for Sicily. The P-40s circled inland twice and headed for home at 4:55 P.M., landing at 5:10 P.M.

In the dogfight, First Lieutenant Lee Rayford's aircraft was hit by machine gun and cannon fire as he chased a pair of Me-109s. More surprised then frightened, he said, "While I was after the two, a third one got on my tail. That's the first time I've ever been shot at."

Combat was what the pilots of the 99th wanted and needed. They were becoming seasoned. Benjamin O. Davis Jr., commanding officer of the squadron, reported, "It was the first time any of them ever shot at the enemy. They gave a good account of themselves considering the odds against them, and, most important, they all came back safely."

The next few days saw more of the same; the 99th performed escort service, flew cover over Pantelleria, and scrambled in response to reported bogies. The missions usually lasted no more than an hour or two.

Mission number thirty-two on June 21 was scheduled for a 7:15 P.M. takeoff. Four P-40s flown by Lawson, Knighten, Bolling, and McCullin were ordered to escort a flight of twelve A-28 bombers to Pantelleria. The P-40s rendezvoused with the bombers near Rasel-Fortass and headed for the target. As the group neared Pantelleria, a flight of four Me-109s took off from the airfield. The bombers continued on their track. Reaching the target, they jettisoned their load. Flying at an altitude of four thousand feet, the bombers headed for home. The German fighters again appeared from below, at three thousand feet and fast approaching. The P-40s broke from the formation and headed off the bandits. Machine guns blazed; the attackers were rebuffed. The P-40s returned to the bombers, and the rest of the flight continued without incident.

Each day was much the same. The Trooper P-40s patrolled to the tip of Cape Bon, Kelebia, and near the south and southeast sector of Sicily. They provided bomber escorts to Sicily, Milo, Sciacca, and Trapani. The skies were always dangerous; the intensity of antiaircraft fire varied from day to day. It had become the norm to expect biting attacks from the Messerschmitts or Focke-Wulfs in the target area. Usually they would make a pass at the formation, be driven off, and run for cover.

Following the attack on Pantelleria, Secretary of War Henry Stimson lauded the 99th. He reported, "We are all very proud of the splendid activity of a fighter squadron commanded by Lt. Col. Benjamin O. Davis Jr. over Pantelleria." The aerial warfare over Pantelleria had been described in the June 26, 1943, issue of the *Pittsburgh Courier* as "one of the heaviest air operations in the history of warfare."

Twelve pilots of the 99th climbed into the tiny cockpits of their silver P-40 Warhawks early on the morning of July 2. Armorers and mechanics had worked through the night to get the squadron's airplanes ready for the day's mission scheduled for a 6:50 A.M. takeoff. Soon the P-40s were in the air en route to a rendezvous with a dozen North American B-25 bombers. Headed to Sicily, after their rendezvous near Kelebia, they flew in close formation above the Mediterranean Sea. Their mission had one objective—to protect the flight of slow-moving bombers.

Near the southwest section of Sicily at an altitude of eleven thousand feet, four Me-109s and several Focke-Wulf Fw-190s appeared. Trooper Squadron headed toward the enemy and made one pass. The left elevator and left wing of one of the P-40s was hit by cannon fire. Just as quickly, one of the Me-109s was damaged. The dogfight was over in minutes; the damage to American and German planes was minor.

The bombers had remained in formation and were still on target. The heavy flak coming at them from Agrigento eclipsed the sun. The mission report follows: "Two FW-190s seen after bomb run was made (3rd bomb run) as the bombers turned to the left, the FW-190's turned to them from a height of approximately 8,000 feet. Bombers were at approximately 7,000 feet. The exact time was indefinite. Lieut. Hall of Trooper Squadron put the nose of his plane between the bombers and the ME-109's, and shot at the first FW-190. Puffs of smoke came from the FW 190 as it fell off on its right wing and went into a right hand spin. The FW-190 hit the ground and clouds of dust arose. No fire was observed. This plane crashed in the Southwestern section of Sicily. The pilot was not seen to bail out. One other pilot of Trooper Sqdn. also saw the FW-190 crash. The FW-190's did not have an opportunity to intercept or fire on the bombers. Two probables also claimed. One FW-190 was seen smoking excessively as it headed toward the ground at approx. 6,000 feet."

That day, on only his eighth combat mission, Lieutenant Charles Hall became the first member of the 99th to score a kill when a group of German fighters followed the bombers and attacked. In the ensuing battle, Hall downed a Focke-Wulf Fw-190 and damaged a Messerschmitt Me-109. After his return to the base, Generals Dwight D. Eisenhower, Carl Spaatz, and James H. Doolittle personally congratulated Hall. The first casualties of the 99th tempered the joy of the day. Lieutenants Sherman White and James McCullin died in a midair collision. The mission report stated, "Two planes with tails sticking from the water were seen S W of Agrigento, Sicily at approximately one mile off shore."

Attacked by nearly fifty German Messerschmitt and Focke-Wulf fighters, Charles "Buster" Hall's success and escape was nearly unbelievable. His plane nearly out of gas, Hall thought he might have to ditch into the Mediterranean Sea. After a narrow escape from the Germans, he was mistaken for a German by Allied forces and had to flee.

On July 2, 1943, Lieutenant Charles B. Hall of the 99th Fighter Squadron became the first black flier to shoot down a German aircraft in a dogfight. Following his return to base, he received congratulations from General Dwight D. Eisenhower. (USAF Photo Collection, USAF Neg. #92821AC, courtesy of National Air and Space Museum, Smithsonian Institution.)

In the midst of the attack by the large number of enemy aircraft, Hall managed to look down at the ground. Through the haze, he could see that the bombers they had been escorting had successfully completed their mission. The bombing had taken no more than a few minutes; black smoke rose from the runways of Costelvestrano. The bombers and their P-40 escorts from Trooper Squadron turned to the left and headed for home. Ever vigilant, Hall looked over his left shoulder and spotted a pair of Focke-Wulfs at an altitude of eight thousand feet. It was obvious that the fighters intended to attack the rear end of the convoy of bombers flying just below them at seven thousand feet.

Hall worked the controls of his P-40 and turned toward the attacking German aircraft. As he armed his machine guns and began firing, Hall's .50-caliber bullets hit the first enemy airplane with such force that it appeared to stop in midair. The Focke-Wulf suddenly began its deadly plummet, hitting the ground within seconds and exploding into a fiery ball. Hall felt a sense of elation, but it would be short-lived.

Tracer shells zoomed past the nose of his airplane. A pair of Messerschmitts were on his tail, making him their prey. Unable to outrun the faster German aircraft, Hall maneuvered his P-40 around toward the attackers, beginning a game of cat-and-mouse. Experienced fighter pilots, the Germans jabbed and feinted at Hall, all the while staying out of range of his guns.

Hall was in trouble, and things were getting worse. In the air for a long time, Hall's plane was getting low on fuel. As he tried to make a run for safety, the Germans kept at him, attacking from on high and then quickly vanishing beneath his plane. The situation seemed increasingly hopeless, as the Germans taunted his gas-guzzling P-40. Hall radioed for assistance, giving his position and imploring the controller to send help. All the while, the pair of German attackers kept him in sight, awaiting their chance to pounce.

Hall felt a tremendous surge of relief as he spotted two specks in the distance. The Germans would soon be caught between Hall and the planes coming to his aid as he continued to fly toward his base. Unfortunately, the specks were two additional Focke-Wulfs. As the four attackers came at him from above in a string formation, Hall put his P-40 into a series of turning and banking evasive maneuvers.

Fending off each attack, Hall attempted to move ever closer to Pantelleria where he was certain to find assistance from patrolling

American aircraft. As the Germans made one last attempt to trap him, Hall again successfully evaded them. They had been chasing him for twenty minutes.

As Hall pointed his P-40 toward a formation of Allied bombers in the distance, a pair of escorting American fighters mistook him for an enemy attacker and moved to intercept him. Once again, Hall was in retreat, this time from the Americans. Calling the controller, Hall advised him of the situation. As soon as they learned that Hall was not an attacker, the fighters returned to their formation. Hall quickly joined them.

After his tour of duty ended, Charles Hall returned to Tuskegee and made public appearances as part of a war bond drive. The attitude of whites was far different in Europe than in America. In an interview with the *Pittsburgh Courier* on race relations, he said, "Over there it doesn't make any difference whether a man is from Minnesota or Mississippi, black, brown or grizzly gray. It is the way he flies that counts. Race theories get blasted out of a pilot's mind in the first burst of flak."

At the time of their first encounter with the enemy, Colonel Davis, the squadron commanders, and the flight commanders had no previous combat experience, an always desirable qualification for the men leading inexperienced pilots into battle. While this may have hampered the 99th Fighter Squadron in their first engagement, the unusually extensive training of the men more than compensated for that shortcoming. Referring to that training, Colonel Davis stated, ". . . a young pilot in these days who has 250 hours in a P-40 before he goes into combat is a hard man to find."

Twelve P-40Ls of Trooper Squadron took off from Fardjouna's Zigzag Field at 10:05 A.M. on July 3. George Roberts, John Rogers, Sidney Brooks, L. C. Roberts, Lemuel Custis, Willie Fuller, Herbert Clark, James Wiley, Allen Lane, Graham Smith, Paul Mitchell, and Louis Purnell were the pilots. Along with forty-four other P-40s, they were to provide cover for twenty-four A-20 and A-30 aircraft. The target, as it had been for nearly a week, was the northwest corner of Sicily. From Zigzag Field they flew a course of fifty-five degrees to Sicily. From the Egadi Islands, the formation of bombers executed a gradual right-hand turn and approached their target from the vicinity of the Cape of S. Vito. A light haze hung over the water and the target. The ceiling was low; there were scattered clouds at two thousand feet.

Lieutenant Colonel Benjamin O. Davis Jr. sat in the cockpit of his aircraft prior to a mission escorting Allied bombers. Davis led by example; he did not expect his pilots to fly any mission that he would not fly himself. (USAF Collection, Air University/HO, Maxwell AFB, AL.)

Five enemy fighters, Me-109s and Fw-190s patrolling the target area, appeared at nine thousand feet at 10:45 A.M. When the bogies attacked, they came from below, knowing that the advantage would be theirs; it would take awhile before they were seen. When they attacked, they broke away in a half roll. One P-40 that was directly astern and slightly below tried in vain to intercept two Fw-190s attacking the bomber squadron. No further contact was made. Nine of the pilots landed at Trooper Field; the other three went to Zigzag Field. The enemy flak from the target was heavy. Two of the bombers were shot down; one burst into flames in midair, the other hit the water. At least two parachutes floated toward the water.

Eleven P-40 pilots of Trooper Squadron inspected their aircraft and prepared for a 3:15 P.M. takeoff. Along with twenty-four P-40s of Growl Squadron, they were to escort twelve A-20s to Sciacca, Sicily. They followed a course of fifty degrees to the vicinity of Bianci, Sicily, then broke to the left to Sciacca. At an altitude of approximately ten thousand feet, they dropped their bombs, reversed direction, and left the target area. The antiaircraft fire in the target area had been fierce. The enemy aircraft action over Sciacca was also heavy; eight Me-109s were observed in the distance. A pair of Fw-190s came out of the sun's glare and attacked four of Trooper Squadron's P-40s directly over Sciacca. Lieutenant Herbert Clark maneuvered behind one of the bandits. As the enemy turned in a split "S" movement, Clark fired a burst from his machine guns; pieces of the Messerschmitt splintered into the air. Clark and Herman Lawson each claimed one probable.

The next day's action was a virtual replay of the day before. Eleven P-40Ls of Trooper Squadron and two dozen P-40s of Growl rendezvoused to escort twenty-four A-30s to Milo Airdrome. The formation followed a course of fifty degrees to the Egadi Islands. A slow starboard turn took them directly into the Sicily target area; the time was 11:00 A.M. and they were at eleven thousand feet. Descending to ninety-five hundred feet, they released their bombs. The formation broke to the left and executed a 270-degree turn out to sea. Trooper Squadron then provided close cover for the second formation of bombers at eleven thousand feet. Bomb hits were observed over the target area; the returning flak had been light and inaccurate.

Four enemy aircraft were observed in the vicinity of Milo at an altitude of approximately fifteen thousand feet, but were not engaged. At nine thousand feet, out of the sun, a pair of Focke-Wulf Fw-190s had attacked the first wave of bombers, but were intercepted and flew away. The action departing the target area was heavy. What was probably a bomber was observed in the water three miles north of the Island of Levanzo. Another unidentified airplane was seen on fire five miles northeast of the Milo Airdrome. All pilots returned safely after the nearly two-hour mission.

A second mission of the day had been made up of twelve Trooper P-40s and thirty-six P-40s of Growl. They escorted thirty-five A-20s to Milo, encountering heavy flak and a trio of Messerschmitt Me-109s with contact. Several missions over the three-day period from July 10 to July 12 supported landing forces at Licata. Each day aircraft from Trooper Squadron pulled out of Fardjouna, headed for Pantelleria, then on to Licata. The formation patrolled the beach as landing force 343 attempted to occupy Licata. Several Focke-Wulf aircraft were usually seen in the distance but not engaged.

On the eleventh, twelve P-40Ls of Trooper Squadron took off on yet another mission to Licata to provide aerial cover for the landing and shipping of invasion force number 343. Lieutenant Willie Ashley returned early because of engine trouble. Lieutenant Erwin Lawrence accompanied him as escort. The remaining P-40s took a direct course to Pantelleria, then flew a course of eighty-five degrees to Licata. Between 12:00 P.M. and 12:30 P.M. Trooper Squadron provided aerial cover. Twelve Focke-Wulf Fw-190s were encountered eight miles northeast of Licata. Attacking in formations of two, the enemy aircraft attempted to attack the Allied ships. The P-40s intercepted the Focke-Wulfs and drove them off, but no enemy aircraft were destroyed.

The antiaircraft fire out of Licata was heavy and accurate. Lieutenant George R. Bolling's P-40 was hit. From an altitude of eight thousand feet he went into a dive. At three thousand feet he bailed out. Landing in the water, Bolling climbed into a dinghy where he awaited air-sea rescue. Lieutenant William A. Campbell continued to fly protection for the helpless Bolling until aid arrived.

Chapter Seven

On to Italy

The 33rd Fighter Group, including the 99th Fighter Squadron, moved from North Africa to Licata on the southern coast of Sicily on July 28, 1943. The scope of the missions did not change greatly. Each day, Licata, Joss Beach, Dime Beach, and Willyie Beach were patrolled. Growl and Trooper Squadrons covered Allied ships and provided frequent escorts for transport aircraft. Pilots flew mission after mission. Bogies were spotted and chased away. Routine fighter sweeps were made; fortunately the flak was inaccurate. On an almost daily basis, the enemy underwent brutal strafing of roads, railway targets, trucks, barges, factories, and ground troops.

On August 11, mission number 6C called for twelve P-40s from Trooper Squadron to patrol Cape Orlando. The time of takeoff was 7:45 A.M. Two planes crashed in midair after takeoff. One pilot bailed out; the other did not. The short mission report stated, "The plane in leaving the formation did not lose enough altitude before turning, consequently was overrun by the pilot who bailed out approximately at 1500 ft." Lieutenant Samuel M. Bruce safely parachuted from his crippled airplane; Lieutenant Paul G. Mitchell died. In his honor, a housing project in Washington, D.C., would be named Mitchell Village. Meanwhile, combat aerial patrols, strafing, and transport convoy protection racked up the daily sortie count. Throughout August 1943, the same type of missions continued.

In September, Lieutenant Colonel Davis was reassigned to the United States to be the commander of the all-black 332nd Fighter Group, comprised of the 100th, 301st, and 302nd Fighter Squadrons. The training was taking place at Selfridge Field, Michigan.

Fliers from the 332nd had been at Oscoda, Michigan, for several weeks. Racism was obvious and mean; the local townspeople did not want blacks in their community. The board of supervisors prepared and forwarded to the War Department a formal resolution requesting that the black airmen be removed. The reason given was that they would "create social and racial problems in such a community where no persons of the Negro race have ever lived, and where there are no facilities for the entertainment of such colored persons."[1] Black organizations protested. There was little support for the resolution outside of Oscoda. The governor of Michigan told a reporter, "I have not been officially approached on the matter, but surely I would not be in sympathy with anything like that, because it is definitely contrary to the war effort in which we are all so sincerely interested in at this time."

When Lieutenant Colonel Davis turned over command of the 99th to Captain George Spencer Roberts, a graduate of the first class at Tuskegee, he said, "Spanky, the destiny of the squadron is in your hands." Nicknamed Spanky, Roberts had been serving as the operations officer of the 99th. A hands-on officer, Roberts strongly believed in the welfare of his men. While at a temporary camp at Termini, in northwest Sicily, officers and enlisted men ate at the same mess because there was only one kitchen. Roberts always ate last, after his men were fed; it was not uncommon for Roberts to grab a ladle and serve his troops. Roberts had been both the first African-American accepted for Army Air Corps training and the first to command the 99th before Benjamin O. Davis Jr. had arrived at Tuskegee.

After Lieutenant Colonel Davis had returned to the United States, Roberts went into temporary seclusion. When asked the reason by Edgar T. Rouzeau, a reporter for the *Pittsburgh Courier*, Roberts explained, "How could I celebrate? Actually, I was unhappy. I felt that I had won my promotion at the expense of the squadron. The 99th will never have as fine a commander as Skipper. I hated to see him go."

Roberts, who flew a total of seventy-eight missions, told a reporter from *Time* in 1944, "We have not turned out to be super-duper pilots—but as good as the U.S. Army turns out. That's important. Because we had one handicap: people assumed we were not producing because we were Negroes. Our men have been under a strain because of the civilian attitude. It is remarkable that they kept up their morale. But now that we have produced, things have changed."

George "Spanky" Roberts commanded the 99th on several separate occasions, the second beginning in September 1943. Roberts had the opportunity to assist Toni Frescell, one of America's most famous female photographers, when she visited the 332nd Fighter Group in March 1945, to do a photographic essay on the Red Tails. (USAF Collection, AFHRA, Maxwell AFB, AL.)

Lieutenant Colonel Benjamin O. Davis Jr. had been a strong commander and had frequently been forced to walk a tightrope with white superior officers. Following Davis' departure from Italy, Colonel Momyer, commander of the 33rd Fighter Group, sensed an opportunity to weaken the cause of the black fliers. He complained that members of the 99th "lacked discipline and motivation in the air." His official attack was made in a very negative report about the 99th's combat performance. Momyer's report to General Edwin J. House read:

> The general discipline and ability to accomplish and execute orders promptly are excellent. Air discipline has not been completely satisfactory. The ability to work and fight as a team has not yet been acquired. Their formation flying has been very satisfactory until jumped by enemy aircraft, then the squadron seems to disintegrate. This has repeatedly been brought to the attention of the Squadron, but attempts to correct this deficiency so far have been unfruitful. On one particular occasion, a flight of twelve JU-88s with an escort

of six ME-109s, was observed to be bombing Pantelleria. The 99th, instead of pressing home the attack against the bombers, allowed themselves to become engaged with the 109s. The Unit has shown a lack of aggressive spirit that is necessary for a well organized fighter squadron. On numerous instances, when assigned to dive bomb a specific target in which the antiaircraft fire was light and inaccurate, they chose the secondary target which was undefended. On one occasion, they were assigned a mission with one squadron of this group to bomb targets in the toe of Italy, the 99th turned back before reaching the target and pressed home the attack. As later substantiated, the weather was considered operational. Based on the performance of the 99th to date: "It is my opinion that they are not of the fighting caliber of any squadron in the group. They have failed to display the aggressiveness and desire for combat that are necessary to a first class fighting organization. It may be expected that we will get less work and less operational time out of the 99th than any squadron in the group."

Their bravery had been directly challenged. Momyer had practically called the pilots of the 99th cowards. Momyer's prime example was the episode in which several pilots of the 99th broke from bomber protection to engage the enemy. He recommended that all-black squadrons be assigned noncombatant roles. Momyer's report took on a life of its own as it reached the desks of level after level of military bureaucracy. The report was endorsed by General Edwin House, the commanding officer of the 12th Air Support Command, and sent to General Henry "Hap" Arnold, commanding general of the Army Air Forces. Arnold forwarded the report to the McCloy Committee.

The Momyer Report had potentially grave implications for black fliers far beyond the immediate effect on the 99th Fighter Squadron. Not only would the 99th be removed from the area of combat, but once fully trained, the 332nd Fighter Group would also be assigned to a non-combat area. In addition, plans for the 477th Bombardment Group, an all-black bomber unit, would be scrapped.

Stemming from the unsubstantiated Momyer Report, the September 20, 1943, edition of *Time* presented a story on the black fliers. The author wrote, "In any case, the question of the 99th is only a single phase of one of the Army's biggest headaches: how to train and use Negro troops. No theater commander wants them in considerable numbers; the high command has trouble finding combat jobs for them. There is no lack of work to be done by Negroes as labor and engineering troops—the Army's dirty work. But the American spirit of fair play, which occasionally devotes some attention to Negro problems, would be offended by a policy of confining Negroes to such duty and the Negro press has campaigned against it. There are plenty of Negro combat troops, but almost none of them have been tested under fire." *Time* ended its article by asking, "Is the Negro as good a soldier as the white man?"

Lieutenant Colonel Davis was justifiably outraged by Momyer's charges and went into action to counter the damaging effects. The report was an obvious fabrication backed by little truth. On October 16, 1943, Davis testified before the McCloy Committee and gave his version of the accomplishments of the 99th Fighter Squadron. War correspondent Ernie Pyle publicly defended the African-American squadron. General Eisenhower believed Momyer's charges were inaccurate.

In a letter to the editor of *Time* on October 18, Agatha Davis, wife of Lieutenant Colonel Davis, responded to the earlier *Time* article:

> *Time* has made some definite statements about the 99th Fighter Squadron and unashamedly admitted these statements to be based on "unofficial reports."

> Are you justified in saying that the record of the 99th Fighter Squadron is only fair? My husband tells me that his judgment, based on comparison with the work done by six veteran P-40 squadrons in the same area on the same types of missions over the same period of time, is that the record of the 99th Fighter Squadron is at least worthy of favorable comment.

> My indictment is that by publishing an article based on "unofficial reports" you have created unfavorable public opinion about an organization to which all Negroes point with pride. You should realize that those few printed words in *Time*—words which may be creating a false impression—have struck at one of the strongest pillars upholding Negroes' morale in their effort to contribute to the winning of the war.

Momyer had never wanted the 99th Fighter Squadron attached to his group and had done everything in his power to discredit the squadron. Of Colonel Momyer, Spann Watson related: "During the Sicilian campaign the pilots of the 33rd and 99th sighted, needless to say, encountered, few enemy aircraft. We went for months without seeing enemy aircraft. Colonel Momyer knew it. He waited until all of his squadrons had gained victories in the invasion of Italy, then criticized us. We didn't get a chance to gain victories because we didn't go with the invasion force to Italy. We remained in Sicily, hundreds of miles from the battle zone.

"I will never forget Colonel Momyer. One morning, Colonel Davis dispatched us to fly to Colonel Momyer's headquarters for a combat briefing. You know, Colonel Davis was strict. If he sent you any place, you better be there on time or have a damn good excuse. Anyway, we arrived at the appointed time, only to learn that the briefing was ending. We were surprised because we knew we were on time. Colonel Momyer informed us that the briefing was over and said, 'You fellows follow my men.' Now I ask you, what way was that to brief pilots going on a combat mission where their lives were at stake? Colonel Momyer was just plain prejudiced towards us."

During the Sicilian Campaign, the 33rd and the 99th were assigned to tactical duty, such as dive-bombing, and strafing. The failure of the 99th to gain victories, however, caused some high army officials to suspect its pilots' courage to fight. They charged the 99th with being a failure and clamored for more action. However, while the 99th was being criticized, Lieutenant Colonel Philip C. Cochran, one of the United States Army's greatest dive-bombing experts, was praising the 99th as "a collection of born dive-bombers."

Rumors abounded that the 99th would be disbanded and no further training of black pilots would take place. Momyer's report was put before the Advisory Committee on Negro Troop Policies, a subgroup of the McCloy Committee. The army ordered yet another study on the performance of black pilots; this one was titled "Operation of the 99th Fighter Squadron Compared With Other P-40 Squadrons in the Mediterranean Theater of Operations." Davis again testified. A G-3 investigation was held and concluded that the 99th "performed on a par with other P-40 Squadrons in the Mediterranean Theater of Operations."

Throughout August, September, and early October, pilots from the 99th performed a wide variety of aerial duties. On September 14, a formation of twenty-four Martin A-30 Baltimore and twelve B-25 double-tail-finned Mitchell bombers was escorted to Nola. There were patrols between Agropoli and Salerno. Bogies were sighted without engagement.

After spending just two months at Licata, the 99th moved to Termini Imerese for slightly less then two weeks. Following one month at Barcellona Pozzo di Gotto, on October 17, 1943, the 99th was ordered to Foggia Air Field on the east coast of Italy. There they became the fourth squadron of the 79th Fighter Group that was part of the 12th Air Force. Unlike Momyer, the commander of the fighter group, Colonel Earl E. Bates, not only accepted, but also welcomed the men of the 99th as he integrated the 79th Fighter Group.

There were bombing missions with ammunition dumps, petroleum storage facilities, and bridges as the targets of opportunity. Bridges were bombed and strafed at Lariano. The docks at Francariella were targets for the 99th's bombs and machine guns. Enemy shipping was attacked at Guilanova. Gun positions fell near the town of Furci. Ack-ack and mechanical problems were more prevalent then enemy fighters.

The anticipation of combat was no different for black pilots than for their white counterparts. Sleep deprivation, jangled nerves, anxiety, exhaustion, dry mouths, tension, and fear were shared equally. It was just as bad when the pilots encountered no enemy fighters; there was a sense of frustration and disappointment. At the same time there were thankfulness and elation.

In December the 99th commenced bombing in the area of the Trigno and Sangro Rivers. The German antiaircraft artillery was heavy; sightings of enemy aircraft became frequent, but usually no engagements followed. The 99th flew almost every day between December 1 and 31 out of the Madna Airdrome. The town of Palena was pounded with five-hundred-pound bombs. Sulmona was the target on the last day of 1943.

A United Press dispatch printed by the *Pittsburgh Courier* in early January 1944 discussed the 1,156 occasions during their first six months of combat on which the 99th had flown patrol, escort, strafing, and ground support sorties against the Axis positions. Based just miles behind enemy lines in Italy, the pilots were flying missions in support of the British Army's advance along the Adriatic Coast. The men of the 99th fully realized the importance of their service, as well as the long-term consequences it might have. Captain Lemuel Custis, a Howard University graduate, spoke for the group when he elaborated upon the sense of responsibility that the men felt, knowing that their performance would determine the future military role that African-Americans would be allowed to play. Custis closed the interview by saying, "We think we've proved ourselves. We've fought in Africa, in Sicily, and now in Italy. We've carried out every assignment given us."

In mid-January 1944, the 99th Fighter Squadron as part of the 79th Fighter Group moved its operation to Capodichino Air Field near Naples. Flying out of Capodichino, they supported the battle of Anzio and provided aerial support to Allied ship convoys.

January 27, 1944, was one of the most successful days of the European campaign for the 99th. Sixteen P-40Ls of the 99th Fighter Squadron took off from Capodichino at 7:35 A.M. Clarence Jamison, George McCrumby, Howard Baugh, Clarence Allen, John Rogers, Elwood Driver, Edward Toppins, John Hamilton, Major George Roberts, Albert Manning, Willie Ashley, Pearlee Saunders, Leon C. Roberts, Walter Lawson, Henry Perry, and Robert Deiz could hardly imagine what was in store for them. They flew a direct course to the Ponziane Islands and patrolled at an altitude of eight thousand feet. On a routine morning flight, the pilots spotted a group of German fighters attacking Allied ships. The 99th attacked with a vengeance, going in high and fast. Before the smoke had cleared, Lieutenant Howard Baugh and Lieutenant Clarence Allen had each destroyed one German attacker. Lieutenant Willie Ashley destroyed another. Lieutenant Robert Deiz another. Lieutenant Henry Perry shot down yet another! Lieutenant Leon Roberts chased an enemy fighter at low altitude before shooting it down. Roberts recalled, "I was following a 'Jerry' and was weaving a lot, but I got a burst into his right wing. He flopped over on his back and headed for the ground."

External belly tanks full of fuel were jettisoned as the P-40 pilots prepared for combat. The fifteen Focke-Wulf Fw-190s hardly knew what hit them as the 99th pounced on them near Peter Beach. Lieutenants Baugh and Allen chased a lone bandit at an altitude of five thousand feet. Four five-second bursts of machine gun fire caught him as he tried to get away. The deadly shells thudded into the fuselage; the plane went into an out-of-control crash. Baugh maneuvered left and immediately let out several bursts of fire at another Fw-190. A hail of bullets ripped into the side of the plane, violently ripping small fragments from the wing and tail.

Lieutenant Ashley jumped a Fw-190 and chased his prey to within a few miles of Rome. The airplane vibrated as the exploding cannon fire tore into the fuselage. Streaming acrid black smoke, the enemy airplane then burst into flames. As Lieutenant Roberts pursued his own bogie, the German aircraft flipped over on its back and smashed into the ground. Lieutenant Toppins, the number three man in Red Flight, fired several short bursts into another Fw-190.

Pilots discussed the danger and exhilaration of a dogfight. January 27, 1944, was one of the most successful days for the 99th Fighter Squadron. In just one day, the squadron destroyed or damaged at least eight German aircraft. (National Archives and Records Administration, #208-MO-18H-22051.)

The .50-caliber shells crisscrossed and thudded into the fuselage. The Focke-Wulf spiraled into the ground and exploded on impact. Rogers and Driver chased down a German as he headed for Rome. When last seen, the evader was smoking excessively and diving for the ground. At five thousand feet, McCrumby picked his target and fired at near point-blank range. As the shells tore into the horizontal stabilizer and rudder, pieces of the Focke-Wulf flew into the air.

At no more than two hundred yards, Lieutenant Deiz got off a sixty-degree shot as he closed on a Focke-Wulf below him. As a portion of the engine cowling was torn off, the airplane went into a sharp dive at 750 feet. Perry homed in as one of the Germans attempted to come out of a dive. He raked the German airplane from propeller to tail at a distance of no more than three hundred yards. Pieces of the canopy flew off and the plane seemed to flutter, then head for the ground. Major Roberts, the flight leader, chased another German. His fire ripped into the Focke-Wulf's right wing. The pilots of the 99th claimed six aircraft destroyed, four damaged, and one enemy machine gun nest destroyed.

On a forty-five-minute afternoon patrol of the battle area including Anzio and Nettuno Beaches, twelve pilots of the 99th encountered several Focke-Wulf Fw-190s. Captain Lemuel Custis, the flight leader, spotted a lone Fw-190 on the deck at approximately 2:25 P.M. At close range, Custis fired several bursts; the enemy crashed into a creek. Lieutenant Alwayne Dunlap confirmed the kill. A German pilot came around behind Erwin Lawrence and started diving, looking for an easy shot. Wilson Eagleson closed in on the attacker at 250 yards and fired off a shot into the side of the enemy airplane. The German pilot never knew what hit him as his plane burst into flames and crashed into the ground.

Lieutenant Charles P. Bailey of Punta Gorda, Florida, caught one of the bandits headed for Rome. Bailey blasted the bogie out of the sky, forcing the German to bail out. Lawrence may have destroyed a Fw-190 with a seventy-five-degree deflection shot. Eagleson saw the enemy aircraft roll over at three thousand feet and dive for the ground with a long stream of smoke, but the kill wasn't confirmed.

The successes of the 99th Fighter Squadron continued throughout 1944. In February, flying their P-40s, the African-American pilots frequently encountered German aircraft as they provided cover for Allied forces at Anzio and Nettuno Beaches. (National Archives and Records Administration, #80-G-54413.)

The 99th had met the enemy head on and showed their mettle with eight kills, two probables, and four damaged enemy planes in one day. Considered to be rookies, Allen, Bailey, and Eagleson had only recently joined the squadron in a group of eight replacement pilots. Unfortunately the day was not without loss; Lieutenant Samuel Bruce died in action when his P-40 crash-landed in the Nettuno Beach area.

Heavy action continued the next day. Charles Hall, Curtis Robinson, Edward Toppins, Lewis Smith, James Knighten, Alwayne Dunlap, Robert Deiz, and Wilson Eagleson took off from Capodichino. Following the coast to the vicinity of the Ponziane Islands and inland to the beach area, their mission was a forty-five-minute patrol from 11:12 A.M. to 12:07 P.M. at an altitude of four thousand to five thousand feet. At 11:50 A.M., four Me-109s and at least three Fw-190s flying at four thousand feet came out of the north. The two formations of the 99th were patrolling at five thousand feet. As they jettisoned their belly tanks and dived at the enemy, the Germans turned away. Lieutenant Deiz scored his second kill in as many days, catching a lone Focke-Wulf at an altitude of three thousand feet with a thirty-degree deflection shot above, behind, and to the left; the pilot bailed out. Robert Deiz would become famous not only for knocking down a pair of "Jerries," but also as the handsome young face immortalized on over 200,000 copies of a War Bond poster titled "Keep Us Flying."

Lieutenant Lewis Smith added a destroyed enemy airplane to his credit. Smith chased a fleeing Fw-190, finally running it down and destroying it with a fifty-degree deflection shot. The German lost control of the aircraft at about twenty feet above the ground. It smashed to earth, erupting in flames.

Lieutenant Charles Hall claimed two victories against the Germans. Hall caught his first kill, a Me-109, with a fifteen-degree deflection shot as he closed in at three hundred yards. At first a razor-thin ribbon of white smoke billowed out, followed by heavy streams of slick oil. The Messerschmitt burst into flames and crashed. A Focke-Wulf fell to Hall's guns as he fired with short bursts dead astern while he closed in at two hundred yards. The Fw-190 augured in.

The 99th had been teamed with British Spitfires, the British 75th Squadron, and the Red Guerillas, an American Warhawk Squadron commanded by Colonel Philip "Flip" Cochran, against a powerful

Selected as the model for a War Bond poster titled "Keep Us Flying," Robert W. Deiz of the 99th Fighter Squadron downed two German aircraft within two days in January 1944. (National Archives and Records Administration, #44-PA-121.)

German affront made up of over one hundred Messerschmitts and Focke-Wulf airplanes. The Red Guerillas shot down five of the enemy aircraft, the 75th accounted for one, and the British Spitfires got nine. The 99th's two-day toll was impressive. They had scored twelve kills, three probables, and four damaged enemy aircraft. On the negative side, three P-40s had been damaged and Lieutenant Bruce had died.

Time, which had months earlier printed a questioning and derogatory article based on the Momyer Report, ran an article after the 99th Fighter Squadron distinguished itself on January 27 and 28, 1944. *Time* reported, "Any outfit would have been proud of combat excellence of one of the most controversial outfits in the Army. . . .They had finally got their big chance flying cover for the Allies' Nettuno beachhead and they knew what to do with it. . . .The squadron was veteran, well-led, sure of itself. . . .The Air Corps regards its experiment proven, and is taking all the qualified Negro cadets it can get."

When talking about their common enemy, Charles Bailey said of Hitler, "His goal was to conquer the world. That was his goal. He had a good start at it until we got over there and broke it up." About the more immediate enemy, the German pilots and aerial engagements, Bailey said, "It didn't last long. We only made one pass, then it was time to get together with your group and head back home. You were so far from your base. Sometimes I would fly right along side of a German boy and look at him and say he looks like a third- or fourth-grade boy up there flying. We were almost twenty years old. So I'd wave at him and go on back. They were little boys flying and we knew then that Hitler's best pilots were gone. And we'd get up over there and look down and see all those airplanes parked. We'd get back and report that and they'd say, 'He doesn't have gas for them.'"

A little more than a year later, on May 29, 1945, Charles Bailey received the Distinguished Flying Cross for his efforts. The accompanying citation read:

> For extraordinary achievement while participating in aerial flight in the Mediterranean Theater of Operations. Consistently, throughout many combat missions against highly important and strategic enemy installations, the personnel listed below have demonstrated the highest order of professional skill, heroism, leadership, and devotion to duty. Although regularly and frequently opposed by large numbers of enemy fighters, together with intense, accurate and heavy anti-aircraft fire during which their aircraft were at times seriously damaged, these

During his tour of duty, Charles Bailey flew two different airplanes, My Buddy *and* Josephine, *both of which were named in honor of his parents.* (Private Collection.)

men have fought through to their targets and aided in the destruction of these vital objectives. Despite severe and adverse weather conditions, rugged terrain and many other major obstacles and hazards, these men have gallantly engaged, fought, defeated the enemy without regard for their own personal safety and against great odds. Their conspicuous and extraordinary achievements throughout these many missions against the enemy have been of inestimable value to successful combat operations and have reflected great credit upon themselves and the Armed Forces of the United States of America.

Interviewed in his home in DeLand, Florida, on December 11, 1996, Mr. Bailey reminisced for several hours about his experiences in Europe. Raised in Punta Gorda, Florida, he named his aircraft after his parents; one bore the legend *My Buddy,* the other was *Josephine.* He flew a total of 133 combat missions, more than twice as many as his white counterparts. When asked the reason, he took a chewed up cigar from his mouth, laughed, and said, "Because they didn't want us back."

Barely a week later on February 5, 1944, over the Italian beachhead at Nettuno, Lieutenant Elwood Driver destroyed another enemy aircraft, a Fw-190. It was the thirteenth bogie bagged by the 99th.

A flight of seven P-40s had taken off at 8:30 A.M. headed to the Ponziane Islands. One aircraft had a mechanical failure and was scrubbed. The patrol was to be of forty-five-minutes duration at an altitude of sixty-five hundred feet. At 9:25 A.M. ten Fw-190s were sighted coming out of the sun to attack the harbor at Anzio. The P-40s dived at the Germans flying at one thousand feet. Lieutenant Driver caught one on the deck. He had what he wanted; the straight-up tail and the horizontal wings of the German plane formed a cross in his gunsight. He dived down on it, closing at three hundred yards while firing short bursts. Flames belched from the right side of the Focke-Wulf. Last seen at an altitude of fifty feet, it was still on fire. The 99th did not emerge from this contest unscathed. One pilot was forced to bail out; Captain Jamison and Lieutenant McCrumby were reported as missing.

Two days later Lieutenants Wilson Eagleson, Leonard Jackson, and Clinton Mills each shot down a German fighter. Hall, Rice, Toppins, Smith, Knighten, Jackson, Mills, and Eagleson received their briefing early on the morning of February 7. Eight P-40s were ready for an assault on Ponziane Beach. The flight took off from Capodichino at 7:00 A.M. and headed along the coast to the Ponziane Islands turning inland to the patrol area. The weather afforded unlimited ceiling and visibility.

Mechanics frequently labored around the clock to keep the planes in the air. On one occasion General Nathan Twining personally commended the "untiring efforts of the ground mainte-nance crews in keeping the maximum number of aircraft operational during this important period." (National Archives and Records Administration, #208-AA-49E-1-1.)

At 8:10 A.M. twelve Fw-190s were spotted at a range of twelve thousand to sixteen thousand feet. Belly tanks were jettisoned and the dogfight was on. Jackson caught a Fw-190 at eighteen thousand feet. Closing directly behind at only 150 yards, he fired at the bogie's tail. The Focke-Wulf fell off on the right wing and the pilot bailed out.

Eagleson met the enemy at six thousand feet. As he closed in to one hundred yards, he caught the German in a thirty-degree deflection shot. The plane burst into flames and crashed into the ground. Mills' turn came at six thousand feet as he flamed a Fw-190 at close range. All the aircraft returned safely to Capodichino; one was damaged on landing.

During an amazing two days of intense action, Allied fighter planes had destroyed eighty-seven enemy aircraft and lost only twelve of their own. The 99th had been flying ground support for the combined American Fifth and British armies as they marched toward Rome. The battle cry of the 99th Fighter Squadron had become "Rome, Berlin, Home." General Henry H. Arnold, commander of the Army Air Forces, had become highly complimentary of the African-American fighter squadron. In a message to Lieutenant General Ira C. Eaker, the Allied commander in the Mediterranean Theater of Operations, Arnold wrote: "The results of the 99th Fighter Squadron during the past two weeks, particularly since the Nettuno landing, are very commendable."

Heavy dive-bombing and strafing of the Ponziane Islands took place during the first ten days of February 1944. German antiaircraft fire was heavy and there were frequent sightings of Fw-190s, although the Focke-Wulfs usually turned away when the Americans attempted to intercept. Peter Beach and the Ponziane Islands were frequent targets. Pursuits of the 99th escorted twenty-four A-20 bombers to Receasecca. The towns of Pico and Pontecorvo were dive-bombed. Porto Corbo and the road junctions near Aquino were pounded.

Tragedy struck the 99th on February 21. Eight aircraft left Capodichino at 6:30 A.M. on a forty-five-minute patrol of the coast of Assault Beach at an altitude of eight thousand feet. Lieutenant Alwayne Dunlap's Warhawk began to smoke at eight thousand feet. Suddenly the aircraft was in flames. Captain Charles B. Hall advised him to bail out, but Dunlap attempted to crash land on the beachhead instead. His attempt was long and he overshot. As he was attempting to turn at five hundred feet, his plane stalled in the turn and crashed into the ground.

The mid-morning mission yielded no kills, but the 99th came close. Eight P-40s lifted off at 9:30 A.M. and headed past the Ponziane Islands, then inland. Twenty-two enemy aircraft were observed at eighteen thousand feet on the northern approach to the patrol area. Ten Messerschmitts began a dive-bombing run in the vicinity of Anzio, while twelve more provided top cover for the attackers. The 99th intercepted the Me-109s at six thousand feet. Major George S. Roberts fired short bursts at a lone Messerschmitt, but was forced to execute evasive maneuvers to shake a bogie on his tail. Lieutenants James T. Wiley and John A. Gibson pursued four Me-109s on the deck, firing short machine gun bursts as they closed. The Me-109s evaded and peeled out toward Rome, eventually losing the pair of pursuing P-40s. No claims were made against enemy aircraft, but one unidentified airplane was seen to hit the ground and explode. A Me-109 trailing acrid black smoke was observed headed for the ground at one thousand feet, but verification of its crash could not be made.

Between late January and early February 1944, in spite of the continuing belief that blacks were not qualified for combat, the War Department sent three squadrons of the 332nd Fighter Group overseas to join the 99th. When the 100th, 301st, and 302nd Fighter Squadrons arrived at Taranto, Italy, Montecorvino Air Base, south of Naples, was their new headquarters. Attached to the 62nd Fighter Wing as part of the 12th Air Force, Lieutenant Colonel Benjamin O. Davis Jr. was the 332nd Fighter Group's commanding officer.

The outfit was given Bell P-39Q Airacobras for use in coastal patrol missions. The Airacobra was slightly over thirty feet in length with a thirty-four-foot wing span. Powered by a 1,150-horsepower Allison engine, the Bell aircraft had a maximum speed of 368 miles per hour. When pushed into a steep dive, the Airacobra could attain a speed in excess of six hundred miles per hour. Firepower came from one 37-millimeter cannon that fired through the propeller hub, and two 0.5-inch fuselage-mounted machine guns.

Twelve P-39s from the 332nd lifted off from Montecorvino at 6:52 A.M. on February 19. Lieutenants William Mattison, Walter McCreary, John Briggs, Robert Nelson, Lawrence Dickson, Clemenceau Givings, Melvin Jackson, Beryl Wyatt, Carrol Woods, Walter Palmer, George Taylor, and Captain Robert Tresville were at the controls. The pilots from the 100th Fighter Squadron were assigned convoy protection over Naples harbor. The weather was hazy, the ceiling unlimited. Visibility was good, two to five miles. The twelve aircraft were well armed; according to the mission report, they carried 8,000 rounds of .30-caliber, 11,000 rounds of .50-caliber, 220 rounds of 20-millimeter, and 240 rounds of 37-millimeter ammunition. The P-39s sighted the convoy ship *Vigorous* at 7:05 A.M., twenty-five miles northwest of Licosa Point and escorted it into Naples harbor. Friendly activity was heavy. P-39s provided cover for flights of B-25s sighted at four thousand feet, headed east. Five bogies were sighted below the fourth flight of bombers, but they did not attempt to interfere with the formation.

On February 21, the 301st Fighter Squadron, flying four P-39s, was scheduled to escort the convoy ship *Langfield* but was called back before reaching the point of rendezvous. Throughout the end of February the duty continued the same. Each day flights of P-39s provided air cover for convoys of Allied ships.

Support and ground duty could be just as dangerous as aerial combat. The first member of the 366th Air Service Squadron assigned to the 99th Fighter Squadron to receive a Purple Heart, First Lieutenant Thomas Malone, was wounded while moving supplies to an advanced base. Driving over a shell-pocked road, Malone's truck hit a land mine left behind by the retreating Germans. Knocked unconscious, Malone was transported to a field hospital behind the lines. While recovering at the Army Convalescent Hospital at Coral Gables, Florida, Malone visited Tuskegee in late February 1944

Most of March was also spent providing P-39 coverage for Allied ship convoys. Operating out of Montecorvino Airdrome, members of the 301st and 100th Fighter Squadrons prepared for combat each day. It was not at all unusual to sight and give chase to bogies, only to lose them. Missions included harbor protection at Naples, point-to-point escorts, submarine hunts, and air-sea rescues.

Friendly fire could be just as dangerous as that of enemy aircraft. On a point patrol on March 16, an Allied Douglas A-26 Invader fired upon thirty P-39s; three P-39s returned the fire. Slight damage was received by one P-39. Allied pilots had to be careful approaching bomber formations; the recommended procedure was to slowly move in sideways. If a plane came in nose first, it was fair game for Allied bomber gunners.

Pilots from the 302nd nearly bagged a lone Junkers Ju-88 on point patrol on March 17. A special reconnaissance patrol of six P-39s was called up at 8:15 A.M. by the controller to intercept sighted enemy aircraft. Designated Primus Pink, the flight sighted the bandit at 2:57 P.M. due west. The enemy was on deck and pulled up into the clouds in an attempt to evade the six P-39s. Primus Pink Three pursued the hiding bandit, identified it as a Ju-88, and opened fire. The American pilot emptied his guns into the German bogie, saw metal pieces fly from the ship, and observed the left side smoking. With a thousand rounds of .50-caliber ammunition expended, the American returned to the field. The bandit was last seen headed out to sea.

The 100th Fighter Squadron lost another pilot on March 18. Six P-39s scrambled at 8:15 A.M. in search of a German reconnaissance patrol. Lieutenant Clemenceau Givings, call sign "Rosie Purple," experienced engine trouble at two thousand feet. His aircraft caught fire and crashed into the Gulf of Gaeta.

Junker Ju-88 bomber activity had become increasingly active in the patrol area throughout March. Fliers from the 302nd might have bagged another on March 28, but it couldn't be verified. At 3:30 P.M. two P-39 pilots from a flight of forty gave chase to a twin-engine Ju-88. The two Americans stalking the German fired intermittently and left the bandit only after expending all of their ammunition. When they pulled away, the enemy aircraft was streaming smoke from its right engine.

April was more of the same for the 100th and 302nd Fighter Squadrons. P-39s worked point patrol, harbor patrol over the Gulf of Naples, special reconnaissance patrols, strafing, air-sea rescues, and fighter scrambles. The antiaircraft fire was heavy. From time to time bandits were encountered, but the Germans normally fled. Reported sightings of enemy aircraft frequently turned out instead to be friendlies. On April 3, two P-39s were scrambled to Salerno in response to unidentified aircraft that turned out to be a trio of B-25s. At thirteen thousand feet, northeast of Mt. Vesuvius, the pair came across another unidentified aircraft and fired a burst of machine gun fire off its nose. Its pilot then identified his aircraft as a P-51.

On April 1, 1944, the 99th Fighter Squadron moved its base of operation to Cercola and became part of the 324th Fighter Group. As Major George Spencer "Spanky" Roberts rotated back to the United States, Captain Erwin B. Lawrence took command. At about the same time, the Army's statistical study commissioned the previous fall was finally completed and released. In it, the 99th was officially recognized as a ". . . superb tactical fighter unit." The report stated: "An examination of the record of the 99th Fighter Squadron reveals no significant general difference between this squadron and the balance of the P-40 squadrons in the Mediterranean Theater of Operations."

Chapter Eight

In the Skies Over Europe

In May 1944, the 332nd was transferred to the 306th Wing, 15th Air Force. Serving as bomber escorts, the Fighter Group was now stationed at Ramitelli, Italy. Once the site of a wheat farm, both the flight line and runway at Ramitelli were constructed of perforated steel planking. In dry weather, the base was a field of dust; on rainy days, it was a sea of mud. Benjamin O. Davis Jr. had been promoted to the rank of full colonel. His pilots were now flying Republic P-47 Thunderbolts, in addition to the P-39s and P-40s. The P-47 was one of the top-rated American fighters to see action in World War II. The most widely used of all American-produced fighters during the war, the Thunderbolt was armed with eight 0.5-inch machine guns. Powered by a single 2,300-horsepower Pratt & Whitney R-2800-59 radial engine, the thirty-six-foot fighter's maximum speed was 428 miles per hour. A step up from what the pilots were used to flying and affectionately known as "the Jug," the P-47 offered front and rear armor protection and bulletproof glass. The 332nd was happy to have the Thunderbolt.

A point patrol over the Gulf of Naples was the 302nd's activity for the first day of May. The rest of the month was a carbon copy of the earlier months. There were point patrols, ground strafing, the occasional scramble, and air-sea searches. There were few sightings of enemy aircraft.

The daily operations report for the 100th Fighter Squadron showed activity every day in May. They provided cover for ocean-going convoy ships named *Woolsack, Armour, Stinker, Waggle, Dowager, Bronze, Almanac, Barbecue, Bellamy, Brunette, Dewey, Bayonet, Tiberius,* and *Maggie.* There were also scrambles for enemy aircraft, point patrols, strafing missions, harbor patrols, and air-sea rescues.

On May 1, twelve P-39s fought through antiaircraft fire as they strafed ack-ack positions installed in houses. As they flew from the scene, they saw a brilliant flash from a large building as nearly two thousand rounds of .50-caliber and 37-millimeter fire tore into it. A pair of P-39s strafed railroad targets on May 8 while ten aircraft provided top cover. One P-39 was slightly damaged in the left wing by light and inaccurate ack-ack. Six Spitfires came on the scene and provided additional top cover for ten minutes.

On May 18, four P-39s of the 100th encountered a lone Junkers Ju-88. Headed toward the Naples harbor, one of the P-39s fired at the Ju-88, but missed because of range. The Junkers returned the fire, but there was no further activity.

Eight P-40s of the 99th, each armed with a five-hundred-pound bomb, went out on reconnaissance to a target west of Valmontone on May 26 at 11:30 A.M. Lieutenants Elwood Driver, Henry Perry, Albert Manning, Theodore Wilson, Robert Deiz, Woodrow Morgan, Alva Temple, and Clarence Allen were the pilots. Four of their five-hundred-pound bombs scored direct hits on several military targets. Deiz scored another direct hit on a gun position atop a house in Fiuggi. An armored car was quickly destroyed.

When Lieutenant Woodrow F. Morgan's P-40 was hit by ground fire, he was forced to crash land at an army field northwest of Presinene. Thinking that Morgan was at deck level to strafe, enemy gunners began firing at his crippled aircraft. Lieutenant Deiz, the flight leader, came in firing at a 20-millimeter gun position located in a house at the northwest end of the field, enveloping the gun position in flames. Deiz's plane had been hit by flak in two places. Lieutenant Perry's P-40 was also shot up. Temple's airplane was hit in the left and right wings. The left elevator was damaged, as was the tail section. Despite a completely destroyed elevator control, Temple was able to nurse his wounded airplane back to Pignataro.

Operating out of Pignataro in June, four P-40Ls of the 99th Fighter Squadron performed reconnaissance and strafing over Civitavecchia, Castelleone, Narni, Spoleto, Marciano, and Orvieto. They strafed the roads, bridges, and barges near Lake Brachiano. The Tiber Bridge was dive-bombed, as was the town of Tivoli. Each of the P-40s was armed with a five-hundred-pound bomb that required an almost direct hit to cause any damage.

On June 7, during the Allied invasion of Europe, the 332nd saw its first real aerial action. As B-17 and B-24 bombers headed toward Munich, the 99th and 332nd flew cover for them against heavy attacks by German pilots. General "Hap" Arnold ordered American fighters to go on the offensive. When confronted with a flight of German attackers, Colonel Davis ordered the 332nd Fighter Group to pursue the enemy. On June 9, 1944, the black fliers from Tuskegee scored five victories.

When the Allies decided to go after deliberate German industrial targets such as weapons factories, steel mills, and oil refineries, the 99th Fighter Squadron and the 332nd Fighter Group were part of the action. While among the most dangerous and heavily protected targets, the oil refineries were unarguably some of the most important and sought-after targets.

Mission number three for June 9 called for pilots from the 301st and 302nd Fighter Squadrons to provide penetration escort for the 5th, 57th, 304th, 49th, and 55th Bomber Wings to the always dangerous Munich area. Thirty-nine P-47s took off from Ramitelli at 7:00 A.M. The escort group was quickly reduced by four when three aircraft experienced mechanical trouble and one P-47 was ordered to provide escort back to base. The others rendezvoused with the bombers at 8:30 A.M. at an altitude of twenty-two thousand feet.

While the bombers were on time and in good formation, there were four stragglers, forcing the fighters to spread out to protect the large number of bombers. On approach to the Udine area, four Messerschmitts made a diving attack from five o'clock above the formation of B-24s. Passing at the bombers, they made a diving turn to the left.

Frederick D. Funderburg spied a pair of Me-109s five hundred feet below him. Making sure his gun switches and gunsights were turned on and firing short bursts as his rate of closure increased, he tore into one bogie. Pieces of the airplane shattered into the air. Funderburg maneuvered under the two attackers and put his P-47 into a steep climbing turn. The Me-109s were now eyeball to eyeball with the American. Funderburg fired, and in seconds, one of the Me-109s shuddered and then exploded. The Americans saw two Messerschmitts hit the water; only one chute had opened.

Lieutenant Robert Wiggins spotted a lone German at altitude at the nine o'clock position. Wheeling around so that he was flying head on into the bandit, he fired a burst into the enemy aircraft.

Pieces flew from the Me-109. The smoking Messerschmitt went into a steep dive, gained speed, and pulled away. Wiggins' plane was slightly damaged in the fray.

Lieutenant Wendell Pruitt made a diving turn and locked in on the tail of a bandit. He activated his guns, giving a short burst. Nothing. Seeing no hit, he fired another longer burst. As his bullets hit the Messerschmitt, Pruitt pressed the attack, going in for the kill. With a third burst, the left wing exploded into angry red flames. Pruitt's wingman saw the pilot bail out as the plane crashed.

Lieutenant Charles M. Bussey pulled his eight-plane formation into four Messerschmitts. A German was dangerously close on Lieutenant Melvin Jackson's tail. William W. Green fired a short burst at the attacker who then went into a dive. Bussey fired two more short bursts and the Me-109's tail assembly disintegrated. As the crippled Messerschmitt plunged earthward, its pilot bailed out and the mutilated airplane exploded.

When Jackson heard Colonel Davis's call to attack, he was flying at twenty-seven thousand feet. Jackson ordered his flight to drop their wing tanks and engage the enemy. There were five or six Me-109s at

Prior to a mission, Wendell Pruitt gave his valuables to his crew chief, Staff Sergeant Samuel W. Jacobs, for safekeeping. Over the course of seventy combat missions, Pruitt shot down a trio of enemy aircraft and assisted in the sinking of a German destroyer escort. (National Archives and Records Administration, #208-AA-46BB-4.)

On a routine bomber escort mission on June 9, 1944, 302nd Fighter Squadron commander Melvin Jackson found himself under attack. Turning his P-47 Thunderbolt into the fray, Jackson downed a Messerschmitt Me-109. (USAF Collection, AFHRA, Maxwell AFB, AL.)

eleven o'clock high. He worked the stick and rudder simultaneously as he maneuvered toward one of the Germans. Within range, he began firing. As he fired one burst, the pilot of the Me-109 rolled over and started a simulated spin to the left. Jackson pulled off to the left, with his flight following him. A bogie at eleven o'clock high was making a head-on pass. As Jackson went into a steep climb, he started to stall, and his opponent maneuvered behind him. Jackson outdistanced the German and entered a bank of clouds. Emerging from his hiding place, Jackson saw that the Me-109 was again in sight at eleven o'clock high and pulled in behind the German. Jackson fired burst after burst until his machine guns reduced the Nazi aircraft to flames, its ejecting pilot barely able to clear the plummeting inferno. With the sweet taste of success in his mouth, Jackson recalled that he then ". . . cruised home happy after my victory."

The bombers safely accomplished their mission; the 332nd lost one pilot, Lieutenant Cornelius G. Rogers. Afterward, the 332nd Fighter Group received a short message from one of the white bomber pilots: "Your formation flying and escort is the best we have ever seen." Colonel Davis received the Distinguished Flying Cross for leading the mission.

The 301st and 302nd Fighter Squadrons combined for a joint mission on the morning of June 13. Thirty-six P-47s lifted off the dirt field of Ramitelli at 6:55 A.M. with four spare aircraft returning to base early. The bombers of the 5th and 49th Bomber Wings, on time and in good formation, were met at 7:55 A.M. for penetration to the Munich area. Twenty-six P-47s penetrated to Lienz with the B-24s at 9:25 A.M. Six planes flew to Casarsa della Delizia, leaving the bombers at 8:45 A.M. Two were low on gas, one developed oxygen problems, and three served as escorts.

Eleven Messerschmitt Me-109s were observed in the area of Udine. Seven were at eight o'clock high; four were at the five o'clock high position. Neither flight attacked. Two unidentified enemy fighters chased a B-24 in Ancona, but broke off their attack once the P-47s countered. A pair of Me-109s fired on the P-47s at twenty thousand feet from the five o'clock high position in the area of Udine. They made only one pass and disappeared.

June 24 was a very bad day for the 100th, 301st, and 302nd Fighter Squadrons. Assigned a strafing mission, their target was the Airasca-Pinerale Landing Ground located less than two miles west of Airasca, Italy. Forty-eight P-47s left Ramitelli at daybreak; seven returned early. From Ramitelli they flew to Anzio, Regliano, and Corsina to a point ten miles northeast of Finale Lig. During the flight, there was haze over the water with a very bright glare from the sea. On the mainland of Italy, the cloud base was one thousand feet, obscuring the top of the mountains. Three P-47s lost their way near Cape Corse. Thirty-eight continued on toward the target area until the formation leader became lost ten miles northeast of Finale Ligure at 9:40 A.M. The remaining thirty-seven P-47s failed to reach the target because of low-lying clouds off the northwest coast of Italy. The flak had ranged in intensity from light to heavy.

Lieutenant Earl Sherard's plane caught fire at 9:07 A.M.; he was forced to ditch, but was later picked up. At 9:12 A M. Second Lieutenant Samuel Jefferson of the 100th Fighter Squadron crashed into the sea. Second Lieutenant Charles B. Johnson went into a precipitous dive and his airplane exploded on impact with the water.

Captain Robert B. Tresville, a West Pointer, had his own problems. In a steep dive, he leveled off and skimmed across the water. Finally able to pull the airplane up, he had lost his wing tanks and part of the ailerons. With the propeller blades bent and no longer revolving, his aircraft again crashed into the sea. When it came to rest, the tail was seen protruding from the water. Tresville, the seventh black cadet ever to graduate from West Point, had completed twenty-three missions. Commander of the 100th Fighter Squadron, Tresville had a daughter he had never seen.

The pilots had severely erred. Narrative Mission Report No. 8 reported, "It was stated by all of the pilots that they flew too long at deck level over the water thus causing a tendency to misjudge their height. It is believed by all concerned that had they flown at a greater height there would have been less tendency to misjudge their distance. However, upon arrival at the Italian mainland, clouds were reported at 1000 ft. to approximately 12,000 ft and completely obscured the top of the mountains. Due to the fact that complete radio silence was maintained throughout the route, the deputy formation leader had no knowledge of the loss of the formation leader, thus, he was unable to take over the formation and the weather prevented them from penetrating to the target."

A pair of airmen from the 332nd Fighter Group recorded one of the most dramatic kills of the war on June 25, 1944. Two dozen P-47s took off from Ramitelli at 9:00 A.M. on a mission to strafe troops on roads between Senj and Kralsuvica, Yugoslavia, and Laurane-Albona and Paranzo-Salvatore, Italy. When four spare ships returned early, the remaining twenty P-47s proceeded in five flights of four each. At a predetermined point, two flights of four gained altitude to furnish protective top cover, while three flights of four each continued on deck to their target. There the twelve P-47s strafed ships, radio stations, motor launches, and the shoreline in the Pola, Isola, and Trieste areas when no troops were found at the assigned target.

Crossing the Adriatic Sea, the group of eight P-47s observed a destroyer escort bearing the German Cross on its smokestacks. The first pass at the ship was made by two P-47s piloted by Wendell Pruitt and Gwynne Peirson. As the destroyer escort turned sharply, it was attacked broadside by all eight P-47s in a line. The ship started to smoke, then exploded, and sank off Pirano. On return to base, the men's account was met with disbelief. Fortunately, the wing cameras on Peirson's P-47 proved their accomplishment.

Before the war ended, Wendell O. Pruitt was credited with destroying three enemy aircraft in the air. After flying seventy combat missions, the twenty-four-year-old captain was transferred to Tuskegee Army Air Field as a flight instructor. On April 20, 1945, Pruitt, holder of the Distinguished Flying Cross, was killed in a crash while on a training mission near Tuskegee. Pruitt received a hero's burial at St. Peter's Cemetery in his hometown of St. Louis, Missouri. Several hundred graveside mourners listened as Father Andrews of the St. Elizabeth Catholic Church eulogized Pruitt's good qualities, keen intellect, and varied accomplishments. His daring, sense of humor, energy, citizenship, friendship, and religious faith were praised. The *Chicago Defender* of April 28 reported that Father Andrews concluded the service by saying, "We needed a modern hero for us to pattern our lives so God called him home."

The destroyer escort was not the only target destroyed on June 25. A pair of P-47s had strafed two radar stations at Brioni; several military vehicles and the wharf area were also strafed at Maggio. Twelve seaplanes bearing the German Cross had been observed by the last pilot flying out of the Pirano area. Unfortunately all of his ammunition had already been expended.

In America, the African-American newspapers reveled in the success of the black pilots and shared the tragedy of their deaths. Each week the *Pittsburgh Courier, Chicago Defender*, and several other black-operated newspapers followed the triumphs of their hometown heroes. For the most part, however, white-owned newspapers provided little coverage of the successes of the airmen.

To be sure, racism had not been eliminated, either at home or abroad. The Italians called the black pilots *cacci pilota* or *caccia pilota con piccolo capelli* which meant "hunter pilots" or "hunter pilots with short hair." The black pilots and ground crews were well treated by Italian civilians who paid little heed to the color of their skins. There were always troublemakers, however; many white soldiers did everything they could to make life difficult for the African-Americans. On one occasion in Naples, personnel from the 332nd Fighter Group allowed a group of men from an engineering squadron to use their facility for a social function. As a white band played music, the men danced with a group of local women, all of whom were white. Lieutenant Felix Kirkpatrick Jr., a member of the 332nd Fighter Group, was quoted in the *Chicago Defender* on January 6, 1945, as saying, "One Italian girl, I remember, finished her dance with a colored soldier then marched over to a white lieutenant and gave him hell for telling her lies about the Negro boys."

P-51 Mustangs of the 99th Fighter Squadron were being readied for one of the several different types of missions that the Red Tails would fly. (USAF Collection, AFHRA, Maxwell AFB, AL.)

Chapter Nine

Red Tails

By June 1944, the pilots of the 99th Fighter Squadron had flown more than 298 missions in the Mediterranean Theater of Operation and a total of 3,277 sorties. As the 99th transferred from P-40s into P-51 Mustangs, the 332nd upgraded from the P-47 into P-51s—easily recognizable by their big four-bladed propellers. Arguably the finest American airplane produced for World War II, the P-51 was the hands-down favorite of the fliers. Mechanics quickly painted the tails completely red, causing the 332nd to become known as the Red Tails.

Much of life is dictated by pure coincidence, and thus it was with the red tails on the aircraft. At a roundtable discussion, several airmen were asked, "Who decided to paint the tails red?" Harry Sheppard explained:

"It was a matter of logistics. At the time we began to get the P-47s, we didn't have them long enough to make the transformation; we had some silver, we had some olive drab. We began to get the P-51s in—we had the checkerboards, we had the candy stripes, we got the yellow tails and everything. So we scouted around, we went down to Foggia. And we found out that they had an overflow of what they called red insignia paint. So the convoy started back with red paint. Then we had a little conference. These were all maintenance people. The painters would say, 'Let's not overdo it, this thing.' So we decided to paint the tails red, the empennage and the trim tabs, and the nose spinner, which made the painters happy because they had the work to do. And this was the brightest red that I have ever seen—insignia red."

"Weren't airplanes painted with red tails an easier target?" The answer was a resounding no. The red tails made identification easier for the bomber-gunners being escorted. As the easiest way to recognize a buddy, it also helped the airmen in the thick of a dogfight. The color of the 332nd's aircraft made no difference to the German gunners on the ground, since they saw only silhouettes. Most of the airmen dreaded the German antiaircraft artillery more than engagement with a German fighter at altitude. That was man-to-man, machine against machine. The unknown, hidden in the clouds of gray dirty smoke from flak, was more dangerous.

The 99th Fighter Squadron became part of the 332nd Fighter Group on July 3, 1944. There was no celebration. The 332nd was the only group to have four squadrons. In the 79th Fighter Group, the 99th had broken racial barriers to become part of an integrated unit. With their transfer into the 332nd, the four squadrons of African-American airmen were once again a segregated unit. Relationships were also not good between the members of the 99th and the 332nd; resentment and jealousy permeated both groups. There was no way that the highly experienced fliers of the 99th intended to fly as wingmen for the less experienced pilots of the 332nd. The pilots of the 332nd sought some of the glory that the 99th pilots had achieved. They resented their fame and worried that the pilots of the 99th would get the plum missions. It was a trying task to meld the two units; it's doubtful that any leader other than Colonel Davis could have been successful.

If the segregation bothered the men of the 332nd Fighter Group, it did not affect their prowess in the air. The Red Tails were in demand as escorts for bombing missions for obvious reasons. The coverage they provided to the bombers was unequaled.

Thirty-six mission P-51s and a half-dozen spares lifted off from Ramitelli at 8:30 A.M. on July 6. Pilots of the 100th, 301st, and 302nd Fighter Squadrons were providing penetration, target cover, and withdrawal for the 47th Bomb Wing to Latisana, Tagliamento, and Casarsa. Four spares, two mechanical failures, and one escort aircraft returned early. A pair of P-51s reached landfall in northern Italy and were credited with sorties. Thirty-seven P-51s lined up with the bombers at 9:33 A.M. at varying altitudes. The 100th formed up as lead squadron, covering the first two groups of bombers at twenty-two thousand feet. The 301st was responsible for middle cover for the four bomber groups at twenty-four thousand feet. The 302nd Fighter Squadron brought up the rear of the bomber formation at twenty-nine thousand feet. The formation was well-disciplined but very wide; the bombers appeared to spread across the entire Adriatic, making recognition of the various bomber wings almost impossible. Following disbursement of the bomb loads, the formation returned home without incident.

On July 12, 1944, the 100th, 301st, and 302nd Fighter Squadrons flew an escort mission to France, assigned to provide close cover, escort penetration, target cover, and withdrawal for B-24s of the 49th Bomber Wing. Forty-two airplanes took off from Ramitelli at 7:45 A.M., with six spares and two aircraft with mechanical problems returning early. The escort lined up with the B-24s in fair formation at 10:11 A.M. at an altitude of twenty-three thousand feet in heavy overcast. The 100th was in the middle, the 301st Fighter Squadron led, and the 302nd flew high, as the bombers reached their target. Twenty-five enemy fighters were spotted off the coast.

The bombers had reported an excellent bombing pattern over the target area; direct hits were observed. Twelve enemy aircraft believed to be Fw-190s had been observed but not encountered because of the distance. Thirty enemy vessels had been observed in Toulon Harbor and approximately sixty enemy fighters were in revetments around the Toulon Airdrome. From the ten o'clock high position, six Focke-Wulfs peeled off slowly and in line dived down through the bomber formation at an extremely high rate of speed. The Fw-190s then did a split "S," made tight turns to the left, and split "S" again. Believed to have been hit, one crashed out of its second split "S." In the middle of the fray, Lieutenant Harold Sawyer shot down another Fw-190.

Joseph Elsberry spotted sixteen Fw-190s attacking the bomber formation at the nine o'clock position of the bombers. On orders, his flight dropped their belly tanks and turned into the Germans. The bandits turned tail. Elsberry caught one Focke-Wulf in range and fired a short thirty-degree deflection shot. Elsberry's fire was on the mark. The Focke-Wulf fell off on its left wing, as heavy black smoke poured from the fuselage. No one observed the definite destruction of the aircraft; therefore, it became only a probable. As another Focke-Wulf turned in front of Elsberry, he began firing and hit it in the left wing. The enemy airplane began to roll; Elsberry continued to fire short bursts. The Focke-Wulf went into a split "S" maneuver. As it tried to recover, it smashed into the ground. One definite for Elsberry.

Only a minute later, yet another Focke-Wulf crossed in front of Elsberry's guns and then went into an evasive turn. That was the

German's mistake. Elsberry got off a lead shot, then fired another two-second burst. Lieutenants Charles A. Dunne and Robert Friend watched as the Focke-Wulf crashed and burned. Two definites for Elsberry.

From the enemy's right side, Elsberry caught still another German in a forty-five-degree dive. With only his left wing guns firing, Elsberry kicked right rudder to keep his sights on the Fw-190. The left wing had been hit near the fuselage. The bandit went into a spiral, then a deadly dive. The German pilot attempted to pull out, but it was too late. The aircraft smashed into the ground, making three definites for Elsberry.

The conflict had been quick and vicious. Captain Joseph Elsberry shot down three Germans during the dogfight, and Harold Sawyer scored a lone kill. Elsberry became the first black pilot to score three victories in one day. Eight days later, Elsberry scored his fourth kill while escorting B-24s of the 47th Bomber Wing in the Munich area.

A four-squadron mission which included the 99th, 100th, 301st, and 302nd Fighter Squadrons was assigned on July 15 to provide coverage for four groups of the 55th Bomb Wing attacking the important oil refinery complex at southwest Ploesti. Sixty-six P-51s left Ramitelli at 8:23 A.M.; five returned to the field early. Sixty-one Mustangs continued on line, hooking up with the heavy bombers at 10:23 A.M. at an altitude of twenty-six thousand feet. In a good formation, the bombers continued on to the target through overcast conditions. The flak over the target area was intense and accurate. One B-24 exploded when hit by flak; no parachutes were seen. Eight Messerschmitts attacked three straggling bombers at 12:45 P.M. at Krusevac, but the enemy aircraft were quickly intercepted and driven off.

The next day, fifty-one pilots of the 100th, 301st, and 302nd Fighter Squadrons were assigned a fighter sweep. The P-51s took off from Ramitelli at daybreak headed to Vienna. Flying in a box-type formation, the 302nd flew low, the 100th in the middle, and the 301st top cover as a high-altitude sweep was made over Vienna through heavy flak. In Vienna, the flak was reported to cover an extremely large geographic area.

As the P-51s left Vienna, pilots observed a straggling B-24 being approached by an Italian-made Macchi 205 V Veltro from the five o'clock low position. The flight leader and his wingman attacked the Macchi. When it went into a steep turn, the leader overran the

July 12, 1944, was a banner day for the 332nd Fighter Group and Joseph Elsberry. Attacked by a large number of enemy aircraft while escorting Allied B-24s to France, Elsberry downed three German airplanes. (USAF Collection, AFHRA, Maxwell AFB, AL.)

Macchi. His wingman turned inside the bandit, fired short bursts at intervals, and almost at will, followed the Macchi to the deck. Trailing black smoke, the enemy aircraft attempted to make a low-altitude turn. Its left wing struck the mountainside, the aircraft burst into flames and exploded.

Watching his wingman attack the enemy aircraft, the flight leader climbed to altitude and spied a second Macchi five thousand feet below. The P-51 closed fast, catching the Macchi as it went into a left turn. The American pilot fired sixty-degree deflection shots and observed large pieces fly from the plane. As the Macchi went into a spin to the left, Lieutenant William Green watched it crash.

Late morning on July 17, fifty-three P-51s of the 100th, 301st, and 302nd Fighter Squadrons took off from Ramitelli. Forty-six of the Mustangs met the bombers of the 306th Bomber Wing shortly after noon at an altitude of twenty-five thousand feet, headed to Avignon. The tight formation of the bombers made it easy for the P-51s to provide cover. A loose formation was an open invitation for enemy fighters. The 302nd was lead and flew low. The 100th provided middle cover, while the 301st furnished top cover at thirty thousand feet.

As the formation approached the target, they spotted nineteen enemy airplanes. Three aggressive Me-109s attempted to attack the B-24s in a string formation from the eight o'clock position. They broke off as the P-51s moved in to counter them; no bombers were hit. The trio of Me-109s went into split "S" maneuvers and attempted to dive while making evasive swerving turns to the left. Three P-51s split up from the formation and gave chase—one on the tail of each Me-109. The three bandits smashed into the ground. Lieutenants Ralph Wilkins, Robert Smith, and Luther Smith each claimed one Me-109 as destroyed. The after-mission narrative reported that the aggressor "pilots seemed very inexperienced and did not even attempt to fight back."

Following the mission, Second Lieutenant Maceo A. Harris described the assistance he had rendered to a damaged bomber. From his vantage point, Harris could assess the flak damage to the bomber; weak radio signals prevented communication, however. Using hand signals, Harris informed the bomber pilot that although his number one engine was damaged, it appeared that it would last the forty minutes that it would take to reach Corsica. Harris then led the disabled bomber to the field where it made a successful belly landing, injuring only the bomber's tail gunner in the process. Afterward, Harris met the B-24 pilot, a Lieutenant Loerb from the 459th Bomber Group, who told Harris how much he and his crew had appreciated the assistance. Harris recalled, "He and the copilot appreciated my friendly aid, and kissed me after the manner of the French."

Sixty-six pilots filed in for their morning briefing on July 18, 1944. The formation leader was Lee Rayford. Flight leaders were Elwood Driver, Clinton Mills, Walter Lawson, and Edward Toppins from the 99th; Andrew Turner, Lawrence Dickson, John Briggs, and Jack Holsclaw of the 100th; Rayford, Joseph Elsberry, Claude Govan, and Joseph Gomer of the 301st; and Charles McGee, Felix Kirkpatrick, Frank Walker, and Charles Bussey of the 302nd Fighter Squadron. The mission briefing assigned the pilots to the 5th Bomb Wing for a raid against Memmingen Airdrome.

Sixty-six P-51s lifted off the steel-matted strip of Ramitelli at 7:50 A.M., meeting the late-arriving bombers at 9:35 A.M. at an altitude of twenty-six thousand feet. The 301st flew as the lead squadron; the 99th was low, the 302nd middle, and the 100th high. En route the weather was overcast; at the target, the visibility and ceiling were both unlimited. As the escort flew into the Udine and Treviso areas, thirty to thirty-five Messerschmitts were spotted to the starboard side of the bombers at twenty-five thousand feet. The German aircraft, painted either black or very dark gray with red markings on the engine cowling, formed in units of two and five and flew in at the three and five o'clock locations. Their evasive tactics were poor and unimaginative; each time that they were met by the P-51s, the enemy aircraft attempted split "S" escapes, regardless of altitude. Nine Me-109s fell to the guns of the P-51s in the Udine area. Another was badly damaged. The twenty-one P-51s that had engaged the enemy returned to Ramitelli; thirty-six others continued on to the target.

A large concentration of enemy fighters was spotted southeast of the target; the bandits included both Messerschmitts and Focke-Wulfs. They followed the formation at the bombers' altitude but stayed out of range. At 10:30 A.M. four Fw-190s dived from an altitude of twenty-six thousand feet at the bombers a thousand feet below. This proved to be a mistake. Two P-51s locked onto the tails of two of the Focke-Wulfs and blew them out of the sky. The surviving two Fw-190s fled. Six others had provided top cover for the attackers but made no attempt to engage in battle.

Lieutenants Charles Bailey and Edward Toppins had each destroyed one Fw-190. Lieutenants Hugh Warner, Roger Romine, Lee Archer, and Walter Palmer were each credited with one Me-109. Lieutenant Jack Holsclaw had dispatched two Me-109s, and

Lieutenant Clarence Lester had scored three kills on Me-109s. Captain Andrew Turner was credited with damaging one more. One B-24 exploded after being hit by heavy flak.

Combat was both physically and emotionally draining. Aircraft went through many changes of direction in a dogfight. The pilots wore no "G" suits, and the centrifugal forces exerted as they maneuvered were hard on their bodies. Some days were uneventful and a welcome respite from the rigors of aerial combat. While every combat pilot wanted to achieve the ultimate—to meet the enemy and knock him out of the sky—everyone wanted something more important. They wanted to stay alive and return home.

As if they knew Germany could no longer win the war, much of the aggression was now missing from the tactics of the enemy pilots. With catastrophic losses among their cadre of fighter pilots, Germany was turning out new classes as quickly as possible. As the fierceness and experience levels of the enemy waned, just the opposite was true with the pilots of the 332nd Fighter Group. They were hungry for action. As each day's battle ended, their experience and confidence levels greatly increased.

Fighter pilots of the 332nd shot down eleven enemy planes on July 18, 1944. Pictured left to right, Clarence D. "Lucky" Lester and his crew chief admired the three swastikas signifying the three Messerschmitt Me-109s destroyed by Lester. (USAF Collection, AFHRA, Maxwell AFB, AL.)

Chapter Ten

The War Rages On

All four squadrons of the 332nd Fighter Group were assigned close cover escort for B-24s of the 49th Bomb Wing on July 19. Headed to the always-dangerous Munich/Schleisheim area, fifty-one P-51s departed Ramitelli at 9:23 A.M.; three returned early. Formation and flight leaders were Captain Turner and Lieutenants Driver, Lawson, Briggs, Faulkner, Jefferson, Sawyer, Gleed, Haywood, Wilkins, Kirkpatrick, and Walker.

The group lined up with the bombers at 11:09 A.M. at twenty-four thousand feet and proceeded to the target. The 100th and 99th were low; the 302nd provided middle cover; and the 301st flew high. The bombing patterns were good; large clouds of black smoke were observed on the ground. At noon, four Me-109s were spotted in the target area at twenty-four thousand feet. When they kept their distance, the P-51s made no attempt to engage. The intense, accurate flak northwest of Munich was just as bad over the target area, hitting a pair of B-24s. One exploded in midair; the other continued in formation.

Fifty-three P-51s lifted off the runway at Ramitelli at 8:35 A.M. the next morning. Formation and flight leaders included Colonel Davis, Captains Jackson, Pullam, Elsberry, and Govan, and Lieutenants McGee, Sheppard, Curtis, Briggs, Steward, Toppins, and Baugh. Pilots of the 332nd Fighter Group had been assigned as penetration escort for the 55th, 304th, and 47th Bomb Wings to Friedrichshafen, Germany, and to conduct a fighter sweep northeast of the target. Nine of the P-51s returned early; forty-four P-51s continued on course, lining up with the bombers at 9:47 A.M. Flak was heavy all along the route, but especially so at Brenner Pass, Merano, Munich, and Lowenthal. The bombers flew a good formation but were too numerous to allow adequate coverage.

At approximately 10:45 A.M. in the dangerous southwest Udine area, twenty enemy aircraft attacked the rear wave of bombers from the position of six o'clock low at an altitude of twenty-seven thousand feet. In an effort to act as decoys, groups of four to eight bandits flew duplicate formations on both the port and starboard side of the bombers, all the while remaining out of range. At the same time, several Me-109s, painted black with white trimmings, trailed at altitude, providing top cover. When several enemy aircraft broke from their box formation to attack the B-24s at high speed, the 332nd pilots immediately broke into flights of four to eight airplanes and intercepted the attackers. When the gunfight ended, four Messerschmitts had been destroyed. Captains McDaniel and Elsberry and Lieutenants Johnson and Toppins each claimed one kill. The fighters that had engaged the enemy returned to base, while twenty-four P-51s continued on to the target area with the bombers and then made a follow-up fighter sweep. Two B-24s were lost to intense anti-aircraft fire in the target area. Earlier, another B-24 had also gone down with several chutes seen to open. Two crippled B-24s were picked up in the area of Udine and escorted to Ancone.

Ploesti was the target the next day. The weather had cleared; the ceiling and visibility were unlimited. The 332nd had drawn an assignment to the 55th Bomb Wing. Sixty-one P-51s took off from Ramitelli at 8:53 A.M. for an uneventful rendezvous with the bombers. Heavy flak over the target hit Lieutenant Walker's aircraft at twenty-six thousand feet. Nearly twenty unidentified aircraft were spotted near the target area but at a great distance from the formation and provided no interference.

Genoa Harbor was the mission of the B-24s of the 47th Bomb Wing on July 24. Thirty-five Mustangs of the 332nd rendezvoused with the bombers at 11:37 A.M. at an altitude of twenty-two thousand feet. The bombers were five minutes early but in a good formation, making it easy to provide coverage. Fighters from the 99th and 302nd merged into a single squadron and flew low position. The 100th flew middle cover, while the 301st provided top cover. Despite intensely heavy flak over the target, the bombing went off without a hitch. Smoke was observed rising to eight thousand feet. With no enemy interference, following bombing, the aircraft rallied right and returned abreast to the base.

The 332nd encountered heavy enemy action on July 25 on the same type of mission they had flown for so many days. The group was ordered to provide aerial protection for B-24s of the 55th Bomb Wing as they attacked the Hermann Goering Tank Works at Linz, Germany. The flight joined up with the B-24s at 10:40 A.M. and continued on to the target. The bomber formation was compact in width but strung out in length, making it difficult to cover. To compensate, the fighters divided into three squadrons—one took the head of the formation, one squadron was in the center, and another brought up the rear. Arriving at 11:20 A.M., the formation covered the target for nearly fifteen minutes. The heavy and dangerous flak hit and destroyed three B-24s.

As the bomber formation made its first penetration into the target area, more than forty Messerschmitts attacked units of the rear squadron of bombers. Distinguished by their yellow under-surfaces and a yellow band around their cockpit cowlings, the Me-109s came in groups of three or four making one sweep, while the other 109s provided top cover. Lieutenants Alfred Carroll and Starling Penn were both shot down but were later rescued. Lieutenant Sawyer was busy; he downed one Me-109 and damaged another two.

Missions over Germany and Austria were always especially dangerous. Flak could be counted upon to be heavy and accurate; sightings of enemy aircraft were routine. Sometimes they struck immediately; sometimes they trailed the formation anticipating stragglers and crippled bombers. The pilots of the 332nd usually gave better than they got—July 26, 1944, was one of those days. On escort duty with the 47th Bomb Wing over Markersdorf Airdrome, Austria, the Americans added to their ledger five destroyed, two probables destroyed, and one damaged.

Following a routine takeoff of sixty-eight P-51s from Ramitelli, twenty-one aircraft returned to the field. The remainder proceeded on to Verazdin for rendezvous with the B-24s. Near the target area two different groups of six Me-109s were spotted without engagement. Shortly afterward, another flight of Fw-190s was observed without incident. This group acted as decoys and stayed above and below the bombers at a safe distance.

At 11:00 A.M., at least eighteen Me-109s engaged the P-51s. Nine more Me-109s that had remained at thirty-five thousand feet suddenly came in from the nine o'clock high position in a compact formation. On approach they split into a two-ship tactical formation for their attack on the bombers. The Messerschmitts flew into split "S" maneuvers and sped to the deck when the Mustangs engaged them. One German pilot was described as extremely aggressive. A second attack was mounted by the Germans, but was turned away. Captain Edward Toppins claimed one Me-109 as destroyed and one probable; Lieutenant Freddie Hutchins claimed a definite Messerschmitt and one probable. Lieutenants Claude Govan, Leonard Jackson, and Roger Romine each scored a kill, and Lieutenant Heber Houston damaged yet another Me-109. The toll against the Allies was also heavy. One B-24 was seen spiraling out of the formation in the target area following the attack by enemy aircraft and a lone P-38 Lightning was observed going down trailing a stream of black smoke.

July 27 was a virtual replay of the prior day. Fighters of the 332nd Fighter Group exacted a heavy price from the Germans. The four squadrons again combined to provide cover for the 47th Bomb Wing to the Mannfred Weiss Armament Works in Budapest, Hungary. The B-24s were fifteen minutes late meeting the thirty-seven Mustangs assigned to their escort. Lee Rayford and Claude Govan were flight leaders of the 301st; William Mattison, Walter Palmer, John Briggs, and Lawrence Dickson led the 100th; Albert Manning and Robert Daniels the 99th; and Dudley Watson, Harry Sheppard, Wendell Pruitt, and Felix Kirkpatrick the 302nd. The bombers and P-51s flew on course at an altitude of twenty-four thousand feet. At 9:45 A.M. they observed an enemy aerodrome with thirty-five to forty single-engine fighters.

North of Lake Balaton, more than twenty-five Me-109s and Fw-190s attacked the bomber formation from all positions. A squadron of the P-51s quickly countered and moved in front of the German attackers where they made quick work of the enemy, destroying eight and damaging two, despite heavy flak. Coming out of the target area, the B-24s were set upon by twelve Fw-190s. Another thirty enemy fighters were spotted as the bombers dropped their loads. The P-51s countered, scaring off every attacker. Lieutenants Gleed and Gorham each scored two Fw-190s; Gleed and Manning damaged two more. Captain Govan and Lieutenants Kirkpatrick, Jackson, and Hall were credited with destroying one Me-109 apiece. In the midst of the aerial combat, Jackson mistakenly fired on a plane believed to be a P-51 that was camouflaged in black and tan with yellow stripes on the tail. At 10:50 A.M., one B-24 was seen at Valpova with two engines out.

On July 28, the 332nd was ordered to provide close cover escort for the 55th Bomb Wing. The mission was the Ploesti Oil Fields, an always-dangerous and well-protected target. A flight of fifty-four P-51s lifted off from Ramitelli at 7:40 A.M.; fourteen returned to the field early. The 332nd flew almost a direct line at twenty-six thousand feet to the rendezvous point, but there were no bombers. Two more Mustangs returned to the field. The B-24s were five minutes late but in a good formation and easy to cover. Approaching the target, the groups of bombers made an echelon to the right. Initially in a group "V" formation, the fighters then flew into squadrons atrail to permit good coverage of all of the bombers. For almost thirty-five minutes, the bombers jettisoned their loads over Ploesti. The flak was heavy, the target area covered in wind-blown smoke from south-west of Ploesti.

Eight enemy aircraft were sighted but not engaged. A lone Messerschmitt trailed two P-51s, but wisely broke off when the Americans turned into it. Seven additional unidentified aircraft were observed in the target area but weren't chased because of the distance. It was a routine mission for the 332nd, but not for the 55th Bomb Wing. Enemy flak had taken an exacting toll; at least three B-24s had fallen.

On July 30, the 332nd scored a rare kill—an Italian Reggiane 2001 Ariete. On approach to rendezvous with the bombers, a single-engine Reggiane 2001 attacked a straggling P-51 at 10:10 A.M. at fifteen thousand feet. As the Re-2001 flew parallel to Lieutenant Carl E. Johnson's Mustang, Johnson turned into the stalking bandit and knocked it from the sky with a ninety-degree deflection shot. While the P-51s were providing top cover for a raid of 5th Bomb Wing B-17s over the Tokol Armament Works in Budapest, ten unidentified enemy aircraft were spotted north of Lake Balaton. There was no engagement.

It had been a rewarding day for other American fighter groups as well. A P-51 sporting a checkered tail dived out of the sky in pursuit of a Me-109. As the flight of 332nd Mustang pilots broke off to keep from hitting the diving Mustang, the checkered-tail made the kill. Another Me-109 was destroyed by the fire of a Lockheed P-38 in the target area. By the end of July, the 332nd had destroyed thirty-nine enemy fighters.

During August 1944, the Red Tails destroyed German aircraft with a vengeance. Junker Ju-87 Stukas, Heinkel He-111 bombers, Junker

Ju-52/3m transports, Messerschmitt Me-109s, Dornier Do-217s, and Focke-Wulf Fw-190s all fell before the cannon and machine gun fire of the attacking airplanes of the 332nd Fighter Group. The daily grind of war continued in August much the same as it had in July. There were bomber escorts to Le Pouzin Oil Storage Fields, attacks against the Gyor Car Works and Campina Stevea Roman Oil Refinery.

On August 12, the 332nd strafed enemy radar stations in southern France. At 8:27 A.M. thirty-five Mustangs of the 99th and 302nd took off. Nearly thirty minutes later, thirty-six aircraft of the 100th and 301st Fighter Squadrons sped down the runway. After so many aircraft took off, the surrounding area was totally obscured by the thick dust. A total of seventy-one P-51s split into a trio of attacking sections for pre-selected strafing missions. Sweeping in, the P-51s attacked at levels ranging from two thousand to five hundred to just a few feet from the ground. The flak was as heavy as ever encountered; several men lost their lives.

Several 332nd Fighter Group pilots discussed strategy and tactics in the shadow of a red-tailed P-51 Mustang in August 1944. Left to right are: Dempsey W. Morgan Jr., Carrol S. Woods, Robert H. Nelson Jr., Andrew D. Turner, and Clarence D. Lester. (National Archives and Records Administration, #208-NP-6XXX-1.)

The 99th went after targets at Sète and Montpellier, flying from five hundred feet to the deck. Pilots from the 302nd destroyed targets at Narbonne and Leucate. Captain Pullam and Lieutenants Curtis and Palmer led P-51s of the 100th against targets at Marseilles and Cape Couronne. Radar stations and antenna installations were destroyed by the 301st at Toulon. There was no interference from enemy aircraft, but the ground fire and flak was extremely heavy and deadly.

Recalling the mission, Woodrow W. Crockett said, "We went over at fifteen thousand feet and had to hit the targets inland. We liked to hit the targets going out to sea, but on this mission we had to go inland. After the mission, I called for a ninety-degree turn to the right. We were on deck. I called for the second ninety-degree turn which would take us out to sea.

"Half-way through my turn to get us out of France, I saw a lookout tower in Marseilles Harbor. It looked like that tower on a can of cleanser. I rolled out and said, 'Look what I found.' I sprayed it from bottom to top, then I decided I better break. The controls were awfully stiff. When I did break, it sounded like I went through a tunnel—that's how close I was. I thought that I had lost the scoop of my Mustang, that's how close I was. The instruments were still reading. If I hit the tower, I'd planned on going right on over and crash-landing on land. I went on out to sea and I could see them shooting at me with holes back here in the seven o'clock position. I looked at my airspeed, and I was still doing 425 miles an hour, and I said , 'If I can do this for another minute, I'll be seven miles out to sea, out of range.'

"We came back; we lost six people on that mission. Jefferson from Detroit was one of those guys. We came back to base. Major Mattison got his tail almost shot off; all his cables were exposed. A couple of times they had us as MIAs, but we made it back."

Combat was hell; there were the German fighters, engine failures, and the enemy flak batteries. It was a miracle that more men didn't die. Second Lieutenant Richard D. Macon of Birmingham, Alabama, believed that a series of miracles had saved his life when he ran into a wall of heavy black flak that day. At just three hundred feet above the ground, Macon's plane suddenly ran into heavy flak, cutting the aircraft's aileron controls and overturning the plane. In the September 1, 1945, issue of the *Pittsburgh Courier,* he later recalled: "While fighting to right the Mustang, I suddenly felt a terrific blast of heat and saw my entire engine smothered out in flames. I passed out."

Unconscious, Macon's limp body slumped against the control stick and pushed it forward. As the P-51 went into a loop, Macon was ejected at an altitude of only three hundred feet. When his chute opened, he floated to the ground, landing in a plowed field.

Several other pilots including Joseph E. Gordon, Langdon E. Johnson, Alexander Jefferson, and Robert H. Daniels were also taken as prisoners of war or killed.

August 13 was another bombing mission. B-24s of the 304th Bomb Wing were assigned the Avignon railroad bridges, with the 332nd picked to provide target cover. Sixty-seven P-51s from Ramitelli were required for the mission, departing at 10:55 A.M. and reaching the target at 12:55 P.M. The bombers attacked in waves at an altitude of twenty thousand feet, but the mission was uneventful. The next day would be different.

Another German fighter pilot lost his life to the guns of a 332nd Fighter Group pilot on August 14. Pilots of the group were assigned to strafe targets at Cape Blanc, Camerat Island, and La Ciotat. The 99th and 100th were ordered to undertake a fighter sweep of the Toulon target area. As the sixty-three P-51 fighters approached the target area, the 99th and 100th conducted a peremptory sweep to clear out enemy aircraft; the 301st and 302nd split up to strafe targets on the ground. Pilots of the 301st attacked the first target—a radar station. They flew in from fifteen thousand feet and dropped to the deck. Lieutenants Weathers, Williams, and Smith fired on the base and saw it crumble. A coast watcher verified that the antenna toppled over. The second flight overran their target, strafing six small buildings that were hit but didn't catch fire. The first flight of the 302nd came in on the deck from the southwest and fired on a radar station and took out a gun position. The second flight attacked another radar station and also silenced a .50-caliber gun position.

The last flight of the formation came under enemy attack. Four enemy pursuits attacked at fifteen thousand feet at 10:25 A.M. in the Toulon area. As the bogies slipped in from five o'clock high, the formation immediately turned into the attackers. The number-three man, Lieutenant Rhodes, began firing short bursts. He followed the fleeing Focke-Wulf from fifteen thousand feet to the deck. Rhodes' fire caused the left wing of the German aircraft to disintegrate. Lieutenant Allen had been forced to bail out over Elba, but was rescued. Lieutenant O'Neil went into a spin over Toulon at thirteen thousand feet, but survived.

Radar stations near Marseilles and Toulon were the targets assigned to the 332nd on August 12, 1944. On that day, slightly more than seven months after his graduation from Tuskegee Army Air Field as a single-engine pilot, Alexander Jefferson was shot down by ground fire and captured by German troops. (Private Collection.)

Jefferson became a prisoner of war for the next nine months. Held first at Stalag Luft III, east of Berlin, and then at Stalag Luft VII-A, near Dachau, Jefferson recorded his experiences as a prisoner of war in a series of drawings. (Private Collection.)

The next day the bombers again attacked southern France; Point St. Esprit, Dousere, LeTeil, Bourg, and St. Andeal were the assigned targets for the 55th Bomb Wing. The bombers were twenty miles off course when sixty-four planes of the 332nd arrived for rendezvous.

A pair of Me-109s were observed at 12:30 P.M., heading south-south-east. Since the bandits made no attempt to attack the formation, no attempt was made to intercept them. Following the bombing, the bombers rallied and returned to base.

The 332nd provided escorts for bombers of the 55th Bomb Wing to Ober Raderach Chemical Works, Germany, on the sixteenth. On the seventeenth they were tasked with covering the 304th Bomb Wing as the Ploesti Oil Refineries were again attacked. Over the next several days, attacks were made against the Osivecin, Kornenburg, and Ploesti Oil Refineries. With each passing day, German and Austrian targets received heavy poundings. Just as Allied bombers exacted a heavy toll, Allied fighters destroyed enemy aircraft on the ground. Once again, the 55th Bomb Wing received the assignment to go after Markersdorf Airdrome, Germany, with the 99th, 100th, 301st, and 302nd Fighter Squadrons assigned escort duty. Lieutenant Holsclaw led a flight of sixty P-51s, arriving at the rendezvous point at approximately 11:30 A.M. The B-24s were seven minutes late, requiring the formation of fighters to circle. An hour later, the collection of bombers and fighters was at the target area. At least

Captain Charles E. McGee and his crew chief Nathan B. Wilson discussed McGee's final mission of World War II. McGee also flew as a combat pilot in both Korea and Southeast Asia. (USAF Collection, AFHRA, Maxwell AFB, AL.)

one B-24 went down from the heavy flak and a pair of Me-109s exploded in flames.'

Fourteen Me-109s were observed at an altitude of twenty-eight thousand to thirty thousand feet. Seven in a Lufbery circle dived through the overhead formation. Lieutenants Hill and Weathers jumped a single Messerschmitt, chasing him from twenty-four thousand feet to the deck, all the while firing their guns. Five days later, based on the evidence from his gun cameras, Hill was awarded the kill.

The 332nd scored several kills on August 24, but it was a costly day for Allied bombers. Lieutenants William H. Thomas, Charles E. McGee, and John F. Briggs each knocked a German fighter out of the air. Briggs of the 100th scored a Me-109, and Thomas and McGee of the 302nd each bagged a Focke-Wulf. At least four B-24s and one B-17 fell victim to the accuracy of German 188-millimeter antiaircraft fire.

German aircraft on the ground were no safer from American fighters than were those in the air. Ground attacks on August 27 yielded twenty-two aircraft destroyed and eighteen damaged. Sixteen P-51s strafed the airdromes at Prostejov and Kostelec, Czechoslovakia. There were over 150 aircraft parked at Prostejov and at least another 200 at Kostelec. No flak or fighter opposition was encountered.

The strafing mission to Grosswardein Airdrome took the Germans completely by surprise. Captain Alfonza Davis was formation leader on the August 30 strafing mission to Romania. Flight leaders were Captains Turner and Govan, and Lieutenants Curtis, Briggs, Palmer, Elsberry, Cisco, and Faulkner. Approaching the target, the flak was minimal. Fifty-seven P-51s flew in from an altitude of fifteen thousand feet and dived to the deck. The assault lasted thirty minutes, as each ship made five to six passes against the enemy airfield.

Approximately 150 enemy aircraft of all types, many camouflaged with hay, were seen on and near the airfield. Reconnaissance photographs taken two days earlier had revealed only a portion of the aircraft found on the field on August 30. Pilots of the 302nd made a total of seven passes at the field, the 99th three passes, and the 100th and 301st five passes. No ground fire of any kind was encountered. The Germans made it easy for the attackers, concentrating the parked aircraft in the southwest and eastern sections of the field, with the remainder along the northern and southern sections. After the last pass by the 332nd the entire airfield was in flames. In all, eighty-three aircraft were classified as destroyed and thirty-one were damaged.

September began as August had ended—with coverage of a B-17 bomber strike against Popesti. On September 2, the four fighter squadrons mounted a joint strafing attack against troop movements on the Stalak, Cuprija, and Osipaonica Roads. Sixty-seven Mustangs left Ramitelli at 1:39 P.M., following a route from base to Nis to Stalak. When there was no troop movement at the assigned target area, the flight hit an alternate target at Krusevac. Fifteen aircraft strafed a dozen freight cars at the Krusevac Railroad Station; another Mustang attacked and damaged a truck at Krusevac. A lone P-51 swept across and fired on a thirty-truck convoy, destroying three and damaging another ten vehicles. Two aircraft damaged five box-cars.

First Lieutenant Jack D. Holsclaw, the Assistant Group Operations Officer, reported on the mission of September 2:

> Four squadrons of the Group covered strafing area, highway and RR installations along highway from STALAK to CUPRIJA and North toward BELGRADE. They arrived in the target area North of NIS, followed the NIS-STALAK Highway to STALAK. Two squadrons covered the highway from STALAK to CUPRIJA twice, then covered several highways in the area N of CUPRIJA toward BELGRADE. No

Lieutenant Edward C. Gleed conducted a mission briefing for 332nd pilots. Both the map and briefing chart indicated that the target for the upcoming mission was in Germany. (National Archives and Records Administration, #208-MO-18K-32983.)

Briefings contained information about weather conditions, coordinates, aircraft to be escorted, estimated levels of antiaircraft fire, and expected number of opposing airplanes that was important to the success of the mission, as well as the safety of the fighters and bombers. (National Archives and Records Administration, #208-N-32987.)

troops, truck convoys or railway movements were seen. The other two squadrons turned left and followed the highway from STALAK to KRUSEVAC to KRALJIVO to KRAGUJEVAC. Sighting nothing they took a course E to CUPRIJA and followed the highway N from that point. No enemy traffic was sighted. One pilot taking off late attempted to catch the formation. He never did catch up and flew NE of NIS 10 or 12 miles. He saw a convoy of approximately 30 trucks. He strafed them, setting three on fire and damaged ten more. On his route home on a heading of 245 degrees, he passed by NIS. He turned N and covered part of the assigned target area. He saw no traffic of any kind, troops, trucks, or trains.

Italy was the target for September 4. The pilots of the 332nd went to Tagliamento, Casarsa, and Latisana, Italy, with B-24s of the 304th Bomb Wing. The bombers were fifteen minutes late meeting the forty-five P-51s circling at twenty-two thousand feet. The bomber formation was good, but some of the elements were three thousand feet higher than briefed. Following the rendezvous, the group split off into two sections of two squadrons each. Twenty-three aircraft were over Tagliamento-Casarsa railroad bridges from 1:10 P.M. to 1:30 P.M. The other twenty-two hit the Latisana railroad bridge for six minutes. Direct hits were reported on both bridges; there had been no flak or enemy fighters.

September 5 and 6 were spent providing coverage for B-17s as they attacked railroad bridges crossing the Danube at Budapest and targets in Romania. Attacks against Yugoslavian targets on September 8 yielded excellent results. Forty-two P-51s pulled out of Ramitelli at 8:40 A.M., headed for targets at Ilandza and Alibunar Airdromes. Twenty-three Mustangs strafed the Ilandza Airdrome for nearly an hour, while four P-51s provided protective top cover. Several unchallenged passes were made at the field and the enemy aircraft on the ground. Junkers, Focke-Wulf, Dornier, Heinkel, and Messerschmitt aircraft—eighteen in all—were destroyed. Pilots from the 99th claimed seventeen of them, while Mattison of the 100th claimed a lone Focke-Wulf Fw-200.

The action at Alibunar Airdrome followed the same pattern. While twenty-six aircraft provided top cover, fifteen P-51s attacked the field almost at will. Of the twenty enemy aircraft on the field at Alibunar, eighteen were destroyed and left in flames. One P-51 strafed Zemun Field damaging two additional aircraft. Met with heavy small arms fire, the pilot estimated that nearly two dozen enemy aircraft sat on the ground. Walter Westmoreland of the 302nd had also destroyed a locomotive at Alibunar.

Most of the latter part of September was spent providing escort protection for the 304th and 5th Bomb Wings. B-17 and B-24 bombing runs were made against Blechhammer North Oil Refinery; Rakos; bridges at Budapest; Malacky Airdrome; Athens, Greece; Delreczen, Hungary; and the BMW Engine Works at Munich.

When they were not engaged in missions against the enemy, the men were busy "winterizing" their quarters in preparation for the heavy rains and strong winds of the Italian winter. Utilizing wing tank boxes, cans, and salvaged pieces of lumber, the men transformed the camp. The 332nd Fighter Group Personnel Narrative dated 8 October 1944 vividly described the activity. "The sound of hammer on nail and sometimes on finger were heard and gradually an area of tents became transformed into an area of tents and houses, semi-tents or semi-houses, and in some cases among the tents or houses, a mansion appeared. Some of the men painted their plywood construction, others burned the wood grain to give a rugged design to their huts, others built showers inside of their huts while others installed seats and built-in closets. To see an ordinary tent supported by tent pegs and side flaps was an item of curiosity."

In the first week of October 1944, bad weather precluded flying many missions. The 332nd was in Hungary on October 11, assigned to strafe railroad and river traffic along the banks of the Danube River from Budapest to Bratislava. Seventy-two Red Tails were up around noon, but bad weather and mechanical problems took their toll. Fifty aircraft were forced to return early to Ramitelli.

Only twenty P-51s of the 99th and 302nd were able to find an opening through an overcast along the Yugoslavian coast to Esztergom on the Danube. At deck level, they strafed three landing fields. Seventeen of thirty-six enemy aircraft were destroyed and left in flames by pilots of the 99th Fighter Squadron. P-51s of the 302nd destroyed another four aircraft. At the same time, two aircraft went after six barges on the Danube, encountering heavy automatic weapons fire. All six barges were damaged. In addition, one stable used as an oil dump was bombed and set on fire; two locomotives and one oilcar also met destruction. An additional locomotive and boxcar were damaged in the attack. Following the strafing missions along the Danube, the twenty-two P-51s regrouped and returned on a south-southwest heading to Ramitelli. On landing, Lieutenant George Rhodes crash-landed and destroyed his Mustang. Fortunately, Rhodes was not hurt.

When the weather cleared, action for the 332nd Fighter Group shifted to Greece. On October 4, aircraft of the 99th, 100th, and 301st Fighter Squadrons were ordered to strafe airfields at Tatoi, Kalamaki, and Eleusis. Of the flight of fifty-three P-51s departing Ramitelli at 10:58 A.M., mechanical problems forced fourteen aircraft to abort. From base, the aircraft flew to the boot of Italy, then on to the targets in perfect flying weather. The three squadrons flew in a single group formation, splitting up at the assigned breaking point and proceeding to targets separately.

Captain Lawrence, Lieutenants Gaiter, Lawson, and Thomas were flight leaders for the 99th. Tatoi Airdrome was strafed by the 99th from deck level for fifteen minutes, despite intense ground fire. Twenty-five to thirty enemy aircraft at Tatoi were well dispersed, making strafing difficult. Of the four fires resulting from the initial passes, at least one came from the burning P-51 of Captain Erwin Lawrence of Cleveland, Ohio, which had fallen victim to the accuracy of German gunners and had spun into the ground. Lieutenant

Kenneth Williams' P-51 was also hit by enemy gunners. When his canopy wouldn't open, he was forced to crash-land. Williams was captured and became a prisoner of war. The 99th claimed one destroyed and eight damaged aircraft at Tatoi Airdrome.

The 100th Fighter Squadron led by Captain Pullam and Lieutenants Palmer, Curtis, and Ellington swept across Kalaki Airdrome at 1:00 P.M. at deck level toward twenty grounded enemy aircraft. Two Junkers Ju-52s and one Heinkel He-111 were destroyed. Eight Junkers and Heinkel aircraft were also damaged. More than twenty-five aircraft, most of which were well camouflaged, sat on the ground at Eleusis Airdrome. As P-51s of the 301st Fighter Squadron made two passes against the field, they destroyed five aircraft and damaged five Junkers Ju-52s. Thirty-seven P-51s returned at 4:45 P.M. Lawrence and Williams were missing. Victory had its cost. The death toll among the 332nd was high.

On October 4, 1944, while on a strafing mission, Captain Erwin B. Lawrence fell victim to the accuracy of German gunners. He had previously served as a commander of the 99th Fighter Squadron and had flown ninety-three missions. (USAF Collection, AFHRA, Maxwell AFB, AL.)

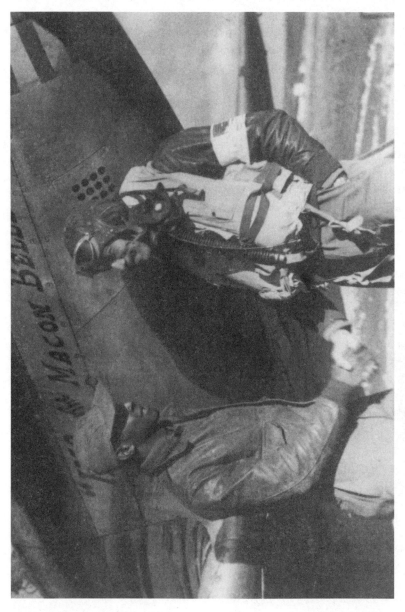

Following a successful mission, Lee A. Archer (right) received congratulations from his crew chief, Staff Sergeant William Carter. Flying his P-51 named Ina, The Macon Belle, Archer was credited with one probable and four definite downings of enemy aircraft. (USAF Collection, AFHRA, Maxwell AFB, AL.)

Chapter Eleven

The 332nd Scores Big

October 12 was one of the most productive days for the 332nd. Led by George Roberts on an escort mission to Blechhammer, Germany, the group scored an impressive nine kills in the air and destroyed another twenty-six aircraft on the ground.

Sixty-eight P-51s lifted off from Ramitelli just after noon. Fourteen P-51s of the 99th Fighter Squadron approached the Kaposvar Airdrome at 2:00 P.M.; for the next quarter hour, they were on the attack. From altitude, nearly forty enemy aircraft were observed on the field below. The Mustangs came swooping in from east to west to attack the German airplanes parked in or near revetments on the field used for pilot training. A large number of the enemy airplanes had swept-back wings with radial engines. Nine subsequent passes were made at the field; each follow-up attack was made in a counterclockwise maneuver with no flak opposition. The pilots of the 99th claimed as destroyed on the ground five Me-111s, four Me-109s, two trainers, five Ju-88s, one Fw-190, and one Fw-200; the eight additional aircraft that were damaged included two biplanes, one Fw-190, one Ju-88, three trainers, and one Ju-87.

Simultaneously, seventeen P-51s of the 302nd Fighter Squadron were attacking another German landing field. A pair of Me-109s, three He-111s, one Ju-88, one Me-110, and one biplane were destroyed on the ground. Six He-111s and a pair of training biplanes were damaged. Between the two squadrons, twenty-six aircraft had been destroyed and another sixteen damaged on the ground.

From 2:30 P.M. to 2:45 P.M., thirteen P-51s of the 100th Fighter Squadron found different targets of opportunity. They damaged three locomotives, three railcars, thirty boxcars, twenty-five trucks on the highway, and a camouflaged factory surrounded by three parking lots holding forty-five trucks and cars. At the same time, eighteen airplanes from the 301st strafed approximately fifty oil barges, destroying four and damaging eleven others.

While en route to a target in a northeasterly direction, Captain Pruitt's flight investigated a lone He-111 at ten o'clock low. As Pruitt peeled off from the formation to attack, nine He-111s and seven Me-109s attacked the flight from five o'clock high. Lee Archer, a highly experienced pilot who had already flown forty-six combat missions and had been awarded the Air Medal with four Oak Leaf Clusters, was the first to spot the enemy Messerschmitts.

Closing on the German's tail, Archer fired short bursts into the Messerschmitt's fuselage. As it spewed a stream of black smoke, the pilot bailed out. Pulling out of a sharp turn, Archer spotted four Me-109s directly below him and dived at them. He stalked the last airplane in the formation, opening fire from a distance of two hundred yards. The Messerschmitt's left wing buckled and broke off, sending the plane into a deadly dive that ended in a fiery explosion upon impact. Archer quickly closed on another enemy aircraft. As its pilot went into acrobatic maneuvers in an effort to escape his pursuer, Archer's bullets found the Me-109's tail. The German's wounded airplane began to emit acrid black smoke and erupted in flames. Seconds later, the pilot opened his canopy and bailed out.

The dogfight lasted fifteen minutes, ranging from seven thousand feet to the deck level. Pilots closed from distances as far as three hundred yards to as close as twenty-five yards. Aerial gunnery ranged from ninety-degree deflection shots to dead astern point-blank. Afterward, Lee Archer expressed the confidence in their P-51 Mustangs that he and the other pilots shared. Feeling that the odds of two Mustangs against more than a dozen German fighters were about equal, he and Captain Wendell Pruitt had had no concerns abut tackling a numerically superior force. He was right—Pruitt shot down two enemy planes while Archer got three. Seven more were downed by the rest of the squadron. As Archer put it, "It was one good fight."

The raids that day had been especially productive; the 332nd Fighter Group had racked up an impressive tally. In addition to nine aircraft destroyed and two probables, fifteen oil-laden barges, three locomotives, thirty boxcars, a factory, and several dozen cars and trucks were also annihilated. As always, victory in war was tempered by defeat. Lieutenant Walter L. McCreary's aircraft had been hit by flak, forcing him to bail out over Lake Balaton. Captured by the Germans, McCreary spent the next nine months as a prisoner of war in the North Compound of Stalag Luft Three. McCreary had successfully flown eighty-nine missions.

The next day eight aircraft of the 302nd Fighter Squadron destroyed seven enemy aircraft on the ground and damaged another half dozen. The 304th Bomb Wing was attacking the Blechhammer Oil Refinery located about 125 miles from Berlin, with the P-51s of the group assigned to provide fighter cover. Afterward, the fighters sought targets of opportunity.

Four P-51s of the 99th located two locomotives heading east from Bratislava. The pair of locomotives and a flatcar loaded with trucks were strafed and damaged. A trio of 100th Fighter Squadron P-51s strafed six boxcars that had suffered earlier damage. Four Mustangs from the 302nd Fighter Squadron went after locomotives, boxcars, coal cars, and a small house beside the railroad tracks. Believed to be an ammunition dump, the house exploded violently when hit. Not to be outdone, eight pilots of the 302nd went after Tapolca landing field. Each time they made a pass from southeast to northwest, they came under small arms fire. By the end of their third pass, they had silenced the guns, destroyed seven aircraft, and damaged six others.

Gunnery school and hundreds of hours of simulated aerial and strafing combat had done much to prepare the fighter pilots for combat. In a dogfight the pilots were taught to ". . . dive to dead astern of the target, attack from dead astern, fire at precisely: 1200 ft.-bead on intersection of horizontal and vertical stabilizer, 450 ft.-bead on top of vertical stabilizer, break off the attack at a minimum range of 300 ft., reduce speed and resume original position for another attack."

In the end, however, the ultimate preparation was combat itself. Hiram Mann, a 302nd Fighter Squadron pilot, recalled his first combat strafing experience:

"Most of our missions were due north and we would rendezvous with the bombers and head on to wherever our target was. We were escort and would always fly above the bombers. When the bombers started their bomb run, we would leave them and fly a wide pattern around their target area, and when they rallied off the target area, we would pick them up again. We were seldom in any position to be shot at.

Hiram E. Mann, a replacement pilot assigned to the 302nd Fighter Squadron, found that the realities of combat differed substantially from the theoretical aspects discussed during training. (Private Collection.)

"On my first strafing mission, I put two sticks of gum in my mouth before I got in the plane. I got in my plane and hooked up my oxygen mask. We took off and were flying over and the flight leader called for us to jettison our external tanks and he picked out a target. He saw a train rolling on the ground. We got into echelon and went in. The leader went for the engine, and as you spread out, you pick out a boxcar and you start firing on the car. I picked out my car and gave my plane full throttle. I'm in my dive and I aimed on this boxcar and I squeezed my trigger.

"We had three .50-caliber guns in each wing and they converged at 250 yards in front. Every fifth bullet in the gun is a tracer. It lights up as it goes out. I could see my tracers as they were going. The adrenaline is pumping. And then I saw tracer marks going past me. The first thought was 'I'm flying faster than my bullets.' Then it occurred to me, 'They're shooting at me!' This was not the scenario that you got in ground school. Luckily, my plane was struck, but I was not shot down. When we got back to the campsite, I got out on the wing. You don't get nervous until after the excitement is over. When I got out, I had literally chewed that gum to the point that there was no cohesion. I had a mouth full of little BBs."

First Lieutenant William W. Green of Staunton, Virginia, came close to losing his life on a strafing mission on October 13 in Yugoslavia. He took out his assigned target, an ammunition dump, but his plane was hit, forcing him to bail out. While the Germans searched for him, Green was rescued and hidden by Yugoslav partisans. After spending four days with the Slavs, he was turned over to the Russians who eventually flew him back to Naples. Over a year later, Green, the holder of the Distinguished Flying Cross with six Oak Leaf Clusters, three battle stars, and a Purple Heart, was awarded Yugoslavia's Partisan Medal Third Class.

First Lieutenant Walter D. Westmoreland, the nephew of Secretary of the NAACP Walter White, was not as fortunate. His family received the news of his death on October 25, in a letter from Major General Nathan F. Twining. Westmoreland had been missing in action since October 13, 1944, when he failed to return from a bomber escort mission to Blechhammer, Germany. Lagging behind the formation as his plane lost altitude on the return flight, Westmoreland attempted a forced landing but hit a tree. Machine gun fire forced the other pilots to regain altitude and leave the scene. Westmoreland's cousin, Frederick Funderburg, also died in combat in Europe.

Fifteen pilots of the 332nd Fighter Group were lost in action or taken as prisoners of war during October 1944. On the 13th, while on a mission to Blechhammer, Germany, Walter D. Westmoreland, nephew of NAACP secretary Walter White, was killed. (Private Collection.)

The Regensburg/Winterhafen Oil Storage facility in Germany was the target for the 5th Bomb Wing on November 4. Seventy P-51s of the 332nd were assigned to provide the bombers with cover. Thirty-two aircraft penetrated to the target area at noon. Another twenty-nine penetrated five minutes later to furnish withdrawal cover. The weather and flak had prevented the rendezvous from taking place as briefed, making the fighters late. Despite the last group of bombers being approximately fifty miles behind the lead group on the return, the fighters managed to provide adequate cover.

On November 16, sixty-two P-51s rolled down the strip at Ramitelli at 10:00 A.M., their assignment—close escort for the 304th Bomb Wing to Munich. Fifty-seven P-51s rendezvoused with the B-24s at Masseria at 11:45 A.M. at an altitude of twenty-four thousand feet. A pair of Messerschmitts attacked six P-51s south of Latisano. The Mustangs had been at twenty thousand feet when the Germans came in from high and six o'clock above. One P-51 was damaged in the attack; two P-51s of the 52nd Fighter Group flying above prevented interception.

At 1:30 P.M. a trio of P-51s were escorting a crippled B-24 of the 304th Bomb Wing when they encountered six Me-109s in the Udine area at an altitude of twenty-four thousand feet. The Germans attacked in a string formation going into a Lufbery Circle for defense. The engagement lasted almost ten minutes and ranged from twenty-four thousand feet to the deck. The B-24 was safely escorted back to its base; the pilots returned to Ramitelli.

Many friendly aircraft in the area contributed to aerial confusion. P-51s of the 52nd Fighter Group had come perilously close to the bomber formation as the 332nd's rear squadron covered the last element of the 304th Bomb Wing. As one bomber began to straggle, four P-51s of the 332nd were detached to furnish escort. They were immediately pounced on by the P-51s of the 52nd before identification was made.

The 332nd lost two men on November 19. A strafing mission of railroad, highway, and river traffic in the Gyor-Vienna-Estergom area ended up with the capture of Lieutenants Roger Gaiter and Quitman Walker. Fifty-seven P-51s took off from Ramitelli in group formation at 11:30 A.M., flying to Sibenik and then to Veszprem at ten thousand feet. At 1:15 P.M., the four-squadron formation split into two sections of two squadrons each. The 99th and 302nd Fighter Squadrons moved northward along the highway and railroad tracks into Gyor. The 99th furnished top cover on the northerly movement while pilots of the 302nd strafed.

On the southward trip along the same route, the roles were reversed. Fourteen aircraft of the 99th Fighter Squadron strafed railway and highway traffic from Gyor to Veszprem. Fifteen horse-drawn vehicles and twenty railroad cars were destroyed. Two locomotives, one hundred horse-drawn vehicles, and forty railroad cars were damaged.

The 301st provided top cover to the 100th as they flew on deck in a northerly direction and strafed in the area of the Danube River. The 100th then furnished top cover for the 301st as they strafed in an easterly direction to Estergom. The 301st and 100th claimed one tank car destroyed and six barges, one tugboat, and over thirty freight cars damaged.

First Lieutenant Roger B. Gaiter had already flown thirty-seven missions over France, Germany, and the Balkans before being shot down that day. Hit by flak, Gaiter was forced to bail out of his flaming airplane. After eluding the enemy for several days, he was captured by the Germans. Herded together with six white captured Allied fliers, Gaiter was force-marched to Gyor.

On more than one occasion along the way, their guards watched as the men were assaulted by Hungarian civilians with clubs and rocks. During one confrontation, a captain from St. Louis was left unconscious by a thrown brick. Denied medical attention, the injured men were forced to treat their wounds and then continue their march to the Gyor train station. Their reception in Vienna was not much better, as revenge-seeking civilians greeted their arrival. Eventually the Allied airmen were rescued by their German guards and transported to a prisoner-of-war camp where they remained until released by Allied forces at the end of the war.

Lieutenant Quitman Walker's P-51 had also been hit by flak near the eastern end of Lake Balaton. As prisoners of war, Gaiter and Walker endured similar hardships. Forced marches, beatings, and malnutrition were routine experiences for captured Allied airmen.

The strafing missions were especially dangerous, as illustrated by a mission flown by Lieutenant Robert J. Friend of Washington, D.C. Spotting an enemy oil barge, Friend dived his aircraft toward the target. As he fired round after round of .50-caliber bullets into the hull, the barge suddenly exploded. Flames surrounded Friend's plane, but fortunately, he was able to pull his P-51 away from the blazing vessel. The October 21, 1944, issue of the *Pittsburgh Courier* reported Friend's recollection of the event, "It was sort of like being in hell."

Captain Armour G. McDaniel experienced a similar situation. Strafing an oil barge, McDaniel watched his phosphorous tracers cut across the hapless vessel. Pulling his airplane out of a dive, he cleared the deck of the barge just as a tremendous explosion ripped the vessel to pieces. The force of the explosion was so great that his guns were ripped from the wings. Somehow he managed to nurse his crippled airplane back to base. On inspection, his crew chief whistled and said, "I don't see what kept her wings on!" With a grin on his face, McDaniel responded, "The power of prayer, Horse, the power of prayer."

In December there were almost daily missions supporting the 5th, 55th, and 304th Bomb Wings. Frequent targets were Moosbierbaum, Vienna, Kolin, Pardubice, Muhldorf, Landshut, and the Brux Oil Refinery. Brux was targeted by waves of B-17 bombers on December 9. In mid-morning, sixty-four P-51s led by Captain Andrew Turner left Ramitelli headed for their rendezvous with bombers from the 5th Bomb Wing. En route pilots reported an encounter with a lone Me-262 jet in the Regensburg area. A highly valued target of the Allied bombers, Regensburg was home to the Messerschmitt fighter plant. The Germans would do all they could to protect it.

Armour McDaniel and his ground crew inspected damage to his aircraft following a strafing mission. McDaniel's luck ran out in March 1945 when he was shot down on a mission to Berlin. Captured by the Germans, he spent the next few months as a prisoner of war. (Air University/HO, Maxwell AFB, AL.)

Described as the world's first operational jet fighter, the Messerschmitt Me-262 was characterized by a knife-like tail. Lean and mean-looking, the jet had a nose that resembled that of an angry shark. Compared to the Focke-Wulf and Messerschmitt 190s, the Me-262 flew with a speed that seemed to be little more than a silvery blur. As the air war wound down and there was little chance for the Third Reich, Hitler's last hope was thought to be the Me-262. Powered by a pair of wing-mounted Jumo 004 jet engines, the Me-262 was one of the greatest threats to the much venerated P-51 Mustang. In spite of their decided speed advantage, however, many German pilots flying the Me-262 found out that they were not immune to the skills of an experienced P-51 pilot.

Painted olive drab, the Messerschmitt Me-262, armed with four fixed MK108 30-millimeter nose cannons, attacked a formation of eight P-51s just before noon at thirty thousand feet. The Me-262 pilot made one blur-like pass from west to east at the formation of northbound fighters, then attempted to turn for combat. In a countering move, one P-51 turned inside the Me-262 and fired off short bursts of .50-caliber machine gun fire. The jet split "S"d into a cloudbank at an altitude of twenty-five thousand feet, then climbed back up through the formation at a terrific rate of speed, disappearing into the overcast at thirty-five thousand feet.

At almost the same time, another P-51 pilot encountered a second Me-262 over Muhldorf, Germany. From an altitude of thirty-one thousand feet, the Me-262 made a head-on pass at the lone fighter, then pulled away. The P-51 pilot fired his guns at a range of one thousand yards without scoring a hit. Like circling sharks, five German jets followed the bombers for several minutes, hanging to the east out of range, then disappeared. A few minutes later, a second group of Me-262s was observed flying in a loose "V" formation in the same position.

By the end of 1944, the black airmen had shot down sixty-two enemy airplanes. As a term of respect, the Germans called the 332nd pilots the *Schwartze Vogelmenschen*—the "black birdmen."

Chapter Twelve

The End in Sight

January 1945 began much as 1944 had ended. Each day the pilots of the 99th, 100th, 301st, and 302nd Fighter Squadrons prepared for aerial combat. Most of their work consisted of providing protective cover for the 55th, 49th, and 304th Bomb Wings as they attacked targets in Moosbierbaum, Vienna, Schewechat, and Regensburg. There were frequent sightings of enemy aircraft, including the sleek, fast, and very dangerous Messerschmitt Me-262 jet fighters. There were sightings, but few engagements as the war continued to wind down.

February was another busy month for the 332nd Fighter Group. Industrial targets were pounded in Germany and Austria on an almost daily basis. Over the area of Munich, Lieutenant William S. Price scored the 332nd's first kill of 1945 when he dispatched a Me-109.

As the war neared its end, Germany's oil production facilities had been virtually destroyed by Allied bombing attacks. A lack of oil forced a drastic reduction in motor transportation, making Germany's war efforts increasingly dependent upon the railroads. Pilots of the 332nd Fighter Group were ordered to make sure that rail traffic did not go through unscathed.

On February 25, fighters from the 99th, 100th, and 301st Fighter Squadrons went after rail traffic in Munich, Linz, Salzburg, and Ingolstadt. They met heavy small arms fire and light flak as they strafed airfields, troop movements, and rail yards. The tally of destroyed and damaged targets was impressive. Ten locomotives and an electric power station were destroyed; five locomotives, ten passenger railcars, forty-four boxcars, six oilcars, four trucks, and one electric power station were damaged. Three He-111s and one Me-109 aircraft were damaged or destroyed on the ground. On the same day, Lieutenants George Iles and Wendell W. Hockaday were lost near Munich. Iles became a prisoner of war. Hockaday was classified as missing in action and subsequently declared dead. In February 1945, the 332nd lost five pilots and their airplanes.

On February 28, 1945, the 332nd Fighter Group was credited with flying its two hundredth bomber-escort mission with the 15th Army Air Force without the loss of an Allied bomber to attacking enemy fighters. To that date, the black pilots had received sixty-three Distinguished Flying Crosses and completed more than eight thousand individual sorties with the 15th.

During the long months of battle, recently made even more unpleasant by the rainy winter climate, those in charge had done what they could to boost morale and help the men escape from the tragedy of war. Boxing matches held throughout the fall culminated in a victory for the 332nd when Technical Sergeant Burnley, 99th Fighter Squadron, won the middleweight championship at the 15th Air Force Boxing Tournament in Bari, Italy. Depending upon the weather, sports included softball, touch football, and basketball. Ping pong and card games were popular indoor activities, augmented by theatrical and choral groups. One squadron began a series of classes on subjects ranging from war news summaries to mathematics and foreign languages. Holiday celebrations included turkey dinners, along with the always-welcome letters and gifts from home. Visiting USO shows were always entertaining. In February, *Light and Fantastic* proved especially popular, while *Panama Hattie* played for several nights at San Severo.

The 99th Fighter Squadron went on a tear on March 14. On one mission, the 99th strafed rail targets on the Bruck, Leoben, and Steyr rail lines. Twenty-one P-51s from Ramitelli arrived at Bruck at 10:00 A.M. with Captain Campbell as formation leader. As four flights flew against the target, the first flight of attackers destroyed two locomotives, three boxcars, and one warehouse. Thirty-three boxcars, eight flatcars, and four oilcars received heavy damage. Three later flights of P-51s destroyed eight locomotives, sixteen boxcars, and twenty-one flatcars. Nearly one hundred targets, including locomotives, boxcars, flatcars, power stations, and railroad structures, were strafed and damaged.

March 16 was more of the same, as pilots from the 99th, 100th, and 301st strafed rail targets and enemy airfields. As the 301st prepared to strafe Mettenheim Airdrome, a lone Me-109 broke ground

Colonel Benjamin O. Davis Jr. and his pilots celebrated following their 200th mission with the 15th Army Air Force. During those missions, the Red Tails had covered territory in Italy, France, Bohemia, Germany, and Greece. (USAF Collection, AFHRA, Maxwell AFB, AL.)

Officers and enlisted men availed themselves of the courses offered by "Naptha University." The objective of the lectures was "to give each man an opportunity to pick up his schooling where he left off and to learn something which may be useful in civilian life." (USAF Collection, AFHRA, Maxwell AFB, AL.)

for takeoff. A P-51 pilot caught it with a rapid burst of machine gun fire sending the ill-fated Messerschmitt cartwheeling into the earth. Nearly 150 targets on the ground were destroyed or damaged, including twelve Focke-Wulfs.

In March 1945, the 302nd Fighter Squadron was deactivated and disbanded. Pilots still ineligible for rotation home joined the three remaining fighter squadrons. Throughout the war, a shortage of replacement pilots had been a continuing problem. Because the black pilot training program took place only at Tuskegee Army Air Field, not enough black pilots could be trained to replenish the ranks and allow the airmen to return home. Replacements should have occurred at a rate of four per month per squadron. It had been far less than that for the four squadrons of the 332nd Fighter Group. Most black pilots had flown an average of between seventy and eighty missions, while their white counterparts had returned home after only fifty missions. Walter Palmer, a member of the 100th Fighter Squadron, had rotated back to the States in November 1944 after flying a total of 158 missions.

Harry Sheppard flew a total of 123 missions, 87 with the 12th Air Force and another 36 with the 15th Air Force. Sharing his feelings about the numerous missions, he stated, "It didn't go over too well with us at first because we did find out that our predecessors had gone home on a strictly mission rotational basis of fifty missions. Since we only had one source of supply coming from Tuskegee, and by this time now they were trying to furnish pilots for the bombardment squadrons, it made replacements hard to come by. We didn't feel it was an impartial way to treat a certain group of people."

During the final week of March 1945, Colonel Davis led the 332nd on a sixteen-hundred-mile round-trip mission to Berlin. Providing cover for B-17 bombers, the 332nd participated in one of the longest missions ever to be carried out by the 15th Air Force.

The sky was full of airplanes belonging to the 332nd. Leaving Berlin, the airmen of the 332nd encountered twenty-five German attackers, many flying jet aircraft. Three of the German jets were shot down; three black pilots also died. The 332nd Fighter Group was awarded the Distinguished Unit Citation for escorting the bombers as they attacked the Daimler Benz Tank Works. The citation read in part:

> On March 23, 1945, the group was assigned the mission of escorting heavy bombardment type aircraft attacking the vital Daimler Benz tank

Flying a P-51 named The Duchess *in honor of his wife, Walter Palmer downed an Me-109 on July 18, 1944. Palmer flew a total of 158 combat missions before returning home to his wife and an infant daughter.* (Private Collection.)

assembly plant at Berlin, Germany. Realizing the strategic importance of the mission and fully cognizant of the amount of enemy resistance to be expected and the long range to be covered, the ground crews worked tirelessly and with enthusiasm to have their aircraft at the peak of mechanical condition to insure the success of the operation.

On March 24, 1945, fifty-nine P-51 type aircraft were airborne and set course for the rendezvous with the bomber formation. Through superior navigation and maintenance of strict flight discipline the group formation reached the bomber formation at the designated time and place. Nearing the target approximately twenty-five enemy aircraft launched relentless attacks in a desperate effort to break up and destroy the bomber formation.

By the conspicuous gallantry, professional skill, and determination of the pilots, together with the outstanding technical skill and devotion to duty of the ground personnel, the 332nd has reflected great credit on itself and the armed forces of the United States.

Fifty-nine P-51s of the 99th, 100th, and 301st Fighter Squadrons took off from Ramitelli at 9:30 A.M. on the twenty-fourth of March. The P-51s were assigned to provide close escort for a 5th Bomb Wing B-17 attack on the Daimler Benz tank assembly plant at Berlin. Thirty-eight aircraft met the bombers at 11:45 A.M. at an altitude of twenty thousand feet. Sixteen additional Mustangs were in the area, but did not yet line up around the B-17s. The escorting P-51s hung close to the formation of bombers as they approached the point of penetration. At 12:05 P.M., a pair of P-51s peeled off from the formation at twenty-six thousand feet. Five minutes later, nine Mustangs withdrew, again at an altitude of twenty-six thousand feet.

Between 12:10 P.M. and 12:15 P.M. thirty-four enemy aircraft at twenty-seven thousand to twenty-eight thousand feet were observed but not encountered. Painted black with German Cross markings, the aircraft, including thirty Me-262s, three Fw-190s, and one Me-163, were preparing to attack the bombers.

Four Me-262s swept against the lower echelon of the lead group of B-17s at 12:08 P.M. from seven o'clock high. The P-51s countered, damaging two of the enemy aircraft. A lone Me-262 made a single pass at the bombers at twenty thousand feet from one o'clock high, but quickly broke off contact. Minutes later, at twenty-six thousand feet, three Me-262s mounted an attack from five o'clock high on the lead group of B-17s. One Me-262 was damaged. As they dived through a formation of B-17s, nine Me-262s and a single Me-163 engaged in a dogfight with seventeen P-51s for nearly fifteen minutes at twenty-seven thousand feet. Three Me-262s were quickly shot down; an additional pair of Me-262s and one Me-163 were believed to have been destroyed. At 12:15 P.M., at an altitude of twenty-six thousand feet, seven Me-262s made passes against the formation from nine o'clock low and six o'clock high. The Germans flew in formations of four and three aircraft. One Me-262 pilot scored a direct hit on a P-51 and knocked off its right wing. The pilot parachuted out.

The hot and vicious action had lasted almost thirty minutes; the running engagement extended from approach into and over the skies of Berlin. Following the encounters, a fighter sweep was made over the target area. Several P-51s strafed railroad targets damaging two locomotives and three railroad cars.

Almost inevitably, the pilots get all of the credit for the success of the operations. However, without the support of the ground crews, the airplanes would not be flyable. The men of the 366th Service Squadron certainly deserved all of the credit they were accorded for their role in the success of the mission against Berlin. At 10:30 P.M. on the night of March 23, Edward Gleed, the operations officer, contacted all of the squadrons to ascertain how many aircraft were equipped with the large 110-gallon external fuel tanks. The mechanics from the 366th literally spent all night installing the larger tanks on nearly sixty P-51s to allow them the longer range needed for the flight to Berlin. By 8:00 A.M. each Mustang was equipped with the large tanks for the maximum-effort mission to Berlin; otherwise, the mission probably would have been scrubbed.

The P-51s rendezvoused with the B-17s nearly six hundred miles from home base, and stayed with them the remaining two hundred miles to the insertion point at Berlin. They were supposed to be relieved at Berlin by a flight of P-38s, but the relief was late. Having plenty of fuel, the P-51s stayed with the B-17s. Had the relieving unit not been late, the 332nd probably would not have had its chance at the Me-262 jet fighters.

On March 31, 1945, the 332nd was sent on a strafing mission near Linz, Austria. In an encounter with a flight of seventeen Messerschmitts and Focke-Wulfs, thirteen enemy aircraft fell without a loss by the 332nd.

The aerial battle in the Munich area was also an overwhelming success for pilots of the 99th, 100th, and 301st Fighter Squadrons. Forty-seven P-51s were off the blocks at noon; four returned early.

Mechanics of the 332nd Fighter Group labored to install 110-gallon external fuel tanks on the group's P-51 Mustangs. The increased fuel capacity made possible the long-range missions into the heart of Germany. (National Archives and Records Administration, #208-AA-49E-1-3.)

Proceeding on course as briefed, the fighters were flying in group formation. The group leader assigned the 99th a strafing mission against rail traffic in the western third of the target, the 100th the eastern third, and the 301st rail lines in the center of the target area.

Six aircraft of the 99th strafed rail traffic for five minutes, destroying one locomotive and damaging five passenger railcars. The Mustangs then flew northeastward and strafed several other rail targets. One electric locomotive and ten passenger cars were damaged. Fifteen aircraft of the 301st flew to their target area, then split into flights of seven and eight P-51s. The eight halved into two flights of four planes each. As one flight of four strafed a moving train, damaging the electric locomotive and two boxcars, the second flight strafed rail traffic, destroying two boxcars, two locomotives, and several hopper cars.

The flight of seven aircraft strafed and destroyed or damaged several locomotives and rolling stock. One P-51 was hit by flak and forced to return to base. The six remaining aircraft flew southeast and spent the next twenty minutes strafing several trains. Total ground targets claimed as destroyed included seven steam locomotives, two boxcars, eight oilcars, three passenger railcars, one house, one warehouse, and several military targets. Nearly seventy pieces of rolling rail stock were damaged.

At 2:15 P.M. five Me-109s and a lone Fw-190 were encountered at an altitude of three thousand feet. Painted a dark color, with no distinguishing markings, the enemy aircraft came out of a cloudbank to pounce on seven P-51s from the nine o'clock position just as the Mustangs prepared to descend to a rail target. The P-51s quickly engaged the bandits, destroying all six. Major William Campbell was credited with one Me-109; First Lieutenant D. L. Rich was credited with another, as were Second Lieutenants Hugh White, James Hall, and John W. Davis. Second Lieutenant Thomas Braswell tallied one Fw-190.

April 1, 1945, turned out to be April Fools' Day for a flight of very unfortunate German pilots. Returning from escort duty for a formation of 47th Bomb Wing B-24s to the St. Pölten marshalling area, pilots of the 332nd were pounced upon by a large number of Me-109s and Pw-190s. Charles White was the first to see the Germans in the vicinity of Vels, Austria. The American P-51 pilots dropped their external tanks and flew into the attacking Germans. When the smoke had cleared, the Americans had destroyed twelve enemy aircraft. Charles White, Carl Carey, and John E. Edwards were each credited with a pair of kills; Harold Morris, Walter Manning, and James Fischer were credited with one each; and Harry T. Stewart had dispatched three Me-109s. The price had been high; Walter Manning and William Armstrong both lost their lives.

Harry Stewart, winner of the Distinguished Flying Cross, remembered the demise of the third German to attack him. After shooting down the first two, Stewart turned around to see an aircraft on his tail. At first he thought the pilot was flashing his lights on and off. Suddenly, he realized that what he thought to be lights were bursts of machine gun fire from a Focke-Wulf that was rapidly closing. Stewart rammed the stick forward and put his P-51 into a steep dive. The German followed. At only forty-five feet above the ground, Stewart pulled back on the stick and headed for blue sky. Unable to pull out of his dive, the German smashed his plane into the ground. An explosion and heavy black smoke streamed toward the sky.

For the mid-morning April 15 mission against rail targets in Salzburg, Linz, Pilsen, Regensburg, and the area surrounding Munich, thirty-seven Red Tails were off the field at Ramitelli at 11:25 A.M. Only one pilot returned early because of mechanical problems. Thirty-six aircraft led by Colonel Davis arrived in the assigned target

*Top honors on April 1, 1945, went to Harry T. Stewart Jr. of the 301st Fighter Squadron.
When eight of the Red Tails encountered sixteen enemy fighters, they shot down twelve and
damaged another two German aircraft. Stewart was credited with destroying three Focke-Wulf
Fw-190s.* (Private Collection.)

area in a three-squadron formation at 1:45 P.M. Cloud coverage en
route had been heavy, forcing the formation to change its course.
Twelve pilots of the 99th Fighter Squadron steered their aircraft from
the group insertion point to their designated section of the target
area. They alternated between flying top cover and strafing rail traffic
for the next fifteen minutes.

A dozen planes from the 100th attacked the rail lines from
Plattling to Passau to Klatovy. Aircraft from the 301st attacked river
and rail traffic, strafing everything in sight. Before the firing stopped
and the smoke cleared, the 332nd had destroyed seventeen steam
locomotives and eight oilcars. Sixteen steam locomotives, two electric engines, seven oilcars, thirty-four boxcars, two passenger railcars,
four barges, one riverboat, one flatcar, one house, two buildings, and
several military targets were damaged.

At 2:40 P.M. at an altitude of two thousand feet, a lone Me-109 was
engaged. The dark blue bogie met two P-51s as they gained altitude
after strafing rail targets. The Luftwaffe pilot attempted to turn just
as the P-51s closed in on him from the rear. As several deflection
shots caught the Me-109 in the engine area, the fleeing aircraft burst
into flames and crashed into the ground.

On June 12, 1945, the 332nd Fighter Group was reassigned to the 305th Bombardment Wing. With the end of the war in Europe at hand, officers and enlisted men alike looked forward to the prospect of returning home. (Private Collection.)

The 15th Air Force flew its last combat mission of World War II on April 26. On this banner day, six P-51s from the 100th and 301st Fighter Squadrons and a single P-38 Lightning took off from Ramitelli at 8:50 A.M. The twin-engine Lockheed P-38 outfitted with a nose camera was on a routine reconnaissance mission to Prague. For nearly two hours, the Mustangs provided escort for the P-38 to Linz, Prague, and Amslettin.

At high noon, flying at twenty-three thousand feet, a lone bogie was spotted. A trio of Mustangs left the P-38 to investigate. The P-51s intercepted and found the aircraft to be a twin-engine British de Havilland Mosquito fighter-bomber flying alone. At 12:05 P.M., as the Americans headed back to escort, they saw five Me-109s. The Germans rocked their wings in an attempt to convince the Mustang pilots that they were friendlies. Just as quickly, the Me-109s took evasive action by executing a series of split "S"s and aileron rolls.

Three of the Messerschmitts were flying at the two o'clock position. Two of the bandits started to turn and one pulled up high as if to dive. One P-51 pulled onto the tail of the climbing German and let loose two quick bursts. The bandit flipped over, went into a deadly spiral, and crashed. A pair of Mustangs closed on the other

Thirty-three members of the 332nd Fighter Group spent part of their tour of duty as prisoners of war. Shot down while on a strafing mission over Greece, Andrew Marshall was more fortunate than most in that he was rescued by Greek partisans and returned to base only weeks later. (National Archives and Records Administration, #208-AA-102E-5.)

Messerschmitts and fired short bursts across their fuselages. One German pilot bailed out. The other rode his crippled aircraft to earth, where it crashed in a red fireball. Of the remaining two Messerschmitts, one was definitely shot down. The other probably met the same fate, but the kill couldn't be verified.

A portion of the airmen of the 332nd Fighter Group headed for home in July 1945, nearly two months after the Germans had surrendered on May 8, 1945. The majority followed in October. The record the pilots of the 332nd Fighter Group and the 99th Fighter Squadron left behind was magnificent. The 450 pilots had flown more than 1,500 missions in their vaunted P-51 Mustangs and had destroyed 111 enemy airplanes in the air and another 150 on the ground in strafing missions. One destroyer escort and fifty-seven locomotives had also been put out of commission.

In the service of their country, these brave men were awarded 150 Distinguished Flying Crosses, plus numerous other medals. Sixty-six pilots had died; another thirty-three had been captured as prisoners of war.

Chapter Thirteen

The Birth of the 477th

Parallel to the formation of the 332nd Fighter Group, the all-black 477th Bombardment Group (Medium) was first activated in mid-1943. Deactivated just two months later, the group was reactivated in January of 1944. The leaders of the Army Air Corps and the War Department had no more interest in black pilots commanding bombers than there had been in the program that put African-Americans into the cockpits of sleek fighter aircraft. The 477th Bombardment Group was formed because of an undiminished public pressure exerted by African-American leaders, newspapers, unions, and civic groups.

Originally based at Selfridge Field, Michigan, the 477th was supposed to have a complement of twelve hundred officers and men. Sixty B-25 twin-engine Mitchell bombers, each capable of carrying a bomb load of three thousand pounds, would perform the medium-range bombing mission of the 477th. The 477th Bombardment Group was an expensive proposition. With B-25 bombers costing $175,000 each and an estimated training expense of $35,000 for each officer, the cost of putting the sixty medium bombers in the air was estimated at $20,000,000.

The men of the 477th paid dearly for the privilege of breaking down yet another military barrier to African-Americans. The group never made it to the war; their losses came not at the hands of an enemy, but from the military leadership of their own country. Pilots and crew members of the 477th experienced some of the most bitter racism of any of the black units ever formed, constantly confronted with bigotry, segregation, and frustration from its activation to war's end. War Department rationales to the contrary, the 477th Bombardment

A pair of B-25 bombers of the 477th Bombardment Group (Medium) flew high above the farmland of Michigan. Just as the 99th Fighter Squadron had opened the door for black single-engine pilots, the formation of the 477th allowed African-Americans to command and crew bomber aircraft. (Private Collection.)

Although the operations building at Selfridge Field, Michigan, was somewhat unimposing, the base was better equipped than many at which the 477th Bombardment Group would be stationed. (USAF Collection, AFHRA, Maxwell AFB, AL.)

The 477th Bombardment Group (Medium) was comprised of four squadrons—the 616th, 617th, 618th, and the 619th. Although the 477th was to be an all-black unit, white officers initially staffed positions of authority. (USAF Collection, AFHRA, Maxwell AFB, AL.)

Group was transferred from base to base as punishment, and in an effort to destroy an already lagging morale. Between May 1944 and June 1945, the 477th endured thirty-eight unit moves. Twenty-three were called permanent changes of station. On the average, one squadron or base unit changed bases every ten days of the period.[1] The effect was devastating to the success of the training program.

Just as in the case of the Tuskegee Experience, the 477th Bombardment Group was an experiment whose failure was desired by the military hierarchy. Prior to the activation of the 477th, the Army Air Corps issued a negative report on the proposal that was rife with the language of failure. The report concluded, "It is common knowledge that the colored race does not have the technical nor the flying background for the creation of a bombardment-type unit." The formation of a bomber group, because of its scope and scale, dwarfed the creation of a much smaller fighter squadron. A fighter plane needed only a pilot and a small ground crew. Bombers required a crew of twelve men including pilots, navigators, bombardiers, gunners, and ground crew.

Airmen assigned to the 618th Bombardment Squadron updated the engineering status board that tracked the readiness of each of the squadron's aircraft. The squadron's training was frequently disrupted as it rotated between Selfridge, Atterbury, Freeman, Walterboro, and Godman Fields. (USAF Collection, AFHRA, Maxwell AFB, AL.)

While the home base of the 477th was Selfridge Field, the training took place at airfields throughout the United States. Pilots would first be trained at Tuskegee Army Air Field on twin-engine airplanes; the first combined class of single and twin-engine pilots received their wings in a graduation ceremony in December 1943. Following Tuskegee, the flight crews learned to fly B-25 bombers at Mather Field, California. Ground crews also trained at Mather, then rotated to Inglewood, California.

When the first class of black pilots arrived at Mather, there was no segregation. All airfield facilities were open to everyone, black or white, until Major General Ralph P. Cousins visited the Central Flying Command's B-25 Transition School on an inspection tour. When General Cousins ordered the base commander to establish segregated mess facilities, the black pilots protested by not eating in the mess hall. Instead, they took all of their meals in the post exchange and paid to do so. On February 10, 1944, eighteen trained

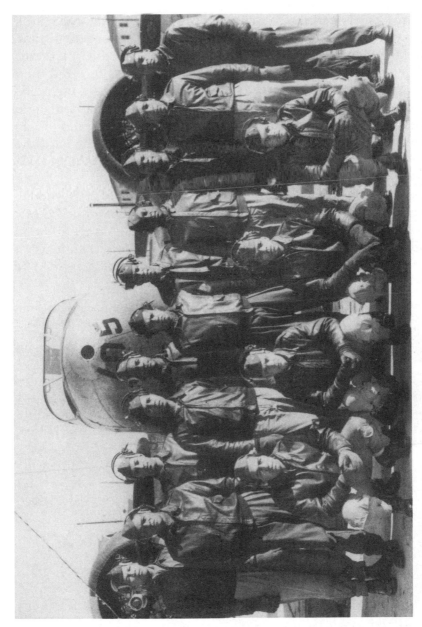

Although Selfridge Field, Michigan, served as the home base of the 477th Bombardment Group, initial pilot training took place at Tuskegee Army Air Field, followed by transition training at Mather Field. (Private Collection.)

bomber pilots graduated from the first Mather Field training course and received their wings; additional B-25 pilot classes were in the pipeline.

Gunners learned their craft at Eglin Field, Florida. Navigator-bombardiers were trained first at Hondo Field, Texas, then transferred to other bases in Texas and New Mexico for bombardier training. On February 26, twenty-four navigation cadets received their wings at Hondo. The next day, sixty-seven black airmen, including the first twenty-four to graduate from Hondo, boarded eight Lockheed Lodestar training airplanes and flew a celebration flight to Pittsburgh where they were honored by the editor of the *Pittsburgh Courier*. Several of the men qualifying as navigators had previously washed out of fighter training at Tuskegee.

By early 1944, hundreds of black men had also been trained at Sioux Falls Army Technical School, Sioux Falls, South Dakota; Lincoln Field Air Forces School at Lincoln, Nebraska; and Scott Field at Bellevue, Illinois. The final training would take place at Selfridge Field, Michigan, where the individual members would be meshed into a complete crew.

An enlisted man got the feel of a turret gun during training. Manpower shortages were always a serious problem for the 477th. In January 1945, the group was lacking all of its mandated 288 gunners. (USAF Collection, AFHRA, Maxwell AFB, AL.)

A pair of 477th Bombardment Group navigators studied the globe and wondered if they would ever see combat. Life with the 477th was a study in contradictions; a July 1944 staff report stated, "The lack of navigators and bombardiers is holding up the training program." (Private Collection.)

Bombardiers learned the intricacies of nose and tail fuses on a 500-pound bomb. White officers held most command positions in the 477th Bombardment Group, including serving as instructors. (USAF Collection, AFHRA, Maxwell AFB, AL.)

The choice of a commander for Selfridge could not have been worse. Colonel Robert Selway Jr., a West Point graduate, was not only a strict segregationist, but also a racist of the worst kind. Believing strongly that African-Americans were inferior and lacked the necessary skills to be combat pilots, he did everything in his power to destroy the morale of the men of the 477th. Selway assigned only white men to positions of supervision, reasoning that while he might have to teach blacks to fly, he didn't have to allow them to supervise or be in positions of power.

Selway had been equally prejudiced in his treatment of the men of the 332nd Fighter Group several years earlier. Serving as their commanding officer at Selfridge prior to their overseas assignment, he considered the group to have been in terrible shape. He later justified his policy of prohibiting blacks in positions of leadership by saying:

"Two years ago in May I was ordered to Selfridge Field to reorganize and train the 332nd Fighter Group, which is an all-Negro outfit. Upon my arrival there, there was not one airplane in commission; and the Negro and white personnel who were assigned there as instructors—that is, the white personnel—had ceased to function and everything was at a stalemate. Investigation disclosed that a great percentage of the colored personnel were malassigned, did not have the qualifications, and could not be qualified to successfully perform in the MOS in that Group."[2]

Selway had support from the top for his racist beliefs. Major General Frank O. Hunter, commander of the 1st Air Force to which the 477th was assigned, stated, ". . . racial friction will occur if colored and white pilots are trained together."[3] An ardent segregationist, Hunter backed Selway in his actions against African-Americans.

Lieutenant Daniel "Chappie" James Jr. recalled the atmosphere at Selfridge and his deep distrust and near hatred of General Hunter. The owner of a fiery temper, James had been expelled for fighting while a student at Tuskegee Institute. Joining the Air Corps at Tuskegee Army Air Field, the young man from Pensacola, Florida, was commissioned as a second lieutenant in the 477th in 1943. James ultimately went on to become the first African-American four-star general in the United States Air Force.

During a commander's call, Hunter addressed black personnel and warned that he would not tolerate any attempts to integrate facilities. James recalled, "They [Selway and Hunter] had drawn a

Daniel "Chappie" James (center) personified the determination of African-Americans to overcome the obstacles placed in their path by the United States military establishment. Originally a civilian flight instructor at Tuskegee, James went on to become the first black four-star general in the U.S. Air Force. (USAF Collection.)

The buildings that served as the headquarters of the 477th at Godman Field appeared even more temporary than those at Selfridge Field. Although the official explanation for the transfer was "better flying weather," most regarded it as a further effort to destroy morale. (USAF Collection, AFHRA, Maxwell AFB, AL.)

line down the middle of the theatre, in Selfridge Field, Michigan, and said, 'The blacks will sit on one side of this line, and the whites on the other.' And so when we, with the full cooperation of most of the whites, decided to go on what we called 'Operation Checkerboard' after the lights went out in the movie, they turned the movie off and made us go back to our segregated seats. This was a very stupid thing to do, but they did it two or three times a night."

After only five months at Selfridge, the 477th was transferred to Godman Field, located near Fort Knox, Kentucky. Godman Field was about as close to hell as any place on earth. The barracks were ramshackle, painted battleship gray to hide slipshod workmanship and dirt. Segregation was the norm. The men felt that they had been transferred as punishment, despite the official attribution of the transfer to better flying weather.

The War Department had expected to have the 477th fully manned by November 1944, only ten months after its reactivation the preceding January. Shortages of manpower prevailed, however. By January 1945, it was apparent that the 477th was woefully behind schedule. The group was short 26 pilots, 43 co-pilots, 2 navigator-bombardiers, and all 288 gunners.[4]

Freeman Field, located in Seymour, Indiana, became the new home of the 477th on March 15, 1945, as things went from bad to worse. With Colonel Selway still in command, the situation at Freeman Field was a simmering cauldron, the boil not long in coming. Facilities on the base were separate for whites and blacks. Troop strength was 400 African-American officers and 2,500 enlisted men; the white population was 250 officers and 600 enlisted men.

The citizens of Seymour were hardly more hospitable to the black airmen than Selway was. Many restaurants refused to serve the black airmen stationed at Freeman Field. Some grocery stores refused to sell food to their families. The Seymour Laundry refused to provide service for the black airmen. The irony of the situation was not lost on the airmen; the laundry had willingly washed the clothing of German prisoners of war.

In late March, several black officers spoke to a reporter from the *Pittsburgh Courier* with the proviso that they not be identified. One young lieutenant said, "We are not mad, but just disgusted with the rewards for our efforts." Another said, "We want promotions for our officers and enlisted men when they merit them and when we go across we want to feel that we are laying down our lives for a cause of absolute freedom, freedom for our people here at home."

COL. ROBERT R. SELWAY JR.

Colonel Robert Selway could be described as even-handed in his treatment of African-Americans—he discriminated against all blacks at every opportunity. Whether in charge of the 332nd Fighter Group or the 477th Bombardment Group, Selway was a terrible choice for a commanding officer. (USAF Collection, AFHRA, Maxwell AFB, AL.)

Chapter Fourteen

The Freeman Field Mutiny

On April 1, 1945, an order was posted at Freeman Field that restricted certain buildings to whites only. Club Number Two was designated for the use of base and supervisory personnel. Club Number One, derisively called "Uncle Tom's Cabin," was now categorized as being for use by black training personnel. Since it had been used formerly as the noncommissioned officer's club, NCOs were now left with no facilities for their use.

On April 5, word filtered down to base headquarters that the black officers had formed a plan to enter Club Number Two. In response, the provost marshal was ordered to station a military policeman at the entrance to advise the airmen that it was the commanding officer's order that they could not enter Club Number Two.

Between the hours of 8:30 P.M. and 11:00 P.M., three groups of black officers attempted to enter the "whites only" officer's club. Four black officers were arrested as they sought entrance. Nineteen more were arrested; then three more. Before the night of April 5 ended, more than thirty black officers had been placed under arrest for the offense of trying to use the officer's club.

That same day, Lowell M. Trice, a newspaper reporter from the *Indianapolis Recorder*, had entered the base. The action by the airmen had been well planned, with Trice on hand to report the events. When the intelligence officer informed Colonel Selway that Trice was on the base, Selway immediately ordered the reporter removed from Freeman Field and barred from reentry. When Trice attempted to meet with Selway, he was refused. At the same time, Selway barred all newsmen from the base and ordered the black military policemen to surrender their firearms.

Selway reported the matter to Major General Frank Hunter, who quickly dispatched an inspector, Colonel Wold, to Freeman Field. Selway advised the inspector general that he would not meet with Trice since the reporter wanted an interview and had failed to get clearance from the Bureau of Public Relations in Washington. After meeting with Selway, Hunter's inspector advised that it was his belief that Selway's actions had been proper. On the morning of April 6, Colonel Selway ordered that the officer's club be closed and again communicated with General Hunter. Shortly afterward, however, Hunter directed Selway to reopen the club and order all officers of Squadron E to assemble.

The black officers' protest actions did not end. That same afternoon at approximately 3:15 P.M., twenty-four more African-American officers entered the officer's club and were immediately placed under arrest. At the same time, members of the 477th sent a communication to the Inspector General, War Department, Washington, D.C. Having as its subject "Discrimination Based on Color Against Army Officers. Violation of Army Regulations and War Department Policies," it read:

> Orders given the undersigned by Major A. N. White and Captain A. N. Chiappe in the name of the Commanding Officer, Colonel Robert R. Selway, are in direct violation of War Department policies as set forth in the above mentioned references (AR 210-10 Par. 19, Ltr. AG 353.8, 5 Mar 1943, Ltr. F/Mmd 2B 939 Pentagon 8 July 1943). These orders are in complete disregard of Army Regulations and certain of the customs of the service. Further, these orders are in continuance of a well and repeatedly expressed command policy of discrimination based solely upon racial difference.

> The undersigned are all members of the 118th AAFBU, CCTS. stationed at this Base for training as replacements for the 477th Bombardment Group (M), a supposedly all Negro organization.

> This group found at the time of their arrival at this station two officer's clubs, number one and two; Club No. one for the use of O.T.U. personnel and No. two for use of Base and supervisory personnel. In effect club number two is a White officer's club and number one is a Negro officer's club. In protest against this flagrant and obvious violation of AR 210-10 the Negro officers of the O.T.U., 477th Bombardment Group (M), barred by direct orders of the Commanding Officer from club No. two (White), have refrained from using club No. one (Colored).

General Frank O. D. Hunter, commander of the 1st Air Force, shared the segregationist beliefs of his subordinate, Colonel Selway. That mutual philosophy enabled Colonel Selway to feel certain that his discriminatory actions would be supported. (USAF Collection, AFHRA, Maxwell AFB, AL.)

Officer's club No. one is housed in a building designed and formerly used as a non-commissioned officer's club. The non-coms on this post have no club and have made requests for such facilities.

Approximately seventy five (75) members of the O.T.U. are now under arrest of quarters by order of Colonel Robert R. Selway for having entered Officer's Club No. two. It is quite obvious that color is the sole basis for exclusion from this club although the command presents other reasons. Negro officers who place a foot across the threshold of this building for any reason whatsoever are immediately placed under arrest of quarters.

This group finds the treatment accorded them and the deprivation of full rights as officers make it extremely and unwarrantedly difficult to maintain morale. We further find and feel it calculated to lower our prestige in the eyes of other officers, in the eyes of the enlisted personnel and with civilians.

The continuance of this policy can hardly be reconciled with the world wide struggle for freedom for which we are asked and are willing to lay down our lives.

Unless the situation is met firmly it will spread and thrive. We request, therefore, that this matter receive immediate attention. It is our feeling that, failing to receive the common courtesies extended officers and gentlemen, we be allowed an opportunity to resign our commissions, warrants or appointments as officers in the United States Army.[1]

On April 8, all arrested officers, with the exception of the three men who allegedly had physically forced their way into the officer's club, were released. In concert with General Frank Hunter, on April 9 Selway authored Regulation 85-2, "Assignment of Housing, Messing, and Recreational Facilities for Officers, Flight Officers and Warrant Officers." The regulation specified strict segregation of base facilities. Colonel Selway directed that not only black officers, but all officers on the base, sign a statement verifying that they had read, understood, and accepted the conditions of Regulation 85-2.

The next day, the black officers were called to order and told to read the housing assignment order and sign the endorsement that they had read and fully understood it. The endorsement read, "I certify that I have read and fully understand the above order." Not surprisingly, all of the white base and supervisory officers had signed the endorsement.

One hundred and one black officers, mostly from the CCTS (Combat Crew Training Squadron) and the 619th Squadron of the

477th, refused to sign their acceptance of the discriminatory regulation. For the next several days, each of the passive resisters was individually required to go before his squadron commander, the field's legal officer, and two witnessing officers. Each man was again asked to read the order and sign the accompanying endorsement. When he refused, each man was then ordered to read the Sixty-Fourth Article of War that dealt with the consequences of refusal to obey a direct order.

Training came to an abrupt halt at Freeman Field on Thursday, April 12. The 101 African-American officers of the 477th Bombardment Group who refused to sign the housing order were arrested and confined to quarters under orders from the field's commander, Colonel Robert Selway. On April 13, they boarded six C-47 aircraft and were transferred under armed guard to Godman Field, Kentucky, where they were kept under house arrest.

On May 12, 1945, the *Chicago Defender* quoted an anonymous airman who had managed to get a letter to his brother detailing the events at Freeman Field. The correspondence began, "Now I am a prisoner of war, and I am wondering what, if any, are the differences between the way things are done here, and in Nazi Germany." The airman was imprisoned not in Germany, however, but rather at Freeman Field.

His crime had been his refusal to sign a statement indicating his understanding that access to certain buildings was restricted. He feared that as a result of his refusal, he would be charged with the crime of treason or the lesser offense of failure to obey a direct order. Extremely disheartened, the airman questioned why the necessity of enforcing segregationist policies appeared to be more important that fighting a war against the nation's enemies overseas.

The letter went on to describe the circumstances on the base as well as in the nearby town of Seymour, Indiana. Likening conditions to that of the Deep South, he wrote of the local theater, barbershops, houses, and hotels as all being segregated; only one restaurant would serve black military personnel. He concluded his letter by urging investigation of the matter and expressed the hope that public awareness of the situation, coupled with determined fighting for change, would bring about improvement.

Theopolis Johnson, a member of class 45-B-TE, graduated from the twin-engine pilot training program at Tuskegee Army Air Field on April 15, 1945. Under orders to report to the 477th at Freeman

Theopolis Johnson graduated from the twin-engine pilot training program at Tuskegee on April 15, 1945, just prior to the conclusion of the war in Europe. The war in the Pacific ended just months later. For Johnson, his first opportunity to serve overseas would not come until the Korean Conflict. (Private Collection.)

Field, Johnson arrived by train several days after graduation. Upon his arrival, he was immediately sent to Godman Field. His first knowledge of the Freeman Field activity of the preceding week came as he arrived at Godman and saw guards surrounding the quarters of his fellow officers. Although there had been a certain amount of coverage in the African-American press, for the most part, the military had been successful in keeping knowledge of the incident under wraps.

The offense that brought about Selway's actions was serious—black officers had attempted to enter and use the white officer's club. White military policemen had barred their admission and told the black officers, "We don't let niggers in." The confrontation had been inevitable. Before the dispute was resolved, more than one hundred black airmen had been arrested. Almost immediately, Congressman Adam Clayton Powell, Senator Scott W. Lucas, the Chicago Urban League, black newspapers, and the NAACP all called for an investigation of Selway's actions and his dismissal as commander of the 477th.

On April 16, 1945, Colonel Selway testified about the officer's club incident before Lieutenant Colonel Smith W. Brookhard Jr. of the Inspector General's Office. In his fourteen-page deposition, Selway stated under oath:

> No orders based on any race segregation have been issued by me assigning the use of facilities within this program. Prior to the occupancy of this station, before March 1, orders were issued at my direction at Godman Field assigning all the buildings at this station in preparation for our occupancy on March 1. As far as the assignment and use of club, recreational, and mess facilities for officers, warrant officers, and flight officers, that assignment was based on our customs of the Air Force and in accord with the policy of the commanding General of the First Air Force, that personnel undergoing OTU and combat crew and air and ground replacement for all such trainee personnel, that they use different facilities from those used by the permanent base command, supervisory, or instructor personnel.

> The purpose of this is that during the normal training hours the instructor and the student work together and use the same airplanes, ranges, and other training facilities, and that they be given an opportunity during their social hours to forget the instructor-student official attitude, and that they be permitted to relax from that position of tension from the result of training.[2]

The remainder of Selway's testimony was much the same. Most

The treatment accorded their fellow officers at Freeman Field had to be especially disheartening to those just graduating from the flying program. Nevertheless, Willis E. Sanderlin went on to serve with the 332nd Fighter Group and subsequently with the 477th Composite Group. (Private Collection.)

of Selway's rhetoric was clearly racist and peppered with comments such as ". . . the general discontent always among Negro personnel to be commanded by white or to be supervised by white personnel; and general resentment over the key positions being occupied by white personnel in organizations. . ." and "The apparent attitude of all the officers in the past few months has convinced me personally that they are not in the Air Force to function as officers; they do not desire combat. Instead, I am convinced that they are in this unit to use this unit as a vehicle on which to conduct a race crusade, and that as they approach the POM inspection in combat, I believe that they will make every effort to eliminate themselves, to return among their people as martyrs." Selway further stated, "As this program progresses in the Bombardment Group, there is more evidence of attempts to get in trouble—AWOLs, general indolence, tardiness at classes, disobedience of regulations."

Rumors circulated that Colonel Selway was finally about to be relieved. Meanwhile, Selway continued in command as a team from the Inspector General's office interviewed those involved. Selway had, in fact, received his own command under similar circumstances, and was certainly not the only line officer to practice discrimination. Lieutenant Colonel Charles A. Gayle was the commanding officer of the 553rd Replacement Squadron that took over at Selfridge Field when the 332nd Fighter Group was ordered to Europe. Gayle was charged with abusively ordering black flying officers out of the officer's club on January 1, 1944. Grievances were raised. The then field commander, Colonel William Boyd, was relieved of command as was Colonel Gayle.

By April 20, General Hunter's house of cards was beginning to crumble. With the concurrence of George Marshall, Army Chief of Staff, General Barney Giles recommended that the 101 men be released, and even worse yet for Hunter, that the charges be dropped. In a telephone conversation with Brigadier General Ray L. Owens, Hunter was livid and expressed not only disbelief, but outrage:

General Hunter: "Are those orders to me? They'd better get the Judge Advocate General, they can't issue orders like that, they haven't got the authority."

General Owens: ". . . 'and an administrative reprimand be given to each of these officers instead of a trial.' I know they can't."

General Hunter: "They can't do that. Now if they want to do it, I'm not a guardhouse lawyer, I'll do anything they say. But I will write a letter telling them I cannot command under these circumstances. I have court martial jurisdiction, and they cannot tell me whom I can try and whom I can't. They're backing water."[3]

The War Department could and did tell Hunter what to do. On April 21, the 101 arrested officers were ordered released and officially reprimanded. To be placed in each officer's file, the reprimand read:

> On or about 11 April 1945, at Freeman Field, Seymour, Indiana, you displayed a stubborn and uncooperative attitude towards the reasonable efforts of constituted authority to disseminate among officers and flight officers of the Command, information concerning necessary and proper measures adopted in the administration of the Officers' Clubs of that station. This action on your part indicates that you lack appreciation of the high standards of teamwork expected of you as an Officer in the Army of the United States, and a failure to understand that you should so conduct yourself at all times so as to be a credit and a source of pride to the military service. In these respects, you have failed definitely in your obligations to your command and your country. It is hoped and expected that you will consider this reprimand as a stern reminder of the absolute requirements of prompt and willing compliance with the policies of superior authority, and that there will be no repetition of such regrettable actions on your part.

Lieutenants Marsden A. Thompson, Shirley R. Clinton, and Roger C. Terry continued to be held in jail pending court martial for the offense of jostling white officers at the door of the club when refused admittance. Considered to be troublemakers, the three had been involved previously in a similar incident as they attempted to enter the officer's club at Selfridge Field. The charges brought against the "Freeman Three" were serious—violation of the Sixty-Fourth Article of War—refusal to obey a direct command of a superior officer and offering violence to a superior officer.

On April 26, 1945, in an effort to quell any further dissension, the 477th was transferred back to Godman Field. The training of the unit, still not fully manned, had lagged through no fault of its own. Selway and the Air Corps wanted the 477th Bombardment Group out of business. If it was possible, morale worsened.

Technically, army regulations forbade the action that Selway had taken; no officer could be denied admittance to an officer's club. Regulation AR 210-10, paragraph 19 stated ". . . on every Army Post

The 477th Bombardment Group endured even worse discrimination than the fighter squadrons. Despite such adversity, Lieutenants James A. Hurd and Augustus G. Brown typi-fied the determination and perseverance of all of the African-American participants in the Tuskegee Experience. (Private Collection.)

there shall be an officers' club in a Government building . . . open to all officers of the post." Selway insisted that he had not barred the black officers from the club based on segregation. Instead, he claimed one officer's club was for instructors, while another for trainees, all of whom happened to be black. There were two weaknesses with this argument. It was not the policy at other airfields, and more impor-tantly, many of the black officers had several years of service to their credit and could hardly be classed as boot-camp trainees.

Problems were rife at almost every field in the South and Midwest. Selfridge, Atterbury, Godman, Freeman, and Walterboro Fields all shared one common thread—racism against black officers. All of the problems fell on the doorstep of one man—Major General Frank O'Driscoll Hunter, the commanding general of the First Army Air Force. On one of his field visits, Hunter told black officers, "This country is not ready or willing to accept a colored officer as the equal of a white one. You are not in the Army to advance your race. Your prime purpose should be in taking your training and fighting for your country and winning the war. In that way you can do a deal for both your race and your country. As for racial agitators, they shall be weeded out and dealt with."[4]

There can be little doubt about the intent of both Colonel Selway and General Hunter. They wanted to keep African-Americans down. The following recorded conversation between the two officers is telling:

> Selway: "And we've got to go through with this, General, we can't pull any punches."

> Hunter: "I don't want to pull any punches, that's just what I'm trying not to do . . . "

> Selway: "If we're going to have any discipline in this Army—"

> Hunter: "I'm the one that wants the discipline."

> Selway: "If we run on this, we might as well quit, General."

> Hunter: "I know that. I don't run on anything. I have no idea of running."[5]

In another recorded conversation, Selway was overheard to remark, "There will be no assimilation except over my dead body."[6]

In June 1945, Assistant Secretary of War John J. McCloy forwarded a confidential memorandum to the secretary of war regarding the incident at Freeman Field. A special Advisory Committee on Special Troop Policies had met on May 19 to consider the recommendations that had been made by the Inspector General regarding Freeman Field. The memorandum concluded that ". . . the action of the Commanding Officer taken immediately preceding and during the course of the incident was within his administrative police powers, and that the arrest of three Negro officers and subsequently the arrest and release of 101 other Negro officers was proper." However, the committee did not agree with the separation of facilities or the method by which Selway had contrived to keep the officer's club segregated. They wrote, ". . . such basis was not in accord with existing Army Regulations and War Department policies prohibiting separation in the use of recreational activities on racial grounds."

While they may have believed that Selway was wrong on the issue of segregation, they were not inclined to show Thompson, Clinton, and Terry mercy. In fact, their action was just the opposite. The committee recommended that ". . . the Commanding General, Army Air Forces be advised that the trial of the three Negro officers now in arrest in connection with the Freeman Field incident be expedited."[7]

When the *Pittsburgh Courier* strongly pushed for the removal of Colonel Selway as commander of the 477th Bombardment Group, Under Secretary of War Patterson responded, "You will just have to be patient with us." The McCloy Committee of the War Department was once again convened to study the festering situation. The outcome was shocking and unexpected. Colonel Robert Selway was found to have performed ". . . not in accord with existing regulations." He was removed from command and Colonel Benjamin O. Davis Jr. replaced Selway as commander of the 477th Bombardment Group on July 1, 1945.

Colonel Benjamin O. Davis Jr. and his senior staff posed in front of the Godman Field headquarters in June 1945. Earlier that month, Davis, fifteen officers, and twenty-five enlisted men had boarded a B-17 returning to the United States. They were about to embark upon another first—the all-black command of a military installation. (USAF Collection.)

Chapter Fifteen

The Commander—
Benjamin O. Davis Jr.

By the end of June, it was announced that Colonel Benjamin O. Davis Jr. would replace Colonel Robert R. Selway as commanding officer of the 477th Bombardment Group. In an impressive ceremony, Davis took control of the 477th. Less than an hour later, Davis had orders cut that transferred all white officers out of the group. Under Davis, the command staff of the 477th Composite Group included Vance H. Marchbanks, Edward C. Gleed, Thomas J. Money, Andrew D. Turner, Douglas L. T. Robinson, Charles I. Williams, William A. Campbell, Elmore Kennedy, William B. Thompson, John R. Beverly, Robert L. Smith, Henry V. Moore, Carl B. Taylor, and John D. Silvera. The positions of leadership, long held almost exclusively by whites, were now about to be under black control. Selway had forty-two white officers under his command; obviously, the change of command would bring some problems. Davis recognized that fact and told a *Pittsburgh Courier* reporter, "Yes, we are bound to experience some difficulty for the next few days, but I am certain that these two squadrons will be ready in a surprisingly short time."

Davis made sweeping changes, but he was not able to easily resolve the issue of the three Freeman Field Mutiny leaders still confined to the field and facing serious charges. The order to push the courts martial of Clinton, Terry, and Thompson came from the War Department. On June 26, the War Department directed that the trials "be expedited." The next day, it was announced that the trials would convene on July 2.

A trial board named by General Hunter was manned by ten officers, including Colonel Davis, Captains George L. Knox, James T. Wiley, John H. Duren, Charles R. Stanton, William T. Yates, Elmore

M. Kennedy, Fitzroy Newsum, and First Lieutenants William R. Ming Jr. and James Y. Carter. Captain James W. Redden and First Lieutenant Charles Hall were assigned as trial judge advocates. Captain Cassius A. Harris II and Second Lieutenant William T. Coleman Jr. served as defense counsel. Attorney Theodore Berry, the president of the Cincinnati, Ohio, branch of the NAACP, acted as a civil advisor.

The trials came to a quick conclusion. The three accused told their side of the story. Major Andrew M. White, the club officer on duty, Captain Anthony Chiappe, commanding officer of "E" Squadron, witnesses for the prosecution, and Lieutenant Colonel Robert Selway testified against the three.

Colonel Davis and Captain Charles Stanton had been excused from the board. After deliberating for nearly two hours before reaching verdicts, the board cleared Marsden Thompson and Shirley Clinton of all charges. Second Lieutenant Roger Terry was found not guilty of disobedience but guilty of offering violence and fined $150, payable in three consecutive months. Fifty years later, this travesty of justice brought about by Robert Selway was corrected when, in 1995, the verdict against Terry was overturned.

Few men in the Army Air Corps, white or black, were better suited for the leadership of first the 99th, then the 332nd, and later what would become the 477th Composite Group than Benjamin O. Davis Jr. From childhood, through his years at West Point, and during the training of class 42-C at Tuskegee Army Air Field, he experienced firsthand the awful effects of racism and segregation. With a finely conditioned mind and a backbone of hardened steel, Davis was fully prepared for the difficulties at hand.

Even before Davis went to Tuskegee for flight training, he had a varied military background. He had served with the 24th Infantry Regiment at Ft. Benning, Georgia, in 1936-37 and attended Infantry School at Ft. Benning in 1937-38. From 1938 to 1940, he acted as a Professor of Military Science and Tactics at Tuskegee Institute.

As a young boy, Davis met head-on the cowardice and bigotry of the white-sheeted Ku Klux Klan, as they marched with torches afire in the darkness in front of his house. At the side of his father, resplendent in his military uniform, young Davis watched as men filled with hatred against Southern blacks passed at a distance of no more than twenty feet. Davis knew what it was like to be hated solely because of the color of his skin.

To the men of the Ku Klux Klan, differences in appearance and

Benjamin O. Davis Jr. epitomized the fighting spirit of the American military during World War II. Excelling at leadership, he ensured the success of the 99th Fighter Squadron and, subsequently, the 332nd Fighter Group. (Private Collection.)

custom meant inferiority. As the Second World War approached, African-Americans were scarcely better off then they had been before the Civil War. Decades of punitive government acts had accomplished much to destroy rights gained immediately after 1865. While the Fourteenth Amendment may have guaranteed an individual's civil rights on the state level, it did not provide protection from other individuals. The "separate-but-equal" philosophy served only to develop a government-sanctioned policy of segregation, supported by historic cases such as *Hall v. De Cuir* and *Plessy v. Ferguson.*

Contemporary American magazines and newspapers supported the view that blacks were inferior. In his *The American Commonwealth,* James Bryce wrote that blacks were lacking capacity "for abstract thinking, for scientific inquiry, or for any kind of invention," and were "unfit to cope with a superior race." That was the environment in which Benjamin O. Davis Jr. prepared to enter one of America's most prestigious educational institutions—the United States Military Academy.

Making his way up the majestic Hudson River from New York City in July 1932, Davis was about to make history. West Point, located high above the Hudson River, presented an impressive architecture of cold, solid granite. Designed for purposes of defense, it was a formidable installation.

Davis' four years at the academy were not pleasant. The physical and mental rigors were compounded by the unthinkable social situation. He was forced to endure a cruel veil of silence; fellow cadets would not talk to him because of the color of his skin. In spite of the silencing and lack of support from fellow cadets, Davis thrived. He graduated in 1936 as a second lieutenant, 35th in a class of 276 cadets. He was the first African-American to graduate from West Point in the twentieth century. Many years after his time at the military academy, Davis recalled, "I couldn't believe the way that I would be treated. If ever a man went to West Point with ideals, I was it. Boy, did I have ideals. Did I believe in duty, honor, country. Did I believe that cadets were the greatest people on the face of the Earth. I believed all that."

A splendid academic record such as Davis' should have guaranteed him any advanced assignment he desired. In the foreword to a book about his father, Benjamin O. Davis Jr. recounted one of his earliest disappointments. He wrote, ". . . I requested Air Corps pilot training upon my graduation the following year and had my application disapproved by the Chief of the Air Corps on the stated basis that with no black Air Corps units and none planned, there was no Air Corps requirement for a black pilot. The fact that I was mentally and physically qualified for pilot training apparently was not relevant."

Eventually to become in 1954 the first African-American general in the United States Air Force, Davis took command of the 477th Composite Group on July 1, 1945. With Davis' assumption of command at Godman Field, Kentucky, the base became the first Army installation to be commanded and staffed by all-black personnel.

The 477th consisted of two medium-size bomber squadrons, plus the 99th and 100th Fighter Squadrons that had returned home from overseas. Although the war in Europe had ended, the war raged on feverishly in the Pacific. The 477th never made it to the Pacific; the Japanese surrendered in August 1945 following the dropping of two atomic bombs. Nevertheless, so strong a hold did Colonel Davis have on the 477th that the group was called "Ben Davis's Air Force." The description was both derogatory and complimentary. It was a reference to the segregation that the group was forced to endure. At the same time, it was a testimony to the loyalty that Davis inspired in his troops.

In mid-1945, Godman Field became home to the 477th Composite Group. The 477th was both derogatorily and affectionately referred to as "Ben Davis's Air Force" because of the segregation of the group and the loyalty inspired by Colonel Davis. (Private Collection.)

A flight of 477th Composite Group B-25s flew in formation en route to the target area. This action was part of a joint Army and Navy maneuver in November 1945. (USAF Collection, AFHRA, Maxwell AFB, AL.)

A B-25 bomber crew of the 477th Composite Group left their aircraft following the successful completion of a practice bombing mission. (USAF Collection, AFHRA, Maxwell AFB, AL.)

Nearly a year after Davis took command of the 477th, the group finally broke the deadly spell of Godman Field. In early March 1946, Brigadier General Edward J. Timberlake, adjutant for the Army Air Forces Continental Command, announced in a joint press conference with Colonel Davis that the 477th Composite Group would be transferred to Lockbourne Field, located outside of Columbus, Ohio. The move made sense; the installation for some time had been occupied only by the Army Air Forces' all-weather flying school, making it a very uneconomical operation. Consisting of the 99th Fighter Squadron, 617th Bombardment Squadron, 602nd Engineer Squadron, 118th Base Unit, and a unit of the Army Air Forces band, the 477th moved into Lockbourne on March 13, 1946.

As at Godman Field, African-Americans would command an Army Air Forces base without immediate supervision of whites. Treated as conquering heroes by black civilians, the black fliers were regarded as unwanted trouble by the white population. A year later, in July 1947, the 477th Composite Group was deactivated and reorganized as the 332nd Fighter Wing, consisting of the 332nd Fighter Group and several other units. The 332nd Fighter Wing was deactivated in July 1949.

Chapter Sixteen

The War Is Over

Segregation and discrimination continued to be as prevalent as before the war began, and not just at the rank and file level. Assistant Chief of Air Staff Lieutenant General Hoyt Vandenberg drafted an incendiary report to General Henry Arnold in which he wrote: "Due to lower average intelligence, the demonstrated lack of leadership, general poor health, and extremely high elimination rate in training, it is far more expensive to train Negro officer personnel than white. . . ." Vandenberg personally espoused segregation because, like many whites, he believed that blacks were inferior. He also backed segregation from the standpoint of structure and discipline, arguing that by keeping the races segregated there would be fewer discipline problems.

Vandenberg's belief that blacks possessed a lower intelligence than whites was patently false, as was his claim that blacks were less healthy. There was no lack of leadership by black officers as charged. It was, however, more expensive to train black crews and their rate of elimination was definitely higher than that of their white counterparts. Both negative consequences were a direct by-product of segregation, not lack of intelligence or mechanical aptitude.

After their return to the United States, the black airmen found themselves subjected to the same difficulties they had experienced before their service overseas. African-American military personnel returning to the United States by ship were greeted at the foot of the gangplank by signs separating blacks from whites. Once again the former pilots and crewmen had to ride in the segregated Jim Crow coaches of trains, while the other cars were reserved for whites only.

The same prejudices and segregationist practices still existed. Nothing had changed.

As if the War Department was still unable to conclude that segregation was not only evil but nonproductive as well, yet another study was ordered to analyze the combat record of African-Americans. A blue ribbon panel comprised of Lieutenant General Alvan C. Gillem Jr., Major General Lewis A. Pick, Brigadier General Winslow Morse, and Brigadier General A. D. Warnock heard testimony from military and civilian leaders as to how blacks should be used in the American military. Day after day, a string of witnesses passed before the board. Military men giving testimony included General Ira C. Eaker, deputy commander of the Army Air Forces; Brigadier General Benjamin O. Davis Sr.; Major General E. M. Almond; and Colonel Noel Parrish. Secretary of the National Association for the Advancement of Colored People Walter White, Dr. Will Alexander, Charles Houston, and Frank Stanley, as well as many other prominent African-Americans, were also called to testify.

On October 15, 1945, Walter White told the committee, "In the post-war Army, segregation of Negroes should be completely abolished, as it is an expensive and inefficient procedure. Segregation maintains and broadens the chasm between the races, creates resentment of Negroes and unwarranted conviction of their own superiority among whites. Overseas the question was frequently asked: 'If the United States is really fighting for democracy why does it send two armies, one white and one black?'" White also told the board that he ". . . vigorously opposed the 'composite' group at Tuskegee for post-war aviation training of Negroes as being a wrong and dangerous policy." He urged the army to dare to face forward and to encourage development of qualified Negro officers by assignment of qualified officers like Colonel Benjamin O. Davis Jr. to the command of mixed troops. Secretary White pointed out that this was not a new practice because "Colonel Davis' father has commanded white troops."

Colonel Noel Parrish, the white former commander of Tuskegee Army Air Field, also made a plea for integration. He testified, "Whether we dislike or like Negroes and whether they like or dislike us, under the Constitution of the United States, which we are all sworn to uphold, they are citizens of the United States, having the same rights and privileges of other citizens and entitled to the same applications and protection of the laws."

With the war in Europe over, the airmen were finally shipped home. Their reception left much to be desired, however. Segregation and prejudice were still a way of life—little had changed. (Private Collection.)

Following the end of World War II, the War Department commissioned a study of the combat record of African-Americans. General Benjamin O. Davis Sr., Colonel Noel F. Parrish, and Colonel Benjamin O. Davis Jr. testified before the investigating panel. (USAF Collection, AFHRA, Maxwell AFB, AL.)

In spite of the admirable results produced by the 99th and 332nd, Air Corps leaders remained intractable. General Eaker claimed that integration would not work and that white and black service men would not do "their best work when integrated." General Carl Spaatz stated that he doubted blacks "could stand the pace if integrated into white crews."

Titled *Report of Board of Officers on Utilization of Negro Manpower in the Post-War Army*, the ten-page Gillem Report was released on February 26, 1946. The report concluded, "In the placement of the men who were accepted, the Army encountered considerable difficulty. Leadership qualities had not been developed among the Negroes, due principally to environment and lack of opportunity. These factors had also affected his development in the various skills and crafts." In short, the report praised the efforts of African-American troops during World War II, but found a marked lack of black leadership ability. The panel concluded that black and white military men should be kept segregated.

On May 6, 1946, the American Veterans Committee forwarded a rebuke to the War Department. It stated:

> We feel that the primary lesson learned from World War II is that segregation does not provide maximum efficient utilization of our nation's manpower. This must be recognized as a fact if the problem is to be investigated and if the errors of the past are to be corrected. The 'modified Jim Crowism' advocated by the Gillem Report is merely an admission of this, but will in no way insure the elimination of these same errors in our post-war army. Despite evidence of the ability of whites and Negroes to live and work together successfully, as seen in the administration of medical services, Red Cross services, in Officers' Training Schools and on the battlefields when the emergency of the situation necessitated the breaking down of the barriers of racial distinction; and although the Board states: 'During the last few years many of the concepts pertaining to the Negro have shown changing trends. They are pointing toward a more complete acceptance of the Negro in diversified fields of endeavor—with good results,' it is unwilling to consider the Negro as an integrated member of the military. In its recommendations it fails to assume the leadership required by these trends and decides, rather, to move only so far as does the slower section of our national community. By recommending the continuance of the basic policy of segregation and only abolishing the most obvious and degrading manifestations of it, the War Department loses a great opportunity, and it is here that the report fails to live up to advance hopes and expectations.

With the end of the war, demobilization of all branches of the military would soon take place. It was obvious that African-Americans would reap few gains and would benefit least from the reduction in force. In 1940, the strength of the Army Air Corps was 51,165; by 1944, the numbers had grown to 2.4 million. By the end of 1946, Army Air Forces personnel had been reduced to 455,515 members.

In November 1945, the Godman Field Separation Center was established to discharge black airmen. That month, one hundred officers, including pilots, navigators, and bombardiers, were discharged en mass at Godman Field. Chief of Staff General George Marshall sent a message commending the men on their service in the Army Air Forces. The *Pittsburgh Courier* of November 10, 1945, quoted him as saying, "You have been a member of the finest military team in history. You have accomplished miracles in battle and supply. Your country is proud of you and you have every right to be proud of yourselves." He then lauded the men for their labor, skill, patriotism, courage, and devotion—all of which had contributed to America's military successes during the war. Telling the men to apply the same traits in their new roles as civilians, Marshall urged the airmen to speak out in favor of honor and decency and in opposition to intolerance and hate.

Support personnel both at home and abroad played a very important role in the operation of the 99th Fighter Squadron, the 332nd Fighter Group, and the 477th Bombardment Group. These mechanics of the 332nd Fighter Group worked tirelessly to ensure that the group's P-51 Mustangs were always mission-ready. (USAF Neg. #53703AC, Air University/HO, Maxwell AFB, AL.)

Laden with belts of .50-caliber ammunition, armorers assigned to the 332nd Fighter Group prepared to arm waiting aircraft. Pilots depended upon the armorers to ensure that guns were in proper working order and that bombs had been correctly hung. (USAF Photo Collection, USAF Neg. #B24125AC, courtesy of National Air and Space Museum, Smithsonian Institution.)

Chapter Seventeen

The Unsung Warriors

It is easy to heap all of the glory and praise on the men who climbed into the cockpits and faced the enemy at an altitude of thirty thousand feet flying at speeds of three hundred miles per hour. It is easy, but it would be a mistake. An army travels on its stomach, be it a ground or aerial unit. The 366th Air Service Squadron of the 96th Air Service Group was comprised of thousands of men performing support functions. They labored round the clock to keep the pots boiling and the airplanes repaired, frequently under attack from German airplanes.

By V-J Day, September 2, 1945, there were more than six thousand African-Americans serving in the Army Air Forces. There were 563 pilots, 319 navigators and bombardiers, and hundreds of officers in support functions. Several thousand enlisted men serving as communications technicians, radio operators, mechanics, armorers, medics, cooks, etc. were necessary for support. These men on the ground have received little credit, but without them, the pilots obviously could not have functioned. Enlisted men, in effect, were the blood and oxygen of the fliers, and most pilots realized and readily acknowledged their value.

While there are certain common aspects, every man involved in the Tuskegee Experience has his own unique story. The same is true of the women who were part of life at Tuskegee. Women were present in a variety of official roles. On the field itself as part of the training, many women were instrumental. Women served as parachute riggers—Alice Dungey Gray headed the parachute-rigging department. Others served as laboratory technicians and nurses at the field's hospital. Cecilia Dixon of Columbia, South Carolina, served

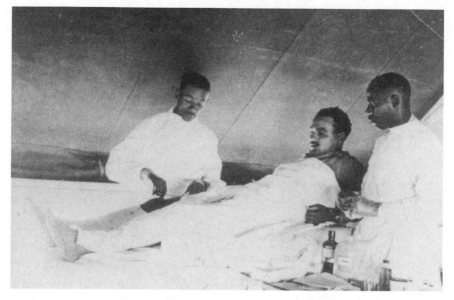

Captain Bascom S. Waugh, 301st Fighter Squadron flight surgeon, dressed the wounds of Captain Lee Rayford. He was assisted by surgical technician Private First Class John H. Patterson. (USAF Collection, AFHRA, Maxwell AFB, AL.)

as an aircraft dispatcher at Tuskegee. Women worked in the fabric repair department and as clerks in the quartermaster corps. Tuskegee had its own dietician—Mrs. Lillie S. Drew.

Women also had an informal presence, providing emotional support as wives and family members. Some served as an attentive audience. Coeds from Tuskegee Institute, Spelman College, and other nearby schools joined the airmen for church services, dances, and other social activities. All shared the triumphs and rejoiced in the accomplishments. Each suffered the sorrows and endured the slights and humiliations.

Peggy Peterman, a former columnist for the *St. Petersburg Times,* recalled how handsome the airmen appeared to a young girl growing up in Tuskegee during the war years. The airmen were an elite group, admired by the local African-American population that shared vicariously in the cadets' accomplishments. Mrs. Peterman told of spending hours at the home of a girlfriend whose older sister was dating a cadet, hoping to see the airman and his friends should they happen to come by. Such admiration could be a two-edged sword, however. One airman told of a fellow cadet who washed out of the program. Severely disappointed by his expulsion, the young man's girlfriend immediately ended the relationship.

There is no refuting the old saw that "an army travels on its stomach." Cooks frequently labored under less than ideal conditions to prepare well-balanced meals. At times, a kitchen was set up in the field with gasoline pump stoves. (Private Collection.)

Alice Dungey Gray, head of Tuskegee's parachute rigging department, posed for a photograph with members of class 44-F-SE. Women served many important roles at Tuskegee, including working as nurses, clerical staff, and guards. (Private Collection.)

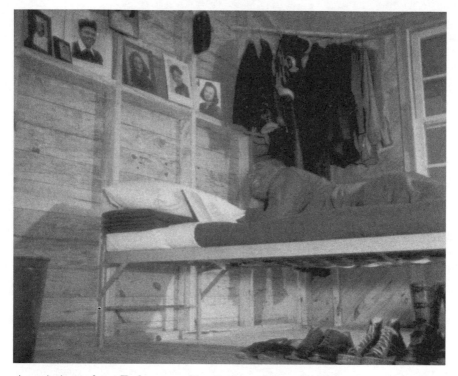

An aviation cadet at Tuskegee gazed longingly at photographs of the young women in his life. Social life on the base was practically nonexistent; the lack of hospitality off-post was worse. Mail from home played an all-important role in the lives of the men. (National Archives and Records Administration, #208-NP-5QQ-9.)

Frankie Minnis met her husband Fred after transferring to Tuskegee Institute from Clark University's music program. Drawn together by a common interest in music, they married in 1944. Fred Minnis became the special services officer at Tuskegee, in charge of arranging the entertainment for the troops. Among the famous female celebrities who visited the base were Ella Fitzgerald, Coral Greer, Dodo Proctor, and the favorite pin-up of the airmen, Lena Horne. Arthur Carter recalled having the chance to drive Lena Horne around the base in his jeep during one of her appearances at Tuskegee, while Harold Gaulden felt sure that the beautiful Miss Horne had been singing especially for him, despite an audience of several hundred. One of the highlights of Cadet Nasby Wynn's time at Tuskegee was his opportunity to dance with Lena Horne; his marriage to Doris Lavarr in the post chapel on March 21, 1944, was another.

Cab Calloway, Ella Fitzgerald, Coral Greer, Rochester, Count Basie, and Joe Louis were among the celebrities who visited Tuskegee Army Air Field. Aviation cadet Nasby Wynn earned the jealousy of most of his classmates when he danced with the beautiful Lena Horne. (Private Collection.)

Bernice "Bunny" Gause Downing came to Tuskegee in 1945 following her marriage to Alvin Downing, adjutant of the 613th Air Force Band. Working first as a substitute high school librarian, she served as a payroll clerk at Tuskegee Institute. In search of higher wages, Mrs. Downing took Civil Service exams and became the Tuskegee Army Air Field cost accounting clerk until the base closing. For four months after her husband's transfer to Lockbourne, she was required to remain at Tuskegee, working eight-to-twelve-hour shifts, seven days a week, to expedite the base closing.

Mrs. Downing recalled Tuskegee Institute and the airfield as being self-contained, totally separate entities from the town of Tuskegee, Alabama, which was implicitly understood to be "off-limits." Tuskegee Army Air Field, with the exception of the white officers, was an all-black community; Tuskegee Institute was the same. To further emphasize the separation, even the local postal designation differentiated from that of the town of Tuskegee. Mrs. Downing lived off base in the home of a black family and confined all of her activities to the black community, rarely if ever venturing into Tuskegee itself.

Kathadaza and Hiram Mann were married and living in Cleveland when he was accepted into the Army Air Corps. Preferring her husband to remain a civilian, Mrs. Mann nevertheless supported his decision to enter the military. As the training at Tuskegee progressed, Mann wrote to his wife asking her to join him there.

"My wife had gotten a job in Chicago in Federal Civil Service. My early part of the training was so rigid that thinking about her up in Chicago and me in Tuskegee, I wrote her and told her that if I was going to make it through this mess, she had better quit her job and come down and be with me, which she did. I got her a room in town and on the weekends that I was permitted to go into town, I'd spend time with her or she would come out to the base and would be there. That eased the rough part of the program for me and she helped me study at the times when we had something in the ground school to do."

Since most of the cadets were unmarried, the small group of wives present at Tuskegee Army Air Field formed a close group, visiting together, playing cards, and reading. Kathadaza Mann remembered that shopping wasn't much fun, since the unwritten but strictly enforced rules of segregation prohibited trying on clothing in the local stores. "It was a rule that black women could not try on clothing in most stores. White women would not buy them [dresses, hats,

While most of the men at Tuskegee Army Air Field were unmarried, Hiram E. Mann, class 44-F-SE, was an exception. His wife Kathadaza left her job in Chicago to accompany her husband to the various bases at which he was stationed prior to shipping overseas. (Private Collection.)

etc.,] if black women had tried them on. Shoes could be tried on in the back of stores," she recalled. Shopping was therefore restricted to the limited selection in the stores in the black community. Having been accustomed to Chicago's giant department stores that lacked similar segregationist policies, she found this an unpleasant surprise. While segregation existed in the North, Mrs. Mann saw it as more subtle there, except when pertaining to the availability of jobs. In that area the story was the same—applications were accepted, only to be thrown into the trash before the eyes of the applicant.

Travel presented similar difficulties for the men and their families. African-Americans riding on trains south of the Mason-Dixon Line were forced to ride in the Jim Crow car. Located at the front of the train just behind the engine where open windows left the travelers covered with soot and cinders from the coal-burning engines, it was the only car on the train available to blacks. The Manns recalled traveling the weekend after graduation ceremonies. When visiting families and friends filled the Jim Crow car to capacity and beyond, an officer asked the train's conductor if the ladies could ride in an adjacent car which was empty except for three white soldiers. After the conductor refused to permit such an action, the women were forced to sit on suitcases in the aisles or in the restroom.

Bus transportation had its humiliations as well. Segregationist policies required African-Americans to ride in the back of the bus, even if the bus was largely unoccupied. Kathadaza Mann recalled making a shopping trip with some friends from Walterboro Army Air Field to Charleston, South Carolina. As the bus filled, a white man forced the women riding on the back seat of the bus to make room for him to sit. If sufficient room hadn't been available, one of the women would have been required to give up her seat for him.

The lack of accommodations that accepted blacks also made automobile travel difficult. While her husband and another officer took turns driving throughout the night on a trip from Florida to Tuskegee, Bunny Downing slept in the back seat of the car. Always careful to obey speed limits and traffic rules in the small Southern towns to avoid possible conflict with police, the travelers were nonetheless stopped by a local sheriff. Even after presenting identification, both men were forced to leave the car for questioning by the sheriff. Shining his flashlight into the back seat where she had been sleeping, the sheriff then demanded that Mrs. Downing also leave the car and questioned her as to why she was traveling with the men.

Female students from Tuskegee Institute endeared themselves to aviation cadets by sewing insignia patches on the men's uniforms. Most of the local black residents held the cadets in high esteem and viewed them as good matrimonial prospects. (USAF Collection, AFHRA, Maxwell AFB, AL.)

Presenting her military identification as an employee at Tuskegee Army Air Field, she explained that one of the officers was her husband. A light-complexioned African-American, Mrs. Downing also recalled two occasions when she was refused admission to the Jim Crow car on a train departing Washington, D.C., for Florida when the conductor mistakenly believed her to be white!

Many difficult times required humor. Alvin Downing recalled that he and his wife were frequently stopped by white policemen who would ask his wife, "What are you doing in this car with those people?" He continued, "Because they didn't realize that she was of the black race and so at times I always would joke and I'd tell my wife, you get in the back seat and I'll get the chauffeur's cap and we'll drive through Alabama."

The lack of military housing for married couples meant that the wives had to live away from the base in the private homes of individuals in the African-American community. While some landlords were only interested in the money to be made from housing the military wives, Kathadaza Mann recalled most as being very kind. Some even allowed the use of other parts of the dwelling and the yard for social activities. In one instance, she recalled a less social use of the yard. Since her husband's monthly cadet pay of fifty dollars did not permit expenditures for laundry, she washed his uniforms with a scrub board in a tin tub in the backyard!

Captain Benjamin O. Davis Jr. was another of the few married men in the aviation program at Tuskegee. While Captain Davis was learning to fly, his wife kept busy at Tuskegee Institute. Elected chairwoman of the knitting production for the Tuskegee Institute chapter of an organization supporting the war effort, she led the group's efforts to provide sweaters, socks, and caps as Christmas gifts for the troops. After her husband was sent overseas, she was employed by the Sperry Corporation in New York.

Many men, while not serving in combat, played vital roles that helped the war effort. Alvin Downing was certainly one of those men. Originally a flying cadet, Downing was eliminated from the program because of asthma. Reassigned to MacDill Field in Tampa, he then attended officer candidate school in Miami, graduated, and was commissioned a second lieutenant. As a special services officer at Tuskegee Army Air Field, Lieutenant Downing was one of the forces behind the *"Roger"* show. The all-soldier show played to thousands across the country as part of the Red Cross War Fund, and

Tuskegee Army Air Field

PRESENTS

"Roger"

A Musical Extravaganza

FEATURING

The T. A. A. F. Glee Club,

The Imperial Wings of Rythm

and a Grand Array of Talent

THURSDAY, MARCH 29, 1945

8 P.M.

MUNICIPAL AUDITORIUM

The program for "Roger" described the show as "a musical extravaganza." The show proved to be so popular that it was performed at bond rallies across the nation to raise funds for the war effort. (USAF Collection, AFHRA, Maxwell AFB, AL.)

included a cast of seventy-five. It featured the Tuskegee Glee Club, the renowned Tuskegee Army Air Field marching band, and the swing band, The Imperial Wings of Rhythm, made up of some of the best-known African-American musicians in show business. The *"Roger"* show was described as being ". . . based on the more or less familiar theme of attempting to portray, with a certain amount of exaggeration and irony, the actual happenings at an army base when an all-star USO troupe is unable to appear for the GI's as publicized. In view of the emergency the disappointed soldiers decide to put on their own variety show, using the names of the previously slated Hollywood stars which they impersonate in the makeshift production. The climax comes when the TAAF Glee Club, swing band and specialty acts present a mock version of the proposed USO show presenting hilarious take-offs on such famous stars as Count Basie, Billie Holiday, Rochester, Louis Armstrong, Ethel Waters, the Peter Sisters, and many others."

Following the deactivation of Tuskegee, Alvin Downing transferred to Lockbourne. Serving as Colonel Benjamin Davis' special services officer, Downing organized on-base entertainment that included Friday night movies and talent shows. Building on the past success of the *"Roger"* show, Downing produced traveling shows as part of *Operation Happiness,* and *Operation Enjoyment.* The star of the show was Private Calvin Manuel, a brilliant entertainer. Daniel "Chappie" James served as the show's master of ceremonies.

Downing remembered the metamorphosis of *Operation Enjoyment* into *Operation Happiness* at the hands of the Pentagon. He recalled, "I wrote that show called *Operation Enjoyment.* Just to show you how, when something nice or big happens, everybody wants to get in on the act. B. O. Davis' show, and I call it his show because it was his base, the Pentagon through the efforts of B. O. Davis heard about it and they sent a man down from the Pentagon to look at the show, and of course, he made some cosmetic changes, a few changes, and it became *Operation Happiness.* In this show that I started was one of the greatest leaders as part of it. That was 'Chappie' James, who was the emcee of this show." The *"Roger"* and *Operation Happiness* shows played before civilian and military audiences, both black and white. It was the first introduction that many whites had to the black community, and they were as surprised to find that African-Americans were talented entertainers as others had been to find that blacks could fly airplanes.

Chapter Eighteen

The Tuskegee Experience

Why would the War Department commence their so-called experiment with pursuit training? As William H. Hastie wrote in his pamphlet *On Clipped Wings*, the program was begun with ". . . pursuit flying, the most difficult type of combat aviation. The single pilot in his pursuit ship has the most exacting of air tasks, handling his fast plane, maneuvering it at terrific speed in actual combat, mastering the technique of accurate and properly directed fire in aerial dogfights, and exercising split-second judgment in unexpected situations and emergencies. Why was the Negro, whose ability was in doubt, not started off with observation flying in bombardment where co-pilots and other crew members assist each other and share and divide responsibility?" The answer was simple—the War Department and the Army Air Corps wanted the experiment to fail!

William Hastie had been a constant and continuous thorn in the side of the War Department. Slightly over a year after the first class entered the training program at Tuskegee, Hastie questioned why there were still so many white officers in positions of command. On July 18, 1942, Hastie corresponded with Lieutenant General Henry H. Arnold:

In a memorandum dated January 30, 1941, and addressed to me by Maj. Gen. George H. Brett, the Assistant Chief of the Army Air Corps, the plan for the development of the Tuskegee Air Base was presented in some detail. It was therein provided as follows:

"In the establishment of the Base Group Detachment the Detachment commander will be a white officer. All other officers will be colored—

"A Base Group commander and Executive Officer may be the same individual.

"The Commanding Officer of the Post will be a white officer. It will be necessary to retain him in this position for an indefinite period of time.

"White officers experienced in the specialties required, assisted by white non-commissioned officers, will be detailed to the school in capacity of instructors similar to that at present set up for the National Guard Squadron, with the exception of Post commander, the Executive Officer, and the Squadron Commander. All other duties will be filled by Negroes and instructors will be relieved at such time as is found the Negro trainees may replace them. Within one year's time 45 officers may be trained to maintain the level of the Pursuit Squadron at 33 per year's time. There become available 12 Negro officers each year to replace officers of both flying and ground school so that within the year's time all white officers, except those three quoted above, may be relieved."

More than a year has now elapsed since the establishment of the Tuskegee Training Base. It is my own observation that a considerable number of white officers have been retained indefinitely and others brought in from time to time for assignments designated for Negro officers in the above plan. It is, of course, desirable that here, as at every other training base, as many officers of the Regular Army as can be spared remain indefinitely and that experienced instructors be retained in combat training as long as possible. It is also recognized that as new functions have been added at the post, officers must be added and replacements trained for new positions. With these limitations, an adequate time would seem to have elapsed for the procurement and training of Negro officers for all assignments designated for them in the basic planning.

May this office be advised what posts at the Tuskegee Base, other than those of instructors and officers of the Regular Army with key administrative and training responsibilities, are now filled by white officers. May it also be indicated what steps have been and are being taken for the procurement and training of Negro officers as replacements and when it is estimated that such replacements will be accomplished.

To be sure, the success of the Tuskegee Experience did not put an end to racism and segregation in the Air Corps. On January 8, 1943, the Army Air Corps put out a call for meteorologists. The announcement stated, "To fill the urgent need for more than 1,000 meteorologists in the Air Forces, men between the ages of 18 and 30, inclusive qualified for meteorological training, will be certified for voluntary induction into the Army as Aviation Cadets in meteorology."

When Robert P. Braddicks of New York City applied for meteorology training, his application was returned with "Colored" penciled in. Major General J. A. Ulio advised Braddicks, "Reference is made to your application for Meteorology training as an aviation cadet. At the present time no specialized training as aviation cadets is being offered to colored men. If such training becomes available due publicity will be given."

Another black applicant for meteorology training was told, "There are at present no Negro Air Force Weather Groups, nor are any contemplated in the near future. However, there is now one Negro meteorologist attached to a Negro Air Force Fighter Group, and six others in training who will be attached to Negro Fighter Groups upon graduation. It is believed by the Army Air Forces that the above mentioned seven Negro meteorologists will take care of their needs for quite some time."

African-Americans had encountered discrimination at the hands of their fellow countrymen for many years. The war now created a new situation that added insult to injury. Due to a lack of stockade space in Europe, many German and Italian prisoners of war were housed at military bases in the United States. Sponsored by local Chambers of Commerce and various fraternal organizations, these enemy soldiers were escorted to USO shows, movies, and dances at which attendance by African-American military personnel was prohibited. Restaurants in the communities were happy to serve the prisoners, while the local laundries willingly washed their clothing. Requests by black soldiers for similar treatment were refused. This occurred not only in the South, but also at bases around the country, prompting prisoners to inquire as to why African-American soldiers would fight to protect a nation which treated them in such a manner.

Nineteen single-engine combat pilots—Richard Armistead, Carl F. Ellis, Charles A. Hill Jr., Lincoln Hudson, Rupert Johnson, George Lynch, Lewis J. Lynch, Hiram E. Mann, James Mitchell, Robert Murdic, Wyrain T. Schell, Leon Spears, Harry T. Stewart Jr., Samuel Washington, Hugh J. White, Yenwith K. Whitney, Frank N. Wright, and James W. Wright Jr.—graduated from Tuskegee Army Air Field on June 27, 1944, and were sent to Walterboro Army Air Field, South Carolina, for overseas replacement training. Upon completion in November 1944, they were granted four days pre-embarkation leave

The 332nd Fighter Group received thirty-four replacement pilots during January 1945. Left to right: Richard Armistead, Robert Lawrence, Harry Stewart, Frank Wright, Yenwith Whitney, Wyrain Schell, and George Lynch were all graduates of class 44-F-SE. (Private Collection.)

to visit their families before shipping out to combat overseas. Hiram Mann recalled an experience they had in Washington, D.C., at National Airport during that time:

"Some class members were close enough to travel by bus or train to get home and back in the four days allotted. Others had to fly because of the distant cities—Los Angeles, Detroit, St. Louis, Chicago, Cleveland, New York, etc. During the war, air travelers were assigned a priority classification for space on airplanes depending upon the urgency. Those of us flying had been assigned A-1 priority, the highest.

"As planes departed with classmates aboard, the wind-down came and only two of us were left: Frank Wright, a very fair-complexioned Negro, who was assumed to be a Caucasian, and me, an unmistakable colored person. We decided we wanted to eat. We located and went into the cafeteria. We hung our coats, placed our caps on the coat rack, and seated ourselves at the counter as any law-abiding American citizen should do.

"The cafeteria was not crowded. About five waitresses huddled in the back by the doors to the kitchen, whispering among themselves.

Additional replacement pilots who joined the 332nd in January 1945 included, left to right: Hugh White, Charles Hill, Lincoln Hudson, and Carl Ellis. Within the next three months, both White and Hudson were reported missing in action. (Private Collection.)

After a while, one came toward us and said to me, 'I'm sorry, we don't serve colored in here.' Frank and I got up, retrieved our garments, and started for the door. The cashier called, 'Lieutenant, Lieutenant!' Both of us turned and looked at her. She beckoned for us to come toward her. Frank went back; I continued to walk ahead. The cashier told Frank she was sorry, but since we were officers in the United States Army she had called upstairs to management and asked them could we be served. Management had said, 'No!'

"Frank asked where could we get something to eat. The cashier told him there was a coffee shop across the lobby. We could eat there. We went in, ordered coffee and donuts, were served, and ate. We departed the D.C. air terminal, Frank going to White Plains, New York, and I went to Cleveland, Ohio.

"The four days passed rapidly, much too fast, and the ten or twelve of us began to filter back into the Washington air terminal. About six or eight of us assembled, and someone suggested we go to the cafeteria to eat. Frank and I told them we would not be served there; we had to go to the coffee shop.

"We entered, as decent people should, ordered coffee and donuts, were served, and were eating when there was a terrible commotion at the entrance doors. There was a little, dried-up old lady standing in the doorway with her hands on her hips shouting, 'I'll be glad when they get signs up saying they can't eat in here. They don't know the Washington air terminal is on the Virginia side of the Potomac River!' Lincoln Hudson spoke up and said, 'I hope those bullets have colored and white on them!' No incident followed the insult. Ironically, however, Frank Wright was killed in aerial combat; Lincoln Hudson, James Mitchell, Leon Spears, and Hugh White were shot down and became prisoners of war."

Flying was always dangerous and not just combat flying. Training could be as dangerous as the real thing. Many accidents happened, and more than a few men lost their lives. Tragedy struck not only on the battlefield, but also on the training field. All accidents are tragic, but one of the worst resulted in the death of Second Lieutenant Wilmeth W. Sidat-Singh of Washington, D.C., in March 1943. Sidat-Singh, a former all-American football star at Syracuse University and a semiprofessional basketball player with the Washington Bears, was one of the most popular graduates of Tuskegee. A member of the 301st Fighter Squadron, Sidat-Singh was assigned to Selfridge Field and had arrived only a few days earlier. Flying his single-engine trainer over Lake Huron, he developed engine trouble and was forced to bail out. Searchers found only an oil smear where his plane had gone down. The body of Sidat-Singh was not recovered until a month later.

In mid-June 1945, a 477th B-25 bomber with seven crew members crashed while on a training mission. The crew had flown the bomber from Godman Field to Gunter Field, Alabama. The bomber had been refueled and was on its return trip home when it went down in a swamp less than four miles east of Gunter Field. The dead included Flight Officers Charles E. Wilson, Edward Glover, Raymond F. Noches, Denny C. Jefferson, Corporals Henry H. Valentine, Luther A. Cox, and Private James H. Ewing. There was only one survivor. Less than a month later, another B-25 crashed into the Ohio River, twelve miles from Madison, Kentucky. First Lieutenant Samuel A. Black, Second Lieutenant Stephen Hotesse, and Flight Officer Glenn W. Pulliam were killed. Two crewmen were thrown clear and escaped injury.

Promulgated by segregation, the treatment that was forced down the throats of well-qualified blacks was certainly an inefficient means of training. Adequate Air Corps training facilities for pilots and ground crews were already in existence when the Tuskegee program began. Fields on the West Coast and in Texas, as well as Maxwell Field not more than forty miles from Tuskegee, were all viable training bases. The approximately $2 million that went into the construction of Tuskegee Army Air Field could and should have been expended on needs other than a segregated airfield.

With few exceptions, the command structure of the American military, from Secretary of War Henry L. Stimson to Chief of the Army Air Corps General Henry H. Arnold, believed that a continuation of segregation and a "separate-but-equal" treatment of blacks was the most efficient policy. While the chiefs might have believed that such treatment was possible, most rank and file military officers did not, and a true "separate-but-equal" policy never existed. As Louis Purnell pointed out, it was a "catch-22" situation: "The same people who were saying that we couldn't do it were the very same people who were in a position to make sure we didn't. We were put in positions where we couldn't score or make kills. We weren't where the action was."

Because of segregation, manpower utilization of the 99th Fighter Squadron and the 332nd Fighter Group was greatly compromised. Shortages of pilots or ground crews could not be as easily filled by the transfer of newly trained pilots as in white squadrons. Because of a shortage of black reinforcements, many black pilots were forced to fly more missions than their white counterparts. Despite the needs of the European Theater for trained pilots, segregation, the reluctance to allow blacks to join the Army Air Corps, and the lag in setting up the mechanism for a segregated base caused delays of nearly a year in sending pilots to the war zone. Segregation obviously obviated any economy of scale that might have been hoped for, and in terms of nothing more than dollars, turned the program into a very expensive proposition. The ratio of support personnel to pilots for the first squadron, for example, was approximately fourteen to one, far above that of white units.

By the conclusion of the Tuskegee Experience, nearly a thousand young black men had graduated from the pilot training program at

234 of these pilots served overseas.

Tuskegee Army Air Field; 450 of these pilots served overseas. Nearly nine hundred awards were earned by these men as they served their country in time of war, including one Silver Star, one Legion of Merit, ninety-five Distinguished Flying Crosses, two Soldiers Medals, fourteen Bronze Stars, eight Purple Hearts, and 744 Air Medals with Oak Leaf Clusters. The accomplishments of the men of the 99th and the other all-black fighter squadrons are unmistakable in the magnitude of social change they helped to achieve. It would be easy to settle for only the quantifiable accomplishments of these brave men such as enemy aircraft destroyed and awards for bravery. But that would be too easy.

The record of the all-black units during World War II was unblemished, although there were many whites in both the lower ranks and upper echelons of the military and civilian leadership who did everything possible to keep African-Americans from realizing their full potential. The Tuskegee Experience proved without a doubt that black pilots were capable not only of training in sophisticated airplanes but were more than capable of performing admirably in combat. Some of these men not only fought in World War II, but also flew combat missions in Korea and Vietnam; Charles Cooper, Hannibal Cox, and Charles McGee were but three.

Much has been made about bomber groups requesting the 99th Fighter Squadron or squadrons of the 332nd Fighter Group to provide escort service for them. The airmen at the flying level did not know if that was, in fact, true or just a story generated by a popular movie. Dr. Florence Parrish-St. John in a telephone interview with Elliott Roosevelt asked that very question. According to Dr. Parrish-St. John, "Roosevelt said, 'We requested the 332nd. Boy, they were terrific. We were just delighted to have them because we needed escorts and there were not enough people doing that.' He praised the 332nd to high heavens. 'Yes,' he said, 'we did request them.'"

The claim that the 332nd Fighter Group never lost an aircraft under their protection to an enemy fighter is difficult to substantiate with certainty. Reading through the thousands of after-action reports shows some close calls; many of the reports are certainly subject to interpretation. It can be said with certainty, however, that they achieved the distinction of never having lost a bomber to enemy fighters in more than two hundred missions with the 15th Air Force. This fact was acknowledged in a letter from Colonel Yantis A. "Buck" Taylor to Colonel Benjamin O. Davis Jr.

In the early days of the war, Allied bomber losses were horrendous; each time the bombers went out, losses of fifteen to twenty percent were routine. Certainly flak was a major cause, but the big, slow-moving aircraft were also lost to the machine guns of enemy fighters. By the waning months of the war, the losses of Allied bombers had greatly diminished to less than five percent. Lieutenant Colonel John Suggs pointed out, "The real tragedy in the thing was that the news media always played up the victories. That was the most important thing, and it sold papers and pictures back in the States, and so forth. And way down at the bottom of the write-up it would say, 'Three bombers failed to return from the mission.' Well, you see, the reason the three bombers failed to return—in many cases, they [the white fighter pilots] didn't take them to the target, and pick them up at the target, and bring them back. They were after victories and individual glory and that was one thing the old man [Benjamin O. Davis Jr.] was on us night and day about. Doing the job, the way it was planned. That's what we were expected to do!"

The program developed hundreds of fine military officers and leaders among the black ranks. Benjamin O. Davis Jr., Daniel "Chappie" James, Coleman Young, William T. Coleman, Lucius Theus, Lee Archer, Roscoe Brown, and Percy Sutton are certainly the best known, but there were many others who labored anonymously to insure that African-Americans had a future in the newly integrated military service of the United States. There can be little argument that the success of the black fliers and the Tuskegee Experience provided the impetus for President Harry Truman's order to desegregate the military. The accomplishments of the black Army Air Corps fliers gave African-Americans something of which to be proud and led to a tremendous boost in the self-esteem of all black men and women. The men of the 99th Fighter Squadron, the 332nd Fighter Group, and the 477th Bombardment Group believed in the dictum that actions speak louder than words. They knew they were capable. Words alone would not convince the doubters; nothing would convince the racists.

President Harry Truman on July 26, 1948, signed Executive Order 9981 striking down segregation in the American military. The order stated, "It is hereby declared to be the policy of the President that there shall be equality of treatment and opportunity for all persons in the armed services without regard to race, color, religion, or national origin. This policy shall be put into effect as rapidly as possible, having due regard to the time required to effectuate any necessary changes without impairing efficiency or morale." The Army Air Corps had been one of the most blatant and strongest defenders of segregation in the military. Conversely and to its credit, after the United States Air Force became a separate branch of the military in 1947, Air Force leaders led the fight to cause the Air Force to be the first to integrate.

The military might have been officially integrated, but things didn't necessarily change. For many years, the *Air Force Almanac* listed the winners of the first United States Air Force Fighter Gunnery Meet held in 1949 as being unknown. Whether a deliberate or accidental oversight, the listing was corrected only after several years of prodding by members of the winning team—the all-black 332nd Fighter Group based at Lockbourne Air Force Base, Ohio!

In early 1949, the Air Force decided to hold its first Air Force Fighter Gunnery Meet at Las Vegas Air Force Base. The goal of the meet was to recognize the top performing fighter group as well as the top performing individual pilot. Each fighter group was invited to nominate three pilots and an alternate. Captain Alva N. Temple of

Surrounded by members of the Fahy Committee, President Harry Truman signed Executive Order 9981 on July 26, 1948. With a stroke of his pen, Truman officially ended segregation in America's military services. (National Air and Space Museum, Smithsonian Institution, SI Neg. #99-15481.)

the 301st Fighter Squadron, First Lieutenant Harry T. Stewart of the 100th Fighter Squadron, and First Lieutenant James H. Harvey of the 99th Fighter Squadron were selected to represent the 332nd Fighter Group. First Lieutenant Halbert Alexander of the 99th Fighter Squadron was to serve as an alternate.

The meet was scheduled to begin on May 2, 1949. Temple, Stewart, Harvey, and Alexander flew their nearly obsolete F-47 propeller-driven airplanes to Las Vegas on April 23. The ground support staff of crew chiefs, mechanics, armorers, and maintenance specialists had arrived the prior day in a C-47 transport airplane. The Air Force had been gradually converting its fighter squadrons from propeller aircraft to jets. Several of the competing groups at Las Vegas were equipped with F-80 and F-84 jets. Others were flying F-51 Mustangs and F-82 Twin Mustangs.

In May 1949, the first Air Force Fighter Gunnery Meet was held at Las Vegas Air Force Base. After several days of intense competition, the 332nd Fighter Group emerged as the winning team. Presentation of trophies was held in a hotel that only one day earlier had refused admittance to several members of the 332nd Fighter Group. (USAF Collection.)

The contest would include aerial gunnery, panel gunnery, dive-bombing, skip bombing, and rocketry. Upon arrival, the pilots of the 332nd Fighter Group spent their time familiarizing themselves with the range over a section of desert called Frenchman Flat, approximately sixty miles from Las Vegas. The ground crews, made up of Wendell D. LaFleur, Kenneth Austin, Fred Archer, Johnathan C. Gibson, Buford A. Johnson, Miles A. Mathews, Willie McNair, Bennie Farmer, Robert L. Moore, Henry Norman, Raymond Rounds, Elijah M. Dyer, James Fleming, Cleveland Thompson, John Otrix, Solomon Oliver, and Reiman P. Rhinehart, worked tirelessly to ensure that the F-47s were in top shape.

By May 2, pilots and aircraft were ready. Because of the desert heat, missions were flown from 7:00 A.M. to 10:00 A.M. Day one was aerial gunnery at an altitude of ten thousand feet. Led by Alva Temple, the flight of three F-47s made contact with the tow target at 7:15 A.M. The Thunderbolts of the 332nd made pass after pass at the target until their guns were empty. As quickly as possible, they returned to base, rearmed, and went in search of the target. After finding it, they again unloaded their guns. By 10:00 A.M. the pilots had finished their work. Ground crews swarmed over the aircraft making sure they were ready for the next day. Day one had been a tremendous success. Alva Temple had been the high scorer.

The next day, the third and fourth missions of the meet were held; the contest was aerial gunnery at an altitude of twenty thousand feet. Once again, Alva Temple was the top scorer. After four missions, the pilots of the 332nd Fighter Group were in the lead. The 332nd fliers were runners-up in the panel gunnery contest to the 82nd Fighter Group. Harry T. Stewart was top scorer for the 332nd Fighter Group. After a total of six missions, the 332nd Fighter Group held a slight lead, but it was still too early for a celebration.

Temple, Stewart, and Harvey excelled in the skip bombing contest. They each had perfect scores putting six out of six bombs dead center through the targets. At meet's end, the 332nd Fighter Group tallied a final team score of 536.588, winning first place. The 82nd Fighter Group was a close second with 515.010. Captain Alva Temple had scored 577.577 in the individual competition, earning him a second place.

Thirteen days had been spent at Las Vegas Air Force Base. The outcome was a tremendous success for the 332nd Fighter Group. When the meet was over, several of the men went to a hotel casino on the Las Vegas strip to celebrate. They were told to leave the casino—no blacks were allowed. The next day, a formal presentation was held; trophies were awarded to the members of the 332nd Fighter Group and Captain Alva Temple. The presentation was held in the same hotel that only one day earlier had refused admittance to several members of the 332nd Fighter Group.

Spann Watson, a man deeply committed to civil rights, related a story of discrimination that occurred several years after the United States Air Force was integrated. Assigned to Command and Staff School at Maxwell Air Force Base in Alabama in 1954, Watson reported for duty. In the tradition of most career military men, he had his hair cut every week at the base barbershop.

Nearly fifty years later, his anger over the incident was still obvious. Watson remembered, "I went to the barber shop and they sent the porter out to tell me that they wouldn't cut my hair here and I would have to go down the street where there was some black man that they had designated to cut black officers' hair. I said to the porter, 'You get the hell out of here and tell your boss to come out here right away.' He came bouncing out and apologized that they could not cut my hair. He said 'Mr. Evans,' who was the black representative, civilian aide to the secretary of war, 'he was here last week and he gave us a clearance as an okay on our progress in integration.' I said, 'I don't care what he said, I want a haircut!' He said, 'Well, we just can't give it to you.' I said, 'Okay, I'm coming here every week and you're going to tell me this every week. I'm going to keep a record of it and when I finish this school, I'm going back to plead the case against you and your barbershop.'

"Right away the commanding general called me in and he said, 'You just can't push. You can't do all these things.' And I said, 'General, are you trying to sell me'. . . I said, 'This is 1954 . . . and we integrated in 1948, and you haven't got your barbershop straightened out yet. Are you trying to sell me integration on a thousand-year endowment?' He hit the ceiling. I smiled. I knew he'd lost his authority then, when he lost his head. After a while he calmed down. He said, 'Well, we'll work on it.' I said, 'In the meantime, I'm going to the barbershop every week.' I said, 'Why in the hell is this university in Alabama in the first place? If you can't do anything, why are we here?' He said, 'You may be right, but I didn't make the plan.'

"So, I kept on going. The porter now has become my friend. 'You got them scared now. They don't know what to do with you,' he said.

He'd come over to my quarters and tell me. I told him, 'I'm going to keep on going.' Finally, he said, 'The barbers all got to discussing you down at the barbershop, and they agreed,' about seven or eight barbers. And one of them was a woman. A white female. He said, 'Guys that came back from Korea, they said they don't mind cutting your hair. They cut black folks hair over in Korea. They don't mind cutting black people's hair.' He said, 'You got them scared.'

"Finally they said, 'You can go down there and get a haircut.' The man running the barbershop was afraid he was going to lose his contract. In the seven times that I was down there, I went to every barber. Every time I went, I went to a different barber to get my hair cut. The last one I went to was the woman. I knew she was the key to the thing. The last one was her. She had this straight razor around my neck and I knew she could do it to me any time. But she went through with it and after that I didn't have any problems at all."

Chapter Nineteen

Black Birds

The black airmen who eventually became known as the Tuskegee Airmen did not simply materialize out of thin air, as if by magic. Many early black fliers had fought the good fight to allow the Tuskegee Experience to happen. It had been a long, hard climb. Blacks in early aviation fought the same biases and stereotypes that blacks were forced to endure when they sought to fly in the military. It was wrongly believed that they simply did not possess the needed level of intelligence. Despite that fallacy, African-American aviators had been around almost from the beginning.

Eugene Jacques Bullard, born in 1894 in Columbus, Georgia, was the first African-American to fly as a military pilot. He did not fly, however, for America. Bullard received flight training in France and ultimately was assigned as a pursuit pilot with the famed Lafayette Flying Corps. Known to the French as the "Black Swallow of Death," Bullard went on to be awarded the coveted Croix de Guerre, the Legion of Honor, and many other military awards.

On a warm April day in 1926, William Wills and Bessie Coleman, in Coleman's well-worn Curtiss JN-4 airplane, headed down the dirt runway at Paxon Field in Jacksonville, Florida. Wills, of Dallas, Texas, sat in front at the controls. Coleman was in back, in order to check out the field for a parachute jump that she intended to make the next day. Since she needed to peer over the side of the aircraft, she didn't fasten her seat belt.

The Jenny slowly picked up speed and took off. Wills labored to take it to an altitude of two thousand feet where he circled for five minutes, then climbed to an altitude of thirty-five hundred feet. Headed back to Paxon Field, Wills was cruising at a comfortable

The first African-American to fly as a military pilot, Eugene Jacques Bullard served as a member of the Lafayette Flying Corps during World War I. Although Bullard was highly decorated by the French for his aviation accomplishments, the United States refused to acknowledge that African-Americans were capable of serving as military aviators. (National Air and Space Museum, Smithsonian Institution, SI Neg. #91-6283.)

speed of eighty miles per hour. Suddenly, the Jenny accelerated to an out-of-control speed of 110 miles per hour. The front-engine tractor airplane went into a nose-dive. At one thousand feet, the aircraft slipped into a deadly tailspin. It flipped upside-down at five hundred feet. Coleman fell from the aircraft, somersaulting head over heels in a free fall until she hit the ground. As it headed toward the ground, the aircraft sheared off the top of a pine tree and crashed into freshly tilled farmland. Wills' body was pinned beneath the overturned fifteen-hundred-pound aircraft. While rescuers attempted to pull the pilot's mangled body from the crashed airplane, an unthinking bystander lit a cigarette. Gasoline fumes hanging heavily over the destroyed aircraft instantly exploded into a ball of orange flame. Almost immediately, the flimsy linen-covered aircraft was a burned-out hulk.

Accidents in aviation were not a rarity. Even in the 1920s it was a rare day when someone didn't die in an airplane crash. Many aviators still refused to use their seat belts, and it was not at all unusual for pilots to fall from airplanes. Wills was not an especially well-known pilot and had probably never received any publicity while living in Dallas. Bessie Coleman had, however, received her fair share of press, mostly in the African-American weekly newspapers of the South and Midwest. What made this fatal crash especially noteworthy was the fact that Bessie Coleman, the holder of a license issued by the Fédération Aéronautique Internationale, was the first African-American to be licensed as an aviator.

On January 26, 1892, Bessie Coleman was born in Atlanta, Texas. Her life in Texas was difficult; she picked cotton to help support her family. At the age of twenty-seven, she moved to Chicago, where she managed to make a living as a beautician, but she wanted more. She wanted to be a pilot. When asked why she had wanted to fly, she responded, "Well, because I knew we [Negroes] had no aviators, neither men nor women, and I knew the Race needed to be represented along this most important line, so I thought it my duty to risk my life to learn aviating and to encourage flying among men and women of the Race who are so far behind the white men in this special line."

Once Coleman decided that she wanted to fly, it was easier said than done. There were few black aviators in the United States. No white flier was willing to take her on as a pupil. Certainly racism was involved, but it was probably as much a case of sexism. Few male

Bessie Coleman was America's first licensed black pilot. An ardent proponent of African-American involvement in aviation, she was quoted as saying that her "great ambition was to make Uncle Tom's cabin into a hangar by establishing a flying school." (National Air and Space Museum, Smithsonian Institution, SI Neg. #99-15415.)

pilots were enthusiastic or even willing to take on any woman as a student. Tony Jannus, the legendary Midwestern flier, had refused to teach Katherine Stinson to fly. She found another instructor and earned her license in 1912. Matilde Moisant, sister of the American aviator and designer John Moisant, recalled, ". . . in those days, well, to put it this way, it was man's work, and they didn't think it was woman's work or that a nice girl should be in it. There were a few fliers that thought we had as much right as they, but most of them didn't. 'Why don't they leave it to us?' was the attitude?" The Wright brothers refused to teach women to fly, and although Glenn Curtiss had female flight students, it had not been an idea he warmly embraced.

Robert Abbott, the editor and publisher of a black newspaper, the *Chicago Defender*, proved to have the answer to Coleman's dilemma. He suggested that she learn to fly in France where the attitude toward blacks was more tolerant. While Coleman warmly embraced Abbott's excellent suggestion, there were problems. Coleman neither had the money to travel to France, nor did she speak French. Never one to allow minor difficulties to stand in her way, Coleman began taking French lessons and saving every penny she could.

By November 1920, she believed that she was sufficiently fluent in French and had accumulated enough money for her transatlantic passage and the cost of the flying lessons. Once in France, however, she found the attitude was not as open as she had expected. She met resistance and was turned down by several flying schools. This actually turned out to be fortuitous, since Coleman was eventually able to convince Gaston and Rene Caudron, managers of the prestigious École d'Aviation des Frères Caudron at Le Crotoy in the Somme, to accept her as a student. Her course of study with the Caudron brothers lasted seven months and featured the basics of flying as well as aerobatic maneuvers such as looping-the-loop and tailspins. She learned to fly in a French Nieuport Type 82, a twenty-seven-foot-long biplane with a forty-two-foot wingspan. The aircraft designed and manufactured by Nieuport had a reputation as a symbol of streamlined and swift flight and had been one of the best-known of all fighter aircraft in the early stages of World War I.

Coleman graduated from the Caudron flying school in June 1921 and on June 15 received her license from the prestigious Fédération Aéronautique Internationale. Three months later, she returned to the United States where Coleman quickly became front-page news in many of America's black newspapers. In November, *Air Service News* wrote that she "had returned as a full-fledged aviatrix, the first of her race." Although Coleman still had little experience in the air, it is understandable why she received such wide coverage. She was a young, attractive, black woman in a business dominated by young white men. Coleman was flamboyant and had learned to manipulate the press early in her career as an aviator. Known as Queen Bess, she developed her own press kit that was full of hyperbole and, at times, outright lies. Coleman also looked the part, outfitted in a military-style uniform. Her flying clothes included knee-high boots, jodhpurs, a leather coat, and a Sam Browne belt.

Coleman's stay in the United States was short-lived; she returned to France in February 1922 for additional training. In spite of the fact that on September 9, 1922, the *Chicago Defender* called Coleman the "world's greatest woman flier," she was still relatively inexperienced and had done very little actual flying in the eight months since she had earned her license. While in Europe for the second time, she visited France, Holland, and Germany, meeting several aircraft manufacturers including Anthony H. G. Fokker. When she returned to the United States in August, the *New York Times* reported that Coleman was "termed by leading French and Dutch aviators as one of the best fliers they had ever seen." The paper stated that she held the "distinction of having piloted the largest plane ever flown by a woman."

On September 3, at the Glenn Curtiss Field at Garden City, Long Island, Bessie Coleman made what *The Call* of Kansas City claimed was the "first public flight of a black woman in this country." In a borrowed Curtiss JN-4, before a mostly black crowd of no more than a thousand people, Coleman made three flights. The *Chicago Defender* claimed that Coleman was going to do "heart thrilling stunts that will be astounding." Coleman's routine was less than spectacular; it included no aerobatic stunts or even routine figure eights. At the same time, the white daily, the *Chicago Tribune*, reported that Bessie Coleman was "the only colored aviatrix in the world."

Queen Bess's first major accident happened at Santa Monica, California, in 1923 when she crashed a recently purchased used Jenny. She was fortunate to escape with her life, sustaining only a broken leg and three broken ribs. After a three-month hospitalization, she returned to Chicago. In the spring of 1924, the *Afro-American* described Coleman as "the colored girl who has been presenting herself as an aviatrix for the last two seasons" with "a long list of incomplete contracts and an almost as lengthy list of managers and agents." There was a certain amount of truth behind the newspaper's sarcasm. In spite of the fact that Coleman was doing little or no flying, she had continued her lecture series.

A strong proponent of black pride, she was undoubtedly a role model for African-Americans, but she was also a threat to black men. At times, her statements seemed to question the masculinity of African-American males. On one occasion she claimed, ". . . we have men who are physically fit; now what is needed is men who are not afraid to dare death." She had a reputation for being difficult and temperamental; however, most of her dealings were with people who knew little about aviation and easily misinterpreted her insistence on doing things her way. At most air shows, black audiences were confined to an area at a distance from whites, with separate admissions gates. Coleman frequently argued against the unfairness of these practices, which did not make her a favorite with managers and promoters.

Coleman traveled to Texas in May 1925. For almost two and one-half years, she had done little or no flying. Although inactive, her sense of accomplishment was hardly diminished. The *Houston Post-Dispatch*, a white newspaper, quoted her as saying her "great ambition was to make Uncle Tom's cabin into a hangar by establishing a flying school." The major success of Coleman's flying career occurred in Houston on June 19, 1925, in her first aerial appearance in Texas. At the Houston Aerial Transport Field, she gave rides to several prominent African-Americans as thousands, both black and white, watched and enjoyed her show. While Coleman has been described as a barnstormer and aerial circus performer, she actually seldom took part in either activity. The few months that she spent flying in Texas were probably the busiest she had ever been. During the summer of 1925, using borrowed or rented airplanes, she flew at Houston, San Antonio, Galveston, Wharton, and Waxachachie. At Wharton she parachuted from an airplane.

Coleman returned to Chicago in the fall of 1925 and fell into one of her periods of inactivity, doing more lecturing than flying. Although she talked of little else but opening her own flying school and owning her own airplane, neither wish had come to fruition. In January 1926, Bessie Coleman headed south. Scheduled for several lectures, she made the circuit, spending time in the Georgia cities of Savannah, Augusta, and Atlanta. By February, she had arrived in Florida. Armed with several newsreels of herself, she lectured in Tampa and at the black Liberty Theater in St. Petersburg. While in Tampa, she tried to persuade the Norman Studios to produce a movie of her life. In a letter to the film studio in February, the self-promoter described herself as "the Most Known Colored person (woman alive) other than the Jazz singers."

While in Dallas the previous summer, Coleman had made partial payment on an old Curtiss Jenny. She still owed money on it as it sat at Dallas' Love Field. Leaving the west coast of Florida, Coleman headed to Orlando and West Palm Beach where she lectured and even flew a couple of exhibition flights in borrowed airplanes. In Orlando, she met Edwin M. Beeman of the Beeman Chewing Gum Company, who offered to give her the money she needed to pay off her airplane. Coleman accepted his offer and made arrangements to have the Jenny flown from Dallas to Jacksonville, the site of her next exhibition. Queen Bess was scheduled to fly on May 1 at the Negro Welfare League's annual Field Day. The *Jacksonville Journal* reported that she was to be the headliner in a flying exhibition, making a parachute jump from an altitude of twenty-five hundred feet.

William D. Wills, a white mechanic and pilot at Love Field, was hired to fly Coleman's Jenny to Jacksonville. Wills arrived in Jacksonville on April 28, after a difficult flight during which he had been forced to make several unplanned stops to work on the airplane. After his arrival in Jacksonville, local pilots Laurie Yonge and W. H. Alexander examined the aircraft. In their opinion, the "OX-5 engine, rated at ninety horsepower, was so worn and so poorly maintained that it could really develop only sixty horsepower at most." Coleman's death on April 30 may have been caused by a loose wrench jammed in the unprotected controls. Five thousand people attended her funeral service on May 2 at Jacksonville's Bethel Baptist Church.

Was Coleman a good pilot? Probably not. She had little actual experience, with few hours in the air. Her career suffered from frequent periods of inactivity, and she was further handicapped by not owning her own aircraft. When she did fly, she did not have the best available equipment, but was usually forced to use borrowed aircraft that were in poor shape and probably should not have been flown. She never opened the flying school for blacks about which she so fervently and frequently talked; she probably never even taught one person to fly. Coleman was certainly not the first woman to pilot an airplane or to be licensed. Baroness Raymonde de

Laroche had been licensed in 1910 in France. Harriet Quimby had received the thirty-seventh license issued by the Aero Club of America in 1911.

Coleman was also not the first woman to die at the controls. That dubious honor went to Madame Denise Moore in France in 1911. What she did accomplish, however, was probably more important. She opened the eyes of many Americans, both black and white, to the possibility of aviation and other careers for blacks. This was accomplished in a country still rigidly segregated, with Jim Crow laws, frequent lynchings, and a prevalent belief among many whites that "blacks are mentally inferior, immoral, predisposed to crime, physically unattractive, and highly emotional." The May 15, 1926, *Norfolk Journal and Guide* summed it up best when the paper reported, "Miss Coleman has taught our women that they can navigate the air, like all pioneers, she has built her own monument."

The early hubs of aviation for African-Americans included Chicago and Los Angeles. As a living memorial to Bessie Coleman, William J. Powell and several others organized the Bessie Coleman Aero Club in Los Angeles in 1929. Powell served as the club's first president, lobbying black businesses and community leaders in Los Angeles in an attempt to raise money to buy the club's first aircraft. They ended up with a well-used Waco 9 that they named the *Oscar De Priest*, in honor of the first African-American to be elected to the United States Congress since Reconstruction. Ironically, it was Oscar De Priest who later appointed Benjamin O. Davis Jr. to the United States Military Academy.

Representative De Priest had worked long and hard to select the right black candidates for American military academies. He succeeded in 1929 in having Alonzo Parham of Chicago admitted to the United States Military Academy. Unfortunately, Parham failed his mathematical course in the spring of 1930, and was forced to withdraw from West Point. De Priest felt so strongly about young African-American men attending the prestigious military academies that he had promised to personally pay for a candidate's preparatory education. At a June 1930 meeting in Nassau, New York, De Priest contended that ". . . if our men are good enough to fight for the United States then they are entitled to the highest military training and commissions. Our youths should be prepared to take command in the event of conflicts in order that our soldiers will not have to go into combat led by white officers who have nothing in common with them." Oscar De Priest strongly believed that his congressional career would have been incomplete if he was unable to select and place qualified black men into the programs at both West Point and Annapolis. With Davis, De Priest picked a winner.

Leon Paris, a black flier from Harlem, New York, made a flight from New York to Port au Prince, Haiti, in May 1932. Paris was accompanied by Eugene Charlton, a white mechanic. Their flight was sponsored by the National Colored Aero Association and the *Amsterdam News*. The two men had originally intended a nonstop flight, but bad weather necessitated stops at Charlotte, North Carolina; Jacksonville, Florida; and Santiago and Havana, Cuba.

Charles E. James, of Jacksonville, Florida, traveled to the Curtiss-Wright school in Long Island, New York, in September 1931. Although he had been flying for several years, he took additional flying lessons and qualified for his pilot's license. His first airplane had been christened *New York City*; he had also conducted a flying school in Atlanta, Georgia. After James received his Department of Commerce license, he opened the James and Nelson Air Circus and toured the country. Less than a year later, he took his circus to Gary, Indiana. Before a crowd of more than fifteen hundred people, James and his white copilot, Eugene Cernhan, took off on September 2, 1932, in a three-year-old Eagle Rock three-seater powered by a Curtiss OX5 engine. Almost immediately after takeoff, the airplane sideslipped out of control. Over the southeast corner of the airport, the airplane went into a steep dive. At only eight hundred feet above the field, the aircraft went into a spin and burst into flames. In seconds, James' airplane smashed into an embankment bordering a small creek. Both men died of their injuries.

In 1929, air shows featuring black pilots and parachutists were frequently held at Checkerboard and Heath Fields in Chicago. Dr. A. Porter Davis of Kansas City was the featured performer. Willie "Suicide" Jones, the black parachute jumper, and Dorothy Darby performed before crowds of blacks and whites in their aerial shows at Markham Field near Chicago. The cost of admission at Markham Field was fifty cents. Jones billed himself as the "Greatest Colored Professional Parachute Jumper." Dorothy Darby of Cleveland was billed as America's only black girl parachute jumper, performing wherever there was a demand for her skills. On September 24, 1933, wearing her trademark knee-high brown boots and riding jodhpurs, she headlined the show at the Second Annual Colored Air and

Ground Show at the Westchester Airport located at Hillside, Illinois. For thirty-five cents, people could view not only Darby's performance, but the daredevil Major George Fisher as well. Fisher's act was described as "a sensational delayed parachute leap from a great plane ten thousand feet up." Rounding out the bill was Peter Consdorf of Mobile, Alabama, and Roy Bridgers of Chattanooga, Tennessee. Only a year earlier, Darby had been injured in St. Louis. Before seven thousand spectators, she had fractured both ankles and suffered internal injuries, requiring nearly a year to recover.

Other Chicago area African-American fliers of note included Harold Hurd, Charles Johnson, Freddie Hutchinson, and Grover Nash, the first black man to fly the United States Air Mail.

John C. Robinson organized the Challenger Air Pilots Association, a black flying club, in Chicago in 1931. Its mission was to stimulate and promote aviation among blacks. The group intended to "create good will among all air pilots and air men regardless of nationality, to uphold and abide by all the rules of aviation for the good of aviation, to try and help promote a landing field or airport in every town where we are represented in any number; and affiliate them all with each other by division, to try and contact positions or connections for qualified members in all lines of aviation and to help make America supreme in the air." As were most black aero clubs, the Challenger Air Pilots Association was kept out of white-owned airports. The group was forced to set up its operation at Robbins Airport in the predominantly black township of Robbins, Illinois.

By the mid-1930s, John Robinson was without a doubt one of the best known and most respected of African-American aviators. Born in Gulfport, Mississippi, Robinson built and flew kites as did most young boys. After studying at Tuskegee Institute, he worked as an auto mechanic for a taxicab company in Chicago, later opening his own shop. After he received his pilot's license, he flew for the Curtiss Flying Service ferrying airplanes from one state to another. While Hubert Fauntleroy Julian called himself the "Black Eagle of Harlem," Robinson was affectionately nicknamed the "Brown Condor."

When the Challenger Air Pilots Association first opened their flying field, Robinson detailed the mission of the fliers in an article in the *Chicago Defender* of April 25, 1936. He began by saying, "We have got to work on a very strict basis because if any kind of accident happens, it will kill everything I have tried to do." As the field operator, Robinson outlined the rules and procedures for the would-be aviators. Insisting on exemplary effort from the students, he went on to detail the requirements necessary for their success.

Janet Bragg, a nurse and student of Robinson's, bought the group's first aircraft. Each day members of the club would travel out to the airport and clear land to make the field usable. They soon built a crude hangar and began to acquire additional airplanes. Bragg considered Robinson to be an excellent pilot and instructor. The *Chicago Defender* of April 25, 1936, reported her comments, "As an instructor, I think he excelled any pilot. He was always anxious about his students. When you did anything wrong pertaining to flying there was no exception to the rules."

In one particular incident during her instruction, Robinson and Bragg had been flying together. As they headed toward the west, Bragg found her vision to be obscured by the setting sun in her eyes. When she attempted to turn in a different direction, Robinson insisted that she maintain her course. When she continued to turn away from the glare of the sun, despite Robinson's instruction to the contrary, Robinson took over the controls, returned to the field, and landed the plane.

Robinson then forcefully suggested that Bragg find another instructor—one from whom she was willing to accept instruction. When she excused her action by stating that the sun had been in her eyes, Robinson countered that such conditions were frequently encountered during flight, and therefore, a necessary part of flying lessons. Seeing the wisdom of Robinson's words and realizing her error, Bragg gave her instructor no further difficulty.

As luck would have it, a windstorm devastated the Challenger's field. The hangar was destroyed and the club's three airplanes were badly damaged. The Challenger Air Pilots Association was forced to relocate to Chicago's Harlem Airport, a field owned and operated by Fred Shumacher, a Caucasian, who befriended the group and allowed them to use his field. They were still segregated, however, since they were assigned to the lower end of the airfield and kept isolated from white pilots. Robinson soon organized a group of young black men and women interested in flying, rented a small storefront in Chicago, and called it the Brown Eagle Aero Club. Things weren't easy; he suffered several setbacks. One day he rented the club's airplane to several young Chinese men. When he returned to the field, the plane was nothing but ashes.

Robinson had become involved in aviation through his association

Well-known black aviator John C. Robinson organized the Challenger Air Pilots Association in Chicago in 1931. Janet Bragg, a member of the Chicago Girls Flying Club and one of Robinson's flying students, purchased the first airplane for the organization. (National Air and Space Museum, Smithsonian Institution, SI Neg. #91-15485.)

with Cornelius R. Coffey. Robinson and Coffey, both auto mechanics, had pooled their money and purchased an airplane from Charles Abbott, a white man who gave them both flying lessons. Flying was only one aspect; they realized that they needed someone to maintain their airplane. White mechanics were not willing to do it. Coffey and Robinson read of the Curtiss-Wright Aeronautical School in Chicago and decided that was the solution for them. Accepted as pupils by mail, each month the pair sent money toward their tuition.

When Robinson and Coffey eventually showed up in person at the Curtiss-Wright school, they found it to be segregated. The school's administration didn't know how to deal with the situation. When they attempted to return the tuition to the two black men, Coffey and Robinson refused to accept the money. They had contracted for instruction in aircraft maintenance, and they intended to get it. The two received the assistance of a pair of white men. Their employer, Emil Mack, offered to provide a lawyer to force the Curtiss-Wright Aeronautical School to accept them as students. Anxious to avoid a lawsuit, the school's administrators agreed to accept the two men. Once in the class, they took verbal abuse from both their fellow students and some of the instructors until Jack Snyder, an instructor and World War I flier, took a liking to the two men, ending the difficulties. Following his training at the Curtiss-Wright school, Coffey opened up his own school of aeronautics at Harlem Airport. He intended to teach blacks to fly.

In May 1934, three black fliers from the Challenger Air Pilots Association set off on a "Good Will" flight from Chicago to Tuskegee, Alabama. Plans had been in the works for a long time. John C. Robinson would fly in one airplane; Grover C. Nash was to pilot his monoplane. The trip began inauspiciously. After inspecting his airplane, Robinson warmed up the engine and headed out. At the end of the runway, he applied more power and the engine stopped. The crowd of friends and well-wishers ran out to the plane to see what was happening. By the time they got there, Robinson had climbed from the airplane and was turning the propeller over. Cornelius Coffey decided to accompany Robinson to Alabama. Off they went. Nash quickly followed.

As they flew due south, their first stop was Evansville, Indiana. After their delayed start at Chicago, things were going well. Montgomery, Alabama, was to be their next stop, then on to Tuskegee. Out of Evansville, the two airplanes flew south-southeast.

When Robinson was forced to make an unscheduled landing for fuel at Decatur, Alabama, he set his airplane down on the grounds of a country club. Nash landed right behind him.

After refueling, they were ready to go. Robinson's airplane headed across the grass, slowly picking up speed. The field was too short; Robinson knew he had a problem. A house loomed in front of him; he pulled back on the stick and the plane's wheels left the ground. As the airplane flew perilously close to the home owned by Fred S. Graves, Robinson's horizontal stabilizer struck the house's chimney. For an instant, the plane was out of control. Robinson tried to straighten it out and headed for a plowed field on the west side of the Bee Line Highway. Robinson and Coffey hit a tree and hurtled toward the ground, crashing to a sudden stop. The lower wings were smashed and the landing gear had been ripped from the fuselage. Coffey and Robinson were unhurt; their airplane was a total wreck. When Grover Nash graciously offered Robinson the use of his airplane, Robinson safely completed the solo flight to Tuskegee. Nash and Coffey followed by bus.

In the early years of manned flight, barely a day passed when there was not a front-page story reporting the tragedy of an airplane crash and horrific death. By the mid-thirties and the "Golden Age of Flight," airplane design and flying skills had greatly improved, but aviation accidents were still a real concern. Black flying clubs were springing up all over the country. In 1933, the Washington, D.C.-based Colored Junior Air League established a flight school at Oxen, Maryland. In Detroit, several men and women organized the Ace Flying Club. A group of blacks formed a flying school in Harlem, New York, and flew out of Floyd Bennett Field. Most of these clubs did not offer the structure, safety, and quality of flight instruction that could be found in Chicago, however.

For weeks, Donald Simmons of Detroit labored on the construction of his own airplane. He had twenty-five hours of dual instruction in his logbook. In early July 1933, he decided to take his wife Katherine for an evening ride in his newly completed airplane. Several people watched him take off from Burns Airport on the edge of Detroit. The plane was barely in the air when its left wing hit the top of a twenty-foot telephone pole. Several motorists narrowly escaped death as the falling airplane and wooden pole crashed into the street. Almost immediately, Katherine Simmons was picked up by friends and transported to the Redford Receiving Station. Within an hour the twenty-year-old woman was dead. Donald Simmons lay in pain for nearly an hour while white sheriff's deputies and Redford Township police chief Jack Bissell argued about how to transport Simmons to the hospital. As the deputies insisted that they needed to wait for an ambulance from Eloise Hospital, Bissell finally lost patience, picked up Simmons, put him into his own car, and sped to the hospital. Simmons survived only an hour longer than his wife, dying of a fractured skull and internal injuries. It had been only his second solo flight.

Police Chief Bissell was unhappy with the bureaucratic treatment of the deputies and vocally lashed out at them. He told reporters from the *Pittsburgh Courier*, "You can't do anything in this county without stumbling over a pack of deputies." Simmons was a member of Detroit's all-black Ace Flying Club. Ronald Chappell, Simmons' instructor, told police that the airplane had been built from secondhand parts. When asked if the airplane had been fit to fly, Chappell hedged and said, "That's a touchy question to answer." Deputy sheriff Joseph P. Creedon was more vocal and declared, ". . . these home-built planes . . . are nothing more than death traps." After Simmons had inspected his airplane, he went to get his wife. In his absence, witnesses reported that they had seen two men tamper with his airplane.

Few men stirred the emotions of African-Americans interested in aviation more than James H. Banning and Thomas C. Allen. As a young man in Oklahoma, Thomas Allen learned to fly by trading his saxophone as a down payment on flying lessons. Hours of hard work at the airport provided the cost of continuing instruction, as Bob Tarbutton taught Allen in a little scrub field near Oklahoma City. When it finally came time to solo, Tarbutton wanted a five-hundred-dollar bond in case the aircraft was destroyed. Since the airplane, a World War I surplus Curtiss Jenny, was worth little more than a few dollars, Allen refused to post the bond. When Tarbutton was out of town, Allen took the plane up without permission, making his first solo flight at the age of seventeen.

On September 18, 1932, Banning and Allen, both members of the Bessie Coleman Flying Club, set out on a transcontinental flight in an eight-year-old airplane. With only twenty-five dollars in their pockets, the pair departed Dycer Airport in Los Angeles. The men were christened the "Flying Hobos," because many times they literally had to pass the hat to collect nickels and dimes to allow their trip to continue. Their flight from Los Angeles to New York took twenty-one

James H. Banning and Thomas C. Allen made aviation history in 1932 as the first African-Americans to make a transcontinental flight. Although the journey lasted three weeks, the actual flying time was forty-one hours and twenty-seven minutes. (National Air and Space Museum, Smithsonian Institution, SI Neg. #99-15420.)

days, but was hardly nonstop; the two men logged forty-one hours and twenty-seven minutes flying time. The transcontinental flight of Banning and Allen had been widely chronicled, not only in black newspapers, but also by white reporters. Dubbed the "Black Birds," they were generally well received by whites along the way.

The Eagle Rock airplane that the pair used for their transcontinental flight cost a mere forty dollars. An enthusiastic crowd of both blacks and whites greeted their arrival at Roosevelt Field in New York. The flight of the "Flying Hobos" had become more than simply an aerial crossing of the United States. It was a symbol of what blacks hoped to achieve, not only in aviation, but also in society. Upon arrival in New York, according to the *Chicago Defender* of October 15, 1932, Banning said, "We left Los Angeles without any publicity, and we arrived in New York minus the ballyhoo. We did not name our plane, or state our intentions." This was not due to superstition, but rather to the fact that Banning and Allen preferred to allow others to publicize their efforts after they had succeeded.

In New York, they replaced the well-worn engine of their airplane

with a Wright Whirlwind J5. Their return to California was calami-
tous. On their way to Pittsburgh where they were contracted to fly an
exhibition, they encountered heavy head winds near Blairsville and
ran out of gas. They were forced to make an emergency landing
and damaged a wing. They went on to Pittsburgh and borrowed an
airplane for their exhibition at Bettis Field. So strapped for cash
were the two pilots that they couldn't afford to pay for repairs to
their airplane. The editor of the *Pittsburgh Courier* provided bus tick-
ets for their trip home to Los Angeles.

On February 5, 1933, James H. Banning died in an airplane crash
at San Diego. Scheduled to fly an exhibition at Camp Kearney Field,
Banning had left his plane at Lindbergh Field; a navy pilot offered to
fly Banning there to pick up his airplane. Banning sat in front, the
pilot in the rear. On the way, at an altitude of one thousand feet,
the plane went into a tailspin and crashed into the ground. Banning
and Albert Burghart, the navy aviation machinist mate second class,
were rushed to the hospital, but it was too late. Banning died an
hour later of a fractured skull and internal injuries. Banning had
planned to take Marie Daugherty, a parachutist, up to four thousand
feet where she would jump. Because he was black, he had been
refused the use of an airplane at the field by the flying instructor of
the Airtech Flying School; the Airtech employee believed that blacks
could not be competent fliers. Banning's wife Mable, a domestic
worker, was left financially destitute. The owner of the Connor and
Johnson funeral home donated the cost of Banning's funeral.
Hundreds of friends as well as strangers sent letters of sympathy
and small monetary gifts.

Born on November 5, 1900, Banning, like most black fliers, had
also been denied aviation training at white flight schools. He was
finally taught to fly by a white army officer. In 1926, when the United
States Department of Commerce began to require the licensing of
pilots, Banning became one of the country's first licensed black
pilots. As qualified a flier as any pilot holding a license, he had studied engineering at Iowa State College. As a member of the Bessie
Coleman Flying Club, Banning had logged hundreds of hours of
flight time.

Meanwhile on the West Coast, William J. Powell was doing his part
for African-American aviators in Los Angeles. Powell's "Craftsmen of
Black Wings" boasted of having seventy-five members, including six
Caucasians and two Mexicans. Among the members were: Bridget

Walton, Latinia Myatt, Ann Jefferson, Willie Mae Sims, Zola Benjamin, Gwendolyn Morton, and Marie Dickerson, wife of Dudley Dickerson, the well-known singer and dancer.

With the publication in 1934 of his book, *Black Wings*, William J. Powell sought to accomplish several purposes. Dedicated to Bessie Coleman, Powell's book proposed that all blacks consider careers in aviation. Powell also produced a short film, *Unemployment, the Negro, and Aviation*, and published a newsletter titled the *Craftsmen Aero News.*

Few black fliers were better known than the duo of C. Alfred Anderson and Dr. Albert E. Forsythe, as they crisscrossed the United States from east to west, north to Canada, and south to Latin America. In July 1933, Anderson and Forsythe completed a round-trip, sponsored by the Atlantic City Board of Trade, between Atlantic City, New Jersey, and Los Angeles. Taking off in their ninety-horse-power Lambert Monocoupe named the *Pride of Atlantic City* on July 17, they hit heavy fog and were forced to make an unscheduled stop at Camden, New Jersey. After stops at Pittsburgh, Indianapolis, St. Louis, Wichita, Kansas City, Amarillo, and Albuquerque, they landed at Grand Central Airport in Los Angeles on July 20. There they were met by thousands of people, including William Powell and representatives from his Black Wings aviation organization. They took little time to rest, departing Los Angeles the next day.

On their return trip, they made stops at Cheyenne, Omaha, Chicago, and New York City. Crowds of jubilant citizens and government officials witnessed their arrival at Atlantic City on July 28. Everywhere they flew, large enthusiastic crowds of blacks and whites greeted them. At Chicago's Municipal Airport, three thousand people, including several hundred members of the Chicago area Elk's Club lodges, met Anderson and Forsythe.

The pair engaged in their Pan-American Goodwill aircraft tour in 1934 after more than a year's preparation. Partnered with the Interracial Goodwill Aviation Committee, the West Indian Federation of America, and the Caribbean Union, their flight was to commemorate the centenary of the emancipation of the British West Indies. The men had collected aerial and weather maps and charts for each country they planned to visit. Passports and visas were acquired. They studied French, Spanish, Dutch, and Portuguese, since at each country, they intended to make a speech in the local language. When the two men met with Charles

Lindbergh in August, he advised them on airports, hazards, and instruments needed for their trip. As a result of their meeting with Lindbergh, they added an inflatable boat to their gear.

Negotiations with the United States and the foreign countries had been long and involved. Finally on October 27, 1934, permission was received from the Department of Commerce authorizing the flight. It read, "Authorization is hereby granted to C. Alfred Anderson and Albert E. Forsythe for a flight to be made in aircraft NR 11745 (the *Booker T. Washington*) over the following countries: Bahama Islands, Cuba, Jamaica, Antigua, Barbados, Haiti, Dominican Republic, Puerto Rico, Virgin Islands, Guadeloupe, Trinidad, British Guiana, Dutch Guiana, French Guiana, Brazil, Venezuela, Columbia, Canal Zone, Costa Rica, Nicaragua, El Salvador, Honduras, British Honduras and Mexico."

The morning of November 9 at the Atlantic City airport was cold. At 5:00 A.M., mechanics and ground crew pored over the *Booker T. Washington*. Everything had to be perfect—there would be a lot of dangerous over-water flying. At 7:30 A.M., Anderson and Forsythe made their own inspection of their airplane. Painted orange and black, the Lambert Monocoupe had a cruising speed of 120 miles per hour and a top speed of 140 miles per hour. With extra fuel tanks, the aircraft had a range of several hundred miles. Anderson had a transport pilot's license; Forsythe held a private pilot's license. They were highly experienced; between them, they had logged several hundred hours of flying time. The trip would be almost fourteen thousand miles in length.

Thousands of people stood outside in the cold November air awaiting their departure. Thirty minutes later, the airplane was in the air. Forsythe and Anderson circled the Atlantic City airport twice, then headed south for Miami. Over North Carolina, a gas line broke in flight, and the fliers were forced to make an emergency landing near Beaufort. Repairs were made overnight. The next morning they were again headed south. Departing from Miami, they flew their second leg of the flight to the Bahamas. Nearly six thousand people waited in the warm, humid Caribbean night for their arrival on November 12. A lack of runway lights forced authorities to illuminate the runway with automobile headlights. Charles P. Bethel, the acting colonial secretary representing Sir Governor Bede Hugh Clifford, extended a royal welcome. That evening, the governor received Anderson and Forsythe at the Government House where they were feted as guests of honor.

Hops throughout the Virgin Islands and the West Indies were made. In Cuba, they were welcomed at Boyeros Airport by Fulgencio Batista. Their trip was considered daring since they frequently flew into uncharted and rugged terrain. After a three-week delay at Santo Domingo, Dominican Republic, they flew to San Juan, Puerto Rico. There they were greeted by thousands of people waving hats and white handkerchiefs. A band played the Tuskegee Institute hymn. Unfortunately, their goodwill tour ended in December 1934 when they crashed at Port of Spain, Trinidad. Though the tour had ended prematurely, it was still an overwhelming triumph. They had successfully promoted aviation for blacks and had fostered goodwill between the people of the Western Hemisphere.

Doris Murphy, Dale L. White, Edward C. Anderson, and Clyde B. Hampton, all African-Americans, passed their flight tests and graduated from Chicago's Aeronautical University on February 28, 1935. John Robinson, the man responsible for breaking segregation at the school, was their instructor and the school's only black staff member. The school now actively recruited both white and black aviation students.

Chauncey E. Spencer and Dale L. White, two National Aeronautics Association pilots, made a three-thousand-mile round-trip flight from Chicago to New York to Washington, D.C., in 1939. The purpose of their extended journey was to promote the Civilian Pilot Training Program and wider aviation opportunities for blacks. With them, they carried a scroll from Mayor Edward J. Kelly of Chicago to Mayor Fiorello La Guardia of New York. Without a doubt, the highlight of their trip took place in Washington, when they met with an up-and-coming senator from Missouri, Harry Truman.

Fliers from the Coffey School of Aeronautics eventually logged thousands of hours in the air. In September 1942, Joseph Hamilton, Charles Smallwood, and Norman Gray, all graduates of Coffey's school, made a two-thousand-mile cross-country trip, flying in Indiana, Ohio, Kentucky, West Virginia, Virginia, and North Carolina. Members of the Civil Air Patrol, the men planned their trip in order to gain more experience flying in mountainous regions as preparation for CAP rescues. The three were all members of the Sixth Squadron of Group 613 of the Illinois Wing of the CAP, commanded by Coffey. In their seventy-five-horsepower Piper Cub Cruiser, painted red and white and named *Wings of Destiny*, their trip had taken six days. Only months after the Civil Air Patrol was organized, the Chicago area Civil Air Patrol Flight Squadron had been organized by Cornelius R. Coffey, William Paris, and Willa Brown. Coffey served as commander; Paris was flight instructor and executive officer. Willa Brown served as the squadron's adjutant. Made up of more than twenty-five pilots, the squadron included both blacks and whites.

The Chicago Girls Flying Club afforded young black women in the Midwest an opportunity to learn to fly. Janet Waterford Bragg, Marie St. Clair, Lois Jones, and Willa Brown were all members. Two of the most famous African-American pilots before World War II were both women. Bessie Coleman was certainly the best known, but Willa Brown was not far behind. In the late 1930s and early 1940s, Brown was unarguably America's most well-known African-American female flier; she perhaps even surpassed black men in reputation and should legitimately be considered the black counterpart to Amelia Earhart. Brown's credentials were unparalleled. Always a trailblazer, she had been the first black woman to work for the Social Security board in the Chicago area. She later transferred to the Immigration and Naturalization Service. Along with Cornelius Coffey and Enoc Walters of the *Chicago Defender*, Brown was a co-founder of the National Airmen's Association in February 1939. She held a limited commercial license with more than five hundred hours of flight time. Willa Brown was a director of the Coffey School of Aeronautics and headed the aviation department at Chicago's Wendell Phillips High School.

Certainly one of the most exciting and enigmatic of early black fliers was Hubert Fauntleroy Julian, self-billed as the "Black Eagle of Harlem." A native of Trinidad, Julian was the epitome of sartorial splendor. His normal dress was a Prince Albert cutaway coat, black trousers, and a white shirt with a wing collar. He was seldom seen without his monocle and black derby. He rode in a chauffeured La Salle convertible. At first, Julian served as a strong inspiration for blacks to become involved with flying. After most of his schemes floundered and he made good on none of his boastful promises, he became a setback to the cause.

Julian's first attempt, or claimed attempt, at a transatlantic flight was in 1919. He claimed also to have been flying since 1918, when he had learned to fly in Canada with the Canadian Air Force. After flying for nearly fifteen years, Julian finally received his pilot's license from the United States Department of Commerce. In August 1931 at New Castle, Delaware, Julian took his flight test. He insisted that he

Willa B. Brown was America's best known African-American female flier during the late 1930s and early 1940s. The first black woman to be commissioned as a lieutenant in the U.S. Civil Air Patrol, Brown was a co-founder of the National Airmen's Association. (National Archives and Records Administration, #208-FS-793-1.)

had been awarded a license in 1924 by the Fédération Aéronautique Internationale and had not needed the license issued by the Department of Commerce. At his press conference in March 1933, Julian promised that there were big things ahead. He planned to fly nonstop from New York to Paris in June. Julian's manager Lonnie Hicks asserted, "The flight across will be completed in about half the time made by Colonel Lindbergh." Julian never improved on Lindbergh's time because he never made the flight.

Only a few months later on September 29, 1933, Hubert Julian called another press conference to announce his planned transatlantic solo flight and to christen his airplane *Abyssinia*. Before a crowd of one thousand people at Floyd Bennett Field, Julian announced that he would fly from New York to Aden, Arabia. Like a strutting peacock posing before newsreel cameras, Julian told reporters, "I am going to take the long distance flight record from the French fliers, Codos and Rossi, and bring it back to the United States. In taking the record I am going to Aden, Arabia, a distance of 7,800 miles, which will be convenient to Abyssinia."

Only a year earlier, on April 15, 1932, Julian and William J. Powell had announced their plans to fly five thousand miles from New York to New Delhi, India, in August of that year. The pair planned to make the trip in a Bellanca fitted with a 650-horsepower Hornet engine. Not surprisingly, the trip never happened.

Taking off from Floyd Bennett Field for his latest venture, Julian ended up in the mud flats of Flushing Bay when he was forced to crash land due to engine trouble. Nearly two months later, Julian still had not made his flight across the Atlantic, but was still talking about it. On November 11, a huge gala was held in his honor at Harlem's Little Theater of the Y.M.C.A. The *Chicago Defender* reported, "Never in the history of Harlem, experts agreed, has there ever been a greater tribute paid to the standing of a Race man in any field of activity. . . ."

Julian did cross the Atlantic—by ship, not air. When war broke out in Africa, Julian traveled to Ethiopia, supposedly as the provisional head of the Ethiopian Air Force. Rumored to have crashed and destroyed Ethiopia's only airplane, he quickly fell into disfavor with Emperor Haile Selassie. By August, the Ethiopian government wanted nothing to do with the "Black Eagle of Harlem." Malak E. Doyen, an Ethiopian representative in Washington, D.C., declared that Julian "is in no way representing the Abyssinian government or any department thereof. . . . Julian has misused the kindness and opportunity the Abyssinian government offered him."

In defiance of orders given by both the king and the minister of war, Julian flew the Abyssinian government's best airplane, only to destroy the aircraft in a disastrous crash. When in November 1930, the *Chicago Defender* reported the incident, the newspaper stated that Julian had been arrested, ". . . but when it was found that it would cost too much to feed him while in prison, he was ordered out of the country." In late November, Julian returned to the United States and declared that the news accounts concerning his imprisonment and banishment were patently false. Julian claimed that he had been the victim of a plot hatched by jealous Frenchmen and that, in fact, he had not smashed the emperor's airplane. His version stated that when he had landed near Makale, tribesmen believing his landing to be a visit from the devil destroyed the airplane.

The "Black Eagle of Harlem" had been back in the United States only a short time and already his troubles were worsening. In early December 1930, Frank P. Oexle Jr. sued Julian for slightly more than five thousand dollars. Oexle claimed that Julian had purchased an engineless airplane from him in 1926, but had never paid for it. In May 1934, Julian again announced his plans for a transatlantic flight from New York to Rome. He intended to fly with Roger Q. Williams in a Bellanca. That transatlantic crossing never happened either.

Somehow, Julian managed to regain his standing with Emperor Selassie and was put in charge of training Ethiopian infantry in 1935. Always the showman, he set out from Addis Ababa to Ambo, a distance of one hundred miles. His mission, he asserted, was to train five thousand Ethiopian soldiers. Regal in appearance and mounted on the back of a snow-white mare, Julian was followed by his own entourage, all dressed in white and wearing no shoes. Prior to the event, he had supposedly been presented with a silver-plated revolver, a gilded sword, and three uniforms by the ministry of war; he also wore three gold ribbons denoting him as a colonel in Ethiopia's army. In reality, he ran guns. In April 1935, Julian supervised the shipment of more than twenty thousand rifles and machine guns from Czechoslovakia to Ethiopia.

Upon his second return from Ethiopia, Julian encountered more difficulties. More a mercenary than a patriot, Julian had few qualms about switching allegiances and was rumored to be working for the Italians. The *Pittsburgh Courier* reported that while Julian was in

London, he had met with an Italian consul and struck a deal for $1,250 and a luxury suite on the *Aquitania* for his return passage to America. In return, Julian was required to denounce Ethiopian emperor Haile Selassie. The newspaper called him "another Benedict Arnold . . . 1936 edition" and a "land aviator." Tongue in cheek, the *Pittsburgh Courier* announced that Julian's new name was Huberto Fauntleroyana Juliano.

At a February 1936 meeting of the National Negro Congress in Chicago, Julian was verbally attacked by E. L. Sullinger, national commander of the War Veterans Association of Brooklyn, New York. Sullinger called Julian a traitor. When Julian protested, he was ejected from the Chicago Armory with a police escort. Only weeks before, when he had announced his plans to travel to Chicago to lecture, the secretary of the Chicago branch of the National Urban League, wrote to Mayor Frederick W. Mansfield asking that Julian be banned because of his betrayal of Ethiopia and his subsequent pro-Italian sentiments. So strong was the public outcry against Julian that he claimed to fear for his life and fled to Paris by ship. Upon his return to the United States on the French liner *Normandie* only a month later, he was refused admittance by immigration officials and was held at Ellis Island for two days.

Four months later, John Robinson sailed to Ethiopia to replace Julian. As had Julian, Robinson wanted to assist Emperor Haile Selassie in the development of a defensive air weapon to rebuff Mussolini's Italian invasion. In January 1935, Robinson had gone to the offices of the *Associated Negro Press* in Chicago, wanting to go to Ethiopia. He asked the director, "Do you think I can get over there, and how?" Eventually invited to Washington to present his credentials to a representative of Ethiopia, Robinson received a cable from the emperor asking him to come to Ethiopia. Despite a recently broken arm, he was ready and willing to go, leaving Chicago on May 2.

In Robinson's absence, the Challenger Air Pilots Association named new officers. Cornelius Coffey became president, Earl Renfroe vice-president, Janet Bragg recording secretary, Harold Hurd financial secretary, and Charles Johnson treasurer. Robinson was named commander-in-chief. Dale L. White, Clyde B. Hampton, Willa Brown, and Preston Bowie served on the advisory board. In August, Haile Selassie appointed John Robinson chief of the imperial air forces of Ethiopia. Robinson quickly gained the favor of the emperor, flying him around Ethiopia, and carrying important dispatches. Robinson's airplane was painted with the emperor's royal symbol, the "Conquering Lion of Judah."

In early October 1935, Robinson arrived in the Ethiopian city of Aduwa with a pouch filled with dispatches from Emperor Haile Salassie to his field commanders. Tired from a long day of flying, Robinson decided to spend the night. The next morning at daybreak, several Italian bombers attacked the city. Most of the sleeping residents of Aduwa were caught unaware and defenseless against the dropping bombs. Many fled to the Red Cross hospital, mistakenly believing that it would be a safe haven. The Ethiopian government later estimated that several thousand people were killed or wounded by bombs hitting near the hospital. Helpless against the aerial attack, Ethiopian soldiers stood in the streets with their swords pointed toward the sky.

At the beginning of the bombing, Robinson, hoping to stave off the attack, headed to a small landing strip where he had hidden his airplane. Unable to take off, he was forced to spend the day next to his plane. In a dispatch to the *Chicago Defender* of October 12, 1935, Robinson recalled, "When I left the city, it wasn't possible to number the dead."

While in Ethiopia, Robinson had faced great difficulties. A broken collarbone resulted from a crash, he was gassed in an infantry attack by the Italians, and was shot twice. Robinson also had an unfortunate encounter with Hubert Fauntleroy Julian. When they met at the Majestic Hotel in Addis Ababa, Julian physically attacked him in the hotel's lobby. After the fray, Julian told reporters, "I knocked Robinson down for sending distorted information about me to America."

In early April 1936, Robinson prepared to return to the United States. He had been away from his wife and business for a year, plus the rainy season was about to begin, making the use of air power less effective. During his absence his wife had managed his automotive garage at Forty-Seventh Street and Michigan Avenue, Chicago. The real reason for his return, however, was the hopelessness of the situation in Ethiopia—the country was about to fall to Italy. After thirteen months in Ethiopia, Robinson returned to the United States on May 22, 1936, arriving aboard the *Europa*. After spending several days in New York, Robinson boarded a scheduled TWA airplane for Chicago.

Twenty thousand people—men and women, adults and children, black and white—anxiously awaited Robinson's arrival at Chicago's Municipal Airport. Several miles from the airport, Dr. Earl Renfroe, a member of the Challenger Air Pilots Association, in his private airplane rendezvoused with the TWA flight to provide escort. As police strained to keep the surging crowd at bay, people fought for the opportunity to touch Robinson, to be near him. Met by members of the Eighth Regiment of the United States Army, the Boy Scouts of America, high school cadets, the American Legion, and members of the Challenger Air Pilots Association, he was greeted with hugs, tears, kisses, handshakes, and words of cheer. A five-hundred-car motorcade led by Robinson wended its way from the airport through the streets of Chicago to the Grand Hotel.

From the hotel's balcony, Robinson was introduced by Robert S. Abbott, editor and publisher of the *Chicago Defender*. Abbott lauded Robinson's effort on behalf of the Ethiopians. He attributed Robinson's success to his ". . . complete preparations through diligent scientific study to properly assume the obligation which awaited him in a foreign country."

Years earlier, Julian, the "Black Eagle," had left Ethiopia in disgrace. Robinson, the "Brown Condor," returned to Chicago as a conquering hero. Robinson was loved, Julian hated, by the Ethiopians. J. A. Rogers, a war correspondent in Ethiopia, frequently was made aware of the intense level of antagonism that Ethiopians felt for Julian. As he learned on several occasions, extremely negative impressions of black Americans were being formed by Ethiopians, based upon the actions of Julian. Rogers reported in the *Pittsburgh Courier*, "If all American Negroes had been like Julian, the Ethiopians were prepared to have nothing to do with them." Hubert Fauntleroy Julian was characterized as one of the most detested men in Ethiopia, ranking with Haile Selassie Gugsa, a traitor to his country. Rogers heard few people say anything good about Julian.

On September 28, 1936, John Robinson opened his John C. Robinson National Air College and School of Automotive Engineering, located on the grounds of Poro College in the south side of Chicago. In addition to Robinson, the staff included Cornelius Coffey, Alexander Seiguff, Homer Lewis, Ray Sawyer, and James Raney. J. A. Rogers said, "One thing is certain. If Col. Robinson is given the support he deserves, he'll see that Negroes take their place among the most capable and distinguished in aviation. Robinson told the group, "This has been my whole life's dream to build a school and the words of encouragement from this group are an inspiration to me."

Following his return to the United States, J. A. Rogers, certainly one of the best-known of all African-American journalists, had suffered the same indignity as ordinary black men and women when his ticket for a flight on Transcontinental and Western Airways service out of Kansas City was refused. Rogers was ejected from the airplane; his seat was given instead to Buddy Rogers, a Caucasian film star.

In November 1936, Hubert Fauntleroy Julian announced another proposed transatlantic flight. This time he claimed that he and Allen Moton, the son of Dr. R. R. Moton, the president of Tuskegee Institute, would make a round-trip flight from New York to Paris to "prove that members of the Race are competent in aviation." As were all of his earlier plans for a transatlantic flight, this one was little more than hot air.

In mid-February 1937, heavy rains and horrific flooding hit the southern part of the United States. People died; homes and personal belongings were destroyed. Agencies from throughout the country tried to provide relief, but the task wasn't easy. The *Chicago Defender* attempted to do its part and sent John Robinson south with six hundred pounds of clothing collected by the newspaper's Flood Relief Committee. On February 17, workers packed Robinson's Curtiss Challenger, powered by a 185-horsepower engine, with more than one-quarter ton of relief supplies. The cargo was one hundred pounds in excess of the aircraft's allowable weight. With the four-passenger airplane packed from floor to ceiling, Robinson could barely move.

The weather out of Chicago was bad; both the ceiling and visibility were poor. After takeoff from Harlem Airport, Robinson climbed through the clouds to blue skies. He leveled off at four thousand feet, one thousand feet above the massive layers of stratus clouds. Near Bloomington, Illinois, the weather worsened, quickly enveloping Robinson in the dark gray clouds. His overloaded airplane fought against a howling forty-mile headwind. Robinson hoped to fly around the bad weather or find an opening in the clouds, but this proved impossible and he continued to fly blindly. When he realized the weather was not improving, Robinson reversed course and headed north, spied a clearing, and dipped through an opening in the clouds. Robinson's plane spiraled down and landed in a cleared field. With the temperature barely above zero, Robinson was forced to sleep in his packed airplane. In the morning, he gathered wood and drained some gasoline to start a fire. Huddled next to the blaze, he attempted to warm his body.

The weather still had not cleared, but Robinson was determined to continue his flight to Memphis. At nine o'clock he lifted off the small field and headed south. Breaking through the clouds at six thousand feet, he found clear sky; things were looking better. Suddenly a sparkplug blew completely out of the cylinder. Exhaust gases and fuel steamed out of the hole in the engine; the pilot worried about fire. Taking a chance, Robinson pointed his airplane's nose down and sliced through the dense clouds. As he poked out of the cloudbank, an open coal mine loomed directly below him. Thirty feet deep, the mine was not an appealing landing site. Robinson steered toward an open space, glided over a small fence, and landed. Several farmers had heard his airplane and headed toward the field. He was lucky, they told him. Several months earlier, another pilot had tried to land at the same field and crashed.

The farmers took Robinson to a telephone to call Edward Anderson, a graduate of the Aeronautical University in Chicago and an old friend. While Anderson drove the twenty-five miles from Braidwood to the pasture, Robinson started working on the engine. Robinson and Anderson cut new threads in the sparkplug hole and used a plug from a Ford Model T. Robinson took off, but at an altitude of five hundred feet, the engine started to backfire and lost power. Robinson glided to the field he had left only minutes earlier, pulled the sparkplug wire, and buttoned up the engine cowling. Once again, he taxied down the field and took off. This time, he climbed to an altitude of nine hundred feet before the engine started to sputter and backfire. He circled around and landed again. The threads on the Ford sparkplug were too small to make a proper fit. They decided to jerry-rig an adapter to the size of an airplane sparkplug.

As it began to snow at near-blizzard force, the temperature plummeted to zero. The pair built a fire in a bucket in an attempt to keep warm, but were forced to stop working. For several days they worked on the cylinder and waited for a sparkplug that Robinson had ordered from Chicago. In a March 3 account in the newspaper for which he was reporting, Robinson recalled the delay, saying, "I was restless and angrily impatient to reach my destination. I had volunteered my services to the *Chicago Defender* in a great cause and I had no intentions of turning back." Robinson had even contemplated leaving without the sparkplug, but fortunately Mr. Sengstacke and Joe Abbott arrived with the needed part. The two men also drove some fifty miles to bring back additional fuel to augment Robinson's diminished supply.

On Friday morning, February 26, Robinson resumed his flight to Memphis. He took off from the farm field at 10:30 A.M. and flew for two hours. At 12:30 P.M., Robinson landed at Lambert Field, St. Louis. Minor engine adjustments were made and the airplane was refueled. Leaving St. Louis at 3:00 P.M., Robinson climbed to an altitude of six thousand feet and leveled out, picked up a headwind, and headed for Memphis. The "Brown Condor" landed at the Memphis Municipal Airport at 5:42 P.M., nine days after his departure from Chicago.

As Robinson taxied toward the hangar, a throng of white men and women broke through the guard ropes and rushed toward his airplane. Again on March 3, he recalled in the *Chicago Defender*, "I felt ill at ease at this sudden rush, not knowing what their intentions were, especially since the women seemed so interested." The crowd couldn't believe that a black man had piloted the airplane. Inundated with questions from the enthusiastic group, Robinson reported that the crowd had demonstrated no prejudice or ill will toward him. Moreover, airport officials treated him in the same manner that they would any pilot, regardless of race.

Robinson's words spoke to a time when all pilots—and all people—would be treated without regard for color, but it was a day to be well in the future. Pioneer African-American fliers were paving the way for black aviators in the U.S. military during World War II. In turn, the groundbreaking achievements, tenacity, and perseverance of the men and women of the Tuskegee Experience led to changes in the United States military and American society in general. Their accomplishments would help to smooth the path for future African-Americans in both military and civilian life, in Korea, Vietnam, America's space program, civil aviation, and society in general. As a result of their efforts, this world is a better place.

Appendix

Roster of Pilot Training Graduates at Tuskegee Army Air Field

Name	Class	Date of Graduation	Grade	Serial Number	City	State
Adams, John H., Jr.	45-B-SE	4/15/1945	2nd Lt.	O842588	Kansas City	KS
Adams, Paul	43-D-SE	4/29/1943	2nd Lt.	O801160	Greenville	SC
Adkins, Rutherford H.	44-I-1-SE	10/16/1944	2nd Lt.	O838152	Alexandria	VA
Adkins, Winston A.	44-B-TE	2/8/1944	2nd Lt.	O821901	Chicago	IL
Alexander, Halbert L.	44-I-SE	11/20/1944	2nd Lt.	O839082	Georgetown	IL
Alexander, Harvey R.	44-D-TE	4/15/1944	2nd Lt.	O828041	Georgetown	IL
Alexander, Robert R.	43-F-SE	6/30/1943	2nd Lt.	O805590	Harrisburg	PA
Alexander, Walter G.	45-D-SE	6/27/1945	2nd Lt.	O842999	Orange	NJ
Allen, Carl V.	46-C-SE	6/28/1946	2nd Lt.	O2102108	Bronx	NY

Allen, Clarence W.	43-C-SE	3/25/1943	2nd Lt.	O799891	Mobile	AL
Allen, Walter H.	44-J-TE	12/28/1944	Flt. Officer	T67978	Kansas City	KS
Allison, James M.	46-C-TE	6/28/1946	2nd Lt.	O210214	Chicago	IL
Alsbrook, William N.	43-I-SE	10/1/1943	2nd Lt.	O814188	Kansas City	KS
Alston, William R.	44-I-SE	11/20/1944	2nd Lt.	O839083	Huntington	WV
Anders, Emet R.	44-H-SE	9/8/1944	2nd Lt.	O838023	Carbondale	IL
Anderson, Paul T.	44-I-1-TE	10/16/1944	1st Lt.	O1294209	Woodbine	NY
Anderson, Rayfield A.	44-K-TE	2/1/1945	2nd Lt.	O841152	Indianapolis	IN
Anderson, Robert D.	44-D-TE	4/15/1944	2nd Lt.	O828034	Indianapolis	IN
Archer, Lee A., Jr.	43-G-SE	7/28/1943	2nd Lt.	O809235	New York	NY
Armistead, Richard S. A.	44-F-SE	6/27/1944	Flt. Officer	T64272	Philadelphia	PA
Armstrong, William P.	44-H-SE	9/8/1944	Flt. Officer	T66139	Providence	RI
Ashby, Robert	45-H-TE	11/20/1945	2nd Lt.	O843351	Jersey City	NJ
Ashley, Willie	42-F-SE	7/3/1942	2nd Lt.	O789641	Sumter	SC
Askins, Montro	44-K-SE	2/1/1945	2nd Lt.	O841156	Baltimore	MD
Audant, Ludovic F.	44-B-SE	2/8/1944			Port au Prince	Haiti
Bailey, Charles P.	43-D-SE	4/29/1943	2nd Lt.	O801161	Punta Gorda	FL
Bailey, Harry L.	43-G-SE	7/28/1943	2nd Lt.	O809437	Chicago	IL
Bailey, Terry C.	45-C-SE	5/23/1945	Flt. Officer	T69972	Richmond	VA
Bailey, William H.	45-E-SE	8/4/1945	2nd Lt.	O843702	Pittsburgh	PA
Baldwin, Henry Jr.	45-H-TE	11/20/1945	Flt. Officer	T70554	Philadelphia	PA
Ballard, Alton F.	43-H-SE	8/30/1943	2nd Lt.	O811773	Pasadena	CA
Barksdale, James M.	46-A-SE	3/23/1946	Flt. Officer	T149586	Detroit	MI

Name	Class	Date of Graduation	Grade	Serial Number	City	State
Barland, Herbert C.	44-H-SE	9/8/1944	2nd Lt.	O1168159	Chicago	IL
Barnes, Gentry E.	44-D-SE	4/15/1944	2nd Lt.	O828045	Lawrenceville	IL
Barnett, Herman A.	45-E-SE	8/4/1945	Flt. Officer	T70221	Lockhart	TX
Bartley, William R.	43-G-SE	7/28/1943	2nd Lt.	O809238	Jacksonville	FL
Bates, George A.	46-A-TE	3/23/1946	Flt. Officer	T149984	Chicago	IL
Baugh, Howard L.	42-J-SE	11/10/1942	2nd Lt.	O793705	Petersburg	VA
Bee, Clarence Jr.	45-B-SE	4/15/1945	2nd Lt.	O842579	Kansas City	MO
Bell, George E.	46-C-SE	6/28/1946	2nd Lt.	O2102113	Altoona	PA
Bell, John J.	44-I-SE	11/20/1944	Flt. Officer	T67141	Jersey City	NJ
Bell, Lloyd W.	44-K-SE	2/1/1945	2nd Lt.	O840735	Pulaski	IL
Bell, Richard H.	44-E-SE	5/23/1944	2nd Lt.	O830780	Chicago	IL
Bell, Rual W.	44-D-SE	4/15/1944	Flt. Officer	T62809	Portland	OR
Bennett, Joseph B.	45-I-SE	1/29/1946	2nd Lt.	O2102013	Halesite	NY
Bibb, William V.	45-H-TE	11/20/1945	2nd Lt.	O843352	Ottumwa	IA
Bickham, Luzine B.	45-A-SE	3/11/1945	Flt. Officer	T68752	Tuskegee Inst.	AL
Biffle, Richard L., Jr.	44-K-SE	2/1/1945	Flt. Officer	T68512	Denver	CO
Bilbo, Reuben B.	45-D-SE	6/27/1945	Flt. Officer	T70093	Fresno	CA
Bing, George L.	44-G-SE	8/4/1944	2nd Lt.	O835406	Brooklyn	NY
Black, Samuel A.	43-K-TE	12/5/1943	2nd Lt.	O817595	Plainfield	NJ
Blackwell, Hubron R.	43-H-SE	8/30/1943	2nd Lt.	O811193	Baltimore	MD

Blaylock, Joseph	45-D-SE	6/27/1945	2nd Lt.	O843000	Albany	GA
Blue, Elliott H.	44-A-TE	1/7/1944	2nd Lt.	O819746	Hampton	VA
Bohannon, Horace A.	44-J-SE	12/28/1944	Flt. Officer	T67963	Atlanta	GA
Bohler, Henry C. L.	44-J-SE	12/28/1944	Flt. Officer	T67964	Augusta	GA
Bolden, Edgar L.	43-K-SE	12/5/1943	2nd Lt.	O439271	Arlington	VA
Bolden, George C.	45-F-TE	9/8/1945	2nd Lt.	O2075526	Pittsburgh	PA
Bolling, George R.	42-F-SE	7/3/1942	2nd Lt.	O789367	Hampton	VA
Bonam, Leonelle A.	44-E-SE	5/23/1944	2nd Lt.	O830782	Pascagoula	MS
Bonseigneur, Paul J., Jr.	44-H-TE	9/8/1944	2nd Lt.	O838936	Chicago	IL
Bowman, James E.	44-K-SE	2/1/1945	Flt. Officer	T68699	Des Moines	IA
Bowman, Leroy	43-C-SE	3/25/1943	2nd Lt.	O798942	Sumter	SC
Bradford, Clarence H.	43-K-SE	12/5/1943	2nd Lt.	O817531	St. Louis	MO
Brantley, Charles V.	44-E-SE	5/23/1944	Flt. Officer	T63110	St. Louis	MO
Brashears, Virgil	44-D-TE	4/15/1944	2nd Lt.	O1313712	Kansas City	MO
Braswell, Thomas P.	44-B-SE	2/8/1944	2nd Lt.	O821907	Buford	GA
Bratcher, Everett A.	43-H-SE	8/30/1943	2nd Lt.	O811220	Poplar Bluff	MO
Brazil, Harold E.	43-K-TE	12/5/1943	2nd Lt.	O817596	Joplin	MO
Brewin, Irvin O.	44-I-SE	11/20/1944	2nd Lt.	O839084	Chicago	IL
Briggs, Eugene A.	46-A-SE	3/23/1946	Flt. Officer	T149957	Boston	MA
Briggs, John F.	43-E-SE	5/28/1943	2nd Lt.	O804556	St. Louis	MO
Bright, Alexander M.	43-F-SE	6/30/1943	2nd Lt.	O805626	Chicago	IL
Broadnax, Samuel L.	45-A-SE	3/11/1945	Flt. Officer	T68752	Oroville	CA
Broadwater, William E.	45-E-TE	8/4/1945	Flt. Officer	T70221	Bryn Mawr	PA

Name	Class	Date of Graduation	Grade	Serial Number	City	State
Brooks, Milton R.	43-E-SE	5/28/1943	2nd Lt.	O804547	Glassport	PA
Brooks, Sidney P.	42-D-SE	4/29/1942	2nd Lt.	O789118	Cleveland	OH
Brooks, Tilford U.	45-B-SE	4/15/1945	Flt. Officer	T69407	East St. Louis	IL
Brothers, James E.	43-D-SE	4/29/1943	2nd Lt.	O801162	Chicago	IL
Brothers, James E.	44-G-TE	8/4/1944	Flt. Officer	T64623	Philadelphia	PA
Browder, Cecil L.	43-I-SE	10/1/1943	2nd Lt.	O814189	Wilmington	NC
Brower, Fred L., Jr.	44-C-SE	3/12/1944	2nd Lt.	O824827	Charlotte	NC
Brown, Augustus G.	44-H-TE	9/8/1944	2nd Lt.	O1038394	Houma	LA
Brown, George A., Jr.	45-E-TE	8/4/1945	2nd Lt.	O843110	Baltimore	MD
Brown, Harold Haywood	44-E-SE	5/23/1944	2nd Lt.	O830783	Minneapolis	MN
Brown, Harold Howard	44-G-TE	8/4/1944	2nd Lt.	O835405	Weeletka	OK
Brown, James B.	43-J-SE	11/3/1943	2nd Lt.	O814825	Los Angeles	CA
Brown, James W.	44-I-1-TE	10/16/1944	2nd Lt.	O838166	Detroit	MI
Brown, Lawrence A.	44-K-SE	2/1/1945	Flt. Officer	T68700	Jamaica	NY
Brown, Reuben H., Jr.	45-F-SE	9/8/1945	2nd Lt.	O843235	Kansas City	MO
Brown, Robert S.	44-H-TE	9/8/1944	2nd Lt.	O1048706	Minneapolis	MN
Brown, Roger B.	43-J-SE	11/3/1943	2nd Lt.	O814826	Glencoe	IL
Brown, Roscoe C., Jr.	44-C-SE	3/12/1944	2nd Lt.	O824828	New York	NY
Brown, Walter R., Jr.	44-C-SE	3/12/1944	2nd Lt.	O824829	Hampton	VA
Browne, Gene C.	43-I-SE	10/1/1943	2nd Lt.	O814190	New York	NY

Name	Class	Date	Rank	Serial No.	City	State
Bruce, Reginald A.	44-G-SE	8/4/1944	Flt. Officer	T64624	Indianapolis	IN
Bruce, Samuel M.	42-H-SE	9/6/1942	2nd Lt.	O792417	Seattle	WA
Bryant, Grady E.	45-D-SE	6/27/1945	2nd Lt.	O843001	Los Angeles	CA
Bryant, Joseph C., Jr.	45-E-TE	8/4/1945	Flt. Officer	T70232	Dowagiac	MI
Bryant, Leroy Jr.	44-J-SE	12/28/1944	Flt. Officer	T67965	Houston	TX
Bryson, James O.	45-D-SE	6/27/1945	Flt. Officer	T70094	Columbus	GA
Burch, John A., III	45-A-SE	3/11/1945	2nd Lt.	O841235	Indianapolis	IN
Burns, Charles A.	46-B-TE	5/14/1946	Unknown	Unknown	Unknown	
Burns, Isham A., Jr.	44-J-SE	12/28/1944	2nd Lt.	O840202	Los Angeles	CA
Bussey, Charles M.	43-E-SE	5/28/1943	2nd Lt.	O804548	Los Angeles	CA
Butler, Jewel B.	46-A-SE	3/23/1946	2nd Lt.	O2078770	Denison	TX
Bynum, Rolin A.	44-A-TE	1/7/1944	2nd Lt.	O819447	Montclair	NJ
Byrd, Willie L., Jr.	43-K-TE	12/5/1943	2nd Lt.	O817597	Fayetteville	NC
Cabiness, Marshall S.	42-I-SE	10/9/1942	2nd Lt.	O792753	Gastonia	NC
Cabule, Ernest M., Jr.	45-A-SE	3/11/1945	2nd Lt.	O841255	Detroit	MI
Caesar, Richard C.	42-H-SE	9/6/1942	2nd Lt.	O792413	Lake Village	AR
Cain, William L.	44-I-1-TE	10/16/1944	Flt. Officer	T66404	London	OH
Calhoun, James A.	44-C-SE	3/12/1944	2nd Lt.	O824830	Bridgeport	CT
Calloway, Julius W.	44-I-SE	11/20/1944	Flt. Officer	T67143	Louisville	KY
Campbell, Herman R., Jr.	43-J-SE	11/3/1943	2nd Lt.	O814041	New York	NY
Campbell, Lindsay L.	44-J-SE	12/28/1944	Flt. Officer	T67966	Washington	DC
Campbell, McWheeler	44-J-SE	12/28/1944	2nd Lt.	O840203	Cambria	VA
Campbell, Vincent O.	45-A-SE	3/11/1945	2nd Lt.	O577235	Corona	NY

Name	Class	Date of Graduation	Grade	Serial Number	City	State
Campbell, William A.	42-F-SE	7/3/1942	2nd Lt.	O790453	Tuskegee	AL
Carey, Carl E.	44-H-SE	9/8/1944	2nd Lt.	O838025	St. Louis	MO
Carpenter, Russell W.	44-I-SE	11/20/1944	2nd Lt.	O839085	Plainfield	NJ
Carroll, Alfred Q., Jr.	43-J-SE	11/3/1943	2nd Lt.	O814827	Washington	DC
Carroll, Lawrence W.	45-H-TE	11/20/1945	2nd Lt.	O843353	Chicago	IL
Carter, Clarence J.	45-D-SE	6/27/1945	Flt. Officer	T70095	Chicago	IL
Carter, Floyd J.	46-A-TE	3/23/1946	Flt. Officer	T146021	Norfolk	VA
Carter, Herbert E.	42-F-SE	7/3/1942	2nd Lt.	O790454	Amory	MS
Carter, James Y.	43-D-SE	4/29/1943	2nd Lt.	O801163	Winston-Salem	NC
Carter, Lloyd A.N.	44-K-SE	2/1/1945	2nd Lt.	O841157	York	PA
Carter, William G.	46-C-SE	6/28/1946	2nd Lt.	O2102109	Pittsburgh	PA
Casey, Clifton G.	45-B-SE	4/15/1945	Flt. Officer	T69738	Birmingham	AL
Cassagnol, Raymond	43-G-SE	7/28/1943			Unknown	Haiti
Chambers, Charles W.	46-A-SE	3/23/1946	2nd Lt.	O2102097	Camden	NJ
Chandler, Robert C.	44-B-SE	2/8/1944	2nd Lt.	O821908	Allegan	MI
Charlton, Terry J.	42-J-SE	11/10/1942	2nd Lt.	O793706	Beaumont	TX
Chavis, John H.	44-D-SE	4/15/1944	2nd Lt.	O828047	Raleigh	NC
Cheatham, Eugene C.	43-K-TE	12/5/1943	2nd Lt.	O817598	Philadelphia	PA
Cheek, Conrad H.	46-C-SE	6/28/1946	2nd Lt.	O2102110	Weldon	NC
Cheek, Quinten V.	45-F-TE	9/8/1945	2nd Lt.	O2075530	Weldon	NC

Name	Class	Date	Rank	Serial	City	State
Chichester, James R.	44-I-1-TE	10/16/1944	2nd Lt.	O131?7?0	Santa Monica	CA
Chin, Jack	46-C-SE	6/28/1946	2nd Lt.	O2102111	Chicago	IL
Chineworth, Joseph E.	44-E-SE	5/23/1944	Flt. Officer	T63111	Memphis	TN
Choisy, George B.	45-E-TE	8/4/1945	2nd Lt.	O2075531	Jamaica	NY
Cisco, Arnold W.	43-D-SE	4/29/1943	2nd Lt.	O801?64	Alton	IL
Cisco, George E.	44-E-SE	5/23/1944	2nd Lt.	O1014831	Alton	IL
Clark, Herbert V.	42-F-SE	7/3/1942	2nd Lt.	O790455	Pine Bluff	AR
Clayton, Melvin A.	45-A-TE	3/11/1945	2nd Lt.	O841263	Salem	NJ
Claytor, Ralph V.	45-C-SE	5/23/1945	2nd Lt.	O842379	Roanoke	VA
Cleaver, Lowell H.	44-K-SE	2/1/1945	2nd Lt.	O841153	Prairie View	TX
Clifton, Emile G., Jr.	44-B-SE	2/8/1944	2nd Lt.	O821309	San Francisco	CA
Cobbs, Wilson N.	45-D-SE	6/27/1945	2nd Lt.	O843002	Gordonsville	VA
Coggs, Granville C.	45-G-TE	10/16/1945	2nd Lt.	O2082572	Little Rock	AR
Colbert, William A., Jr.	44-K-SE	2/1/1945	Flt. Officer	T687??	Cumberland	MD
Cole, Robert A.	44-J-SE	12/28/1944	Flt. Officer	T67957	Northfield	VT
Coleman, James	44-H-SE	9/8/1944	2nd Lt.	O838056	Detroit	MI
Coleman, William C., Jr.	44-D-TE	4/15/1944	2nd Lt.	O828056	Detroit	MI
Coleman, William J.	45-A-SE	3/11/1945	2nd Lt.	O84?257	Columbus	GA
Collins, Gamaliel M.	44-I-1-TE	10/16/1944	Flt. Officer	T66405	Los Angeles	CA
Collins, Russell L.	45-E-SE	8/4/1945	Flt. Officer	T70522	Davenport	IA
Connell, Victor L.	45-D-SE	6/27/1945	2nd Lt.	O843003	Nutley	NJ
Cook, Martin L.	44-D-TE	4/15/1944	Flt. Officer	T62816	Purcellville	VA
Cooper, Charles W.	44-H-SE	9/8/1944	Flt. Officer	T66?40	Washington	DC

Name	Class	Date of Graduation	Grade	Serial Number	City	State
Cooper, Edward M.	45-F-TE	9/8/1945	2nd Lt.	O2080879	Sharon	LA
Corbin, Matthew J.	45-D-SE	6/27/1945	Flt. Officer	T70027	Pittsburgh	PA
Cousins, Augustus	44-D-TE	4/15/1944	2nd Lt.	O1307085	Toledo	OH
Cousins, William M.	44-H-SE	9/8/1944	2nd Lt.	O838027	Philadelphia	PA
Cowan, Edwin T.	44-J-TE	12/28/1944	Flt. Officer	T67986	Cleveland	OH
Cox, Hannibal M., Jr.	44-D-SE	4/15/1944	2nd Lt.	O828048	Chicago	IL
Craig, Charles E.	44-K-SE	2/1/1945	Flt. Officer	T68702	Detroit	MI
Craig, Lewis W.	44-D-SE	4/15/1944	2nd Lt.	O828049	Ashville	NC
Criss, Leroy	45-B-TE	4/15/1945	Flt. Officer	T69752	Los Angeles	CA
Crockett, Woodrow W.	43-C-SE	3/25/1943	2nd Lt.	O798943	Little Rock	AR
Cross, William Jr.	43-I-SE	10/1/1943	Flt. Officer	T61446	Cleveland	OH
Crumbsy, Grover	44-K-TE	2/1/1945	Flt. Officer	T68711	Pensacola	FL
Cummings, Herndon M.	45-A-TE	3/11/1945	2nd Lt.	O841277	Montrose	GA
Curry, John C.	45-E-TE	8/4/1945	2nd Lt.	O843111	Indianapolis	IN
Curry, Walter P.	45-F-SE	9/8/1945	Flt. Officer	T70420	Washington	DC
Curtis, John W.	45-B-SE	4/15/1945	2nd Lt.	O842581	Detroit	MI
Curtis, Samuel L.	43-G-SE	7/28/1943	2nd Lt.	O809239	Yeadon	PA
Curtis, William J., Jr.	45-A-TE	3/11/1945	Flt. Officer	T68763	Pittsburgh	PA
Custis, Lemuel R.	42-C-SE	3/6/1942	2nd Lt.	O441128	Hartford	CT
Dabney, Roscoe J., Jr.	45-F-TE	9/8/1945	2nd Lt.	O843244	Lakewood	NJ

Name	Class	Date	Rank	Serial	City	State
Daniels, Harry J.	43-H-SE	8/30/1943	2nd Lt.	O811240	Indianapolis	IN
Daniels, John	43-G-SE	7/28/1943	2nd Lt.	O1106669	Chicago	IL
Daniels, Robert H., Jr.	43-K-SE	12/5/1943	2nd Lt.	O817582	Corona	NY
Daniels, Thomas J., III	44-I-1-SE	10/16/1944	Flt. Officer	T66359	Wetumpka	AL
Daniels, Virgil A.	44-A-TE	1/7/1944	Flt. Officer	T61867	Jacksonville	FL
Darnell, Charles E.	44-C-TE	3/12/1944	2nd Lt.	O824324	Dayton	OH
Dart, Clarence W.	43-J-SE	11/3/1943	2nd Lt.	O814326	Elmira	NY
Davenport, Harry J., Jr.	44-E-SE	5/23/1944	2nd Lt.	O830784	Beaumont	TX
Davis, Alfonza W.	43-C-SE	3/25/1943	2nd Lt.	O798344	Omaha	NE
Davis, Benjamin O., Jr.	42-C-SE	3/6/1942	Capt.	O20146	Tuskegee	AL
Davis, Claude C.	44-G-TE	8/4/1944	1st Lt.	O441115	Pittsburgh	PA
Davis, Clifford W.	45-F-TE	9/8/1945	Flt. Officer	T70427	Chicago	IL
Davis, Donald F.	45-F-SE	9/8/1945	Flt. Officer	T140090	Detroit	MI
Davis, John W.	44-E-SE	5/23/1944	2nd Lt.	O830755	Kansas City	KS
Davis, Richard	42-G-SE	8/5/1942	2nd Lt.	O790935	Ft. Valley	GA
Davis, Sylvester S.	45-F-SE	9/8/1945	2nd Lt.	O2080383	Cleveland	OH
Dean, Vincent C.	44-C-SE	3/12/1944	2nd Lt.	O824831	Corona	NY
DeBow, Charles H.	42-C-SE	3/6/1942	2nd Lt.	O441130	Indianapolis	IN
Deiz, Robert W.	42-H-SE	9/6/1942	2nd Lt.	O792419	Portland	OR
Derricotte, Eugene A.	46-B-TE	5/14/1946	Unknown	Unknown	Detroit	MI
Desvignes, Russell F.	45-B-TE	4/15/1945	Flt. Officer	T69753	New Orleans	LA
Dickerson, Charles W.	43-J-SE	11/3/1943	2nd Lt.	O814829	New Rochelle	NY
Dickerson, Page L.	45-G-SE	10/16/1945	Flt. Officer	T70546	St. Louis	MO

Name	Class	Date of Graduation	Grade	Serial Number	City	State
Dickerson, Tamenund J.	44-I-SE	11/20/1944	Flt. Officer	T67144	Detroit	MI
Dickson, DeWitt	44-J-SE	12/28/1944	Flt. Officer	T67968	New York	NY
Dickson, Lawrence E.	43-C-SE	3/25/1943	2nd Lt.	O798945	Bronx	NY
Dickson, Othel	43-K-SE	12/5/1943	2nd Lt.	O817583	San Francisco	CA
Diggs, Charles W.	44-B-TE	2/8/1944	2nd Lt.	O821902	Roxbury	MA
Dillard, James M., Jr.	45-I-TE	1/29/1946	2nd Lt.	O2102016	East Beckley	WV
Dillon, Oliver M.	45-I-TE	1/29/1946	2nd Lt.	O2102017	McComb	MS
Dixon, Edward T.	44-G-SE	8/4/1944	2nd Lt.	O835403	Hartford	CT
Doram, Edward D.	44-I-1-SE	10/16/1944	2nd Lt.	O838164	Cincinnati	OH
Dorkins, Charles J.	45-A-TE	3/11/1945	2nd Lt.	O841269	Baltimore	MD
Doswell, Andrew H.	43-H-SE	8/30/1943	2nd Lt.	O811246	Cleveland	OH
Doswell, Edgar A., Jr.	45-A-SE	3/11/1945	Flt. Officer	T68754	Lynchburg	VA
Dowling, Cornelius D.	44-I-1-SE	10/16/1944	2nd Lt.	O1292319	New Rochelle	NY
Downs, Walter M.	43-B-SE	2/16/1943	2nd Lt.	O797218	New Orleans	LA
Driver, Clarence N.	44-A-SE	1/7/1944	Flt. Officer	T61895	Los Angeles	CA
Driver, Elwood T.	42-I-SE	10/9/1942	2nd Lt.	O792781	Trenton	NJ
Drummond, Charles H.	44-I-1-TE	10/16/1944	2nd Lt.	O1289402	Roxbury	MA
Drummond, Edward P.	46-C-SE	6/28/1946	2nd Lt.	O2102112	Philadelphia	PA
Dryden, Charles W.	42-D-SE	4/29/1942	2nd Lt.	O789119	Bronx	NY
Dudley, Richard G.	45-B-SE	4/15/1945	2nd Lt.	O842582	Norristown	PA

Name	Class	Date	Rank	Serial No.	City	State
Duke, Charles H.	44-A-SE	1/7/1944	2nd Lt.	O819455	Portland	OR
Duncan, Roger B.	45-E-SE	8/4/1945	2nd Lt.	O843104	St. Louis	MO
Dunlap, Alwayne M.	43-C-SE	3/25/1943	2nd Lt.	O798046	Washington	DC
Dunne, Charles A.	43-H-SE	8/30/1943	2nd Lt.	O811277	Atlantic City	NJ
Eagleson, Wilson V.	43-D-SE	4/29/1943	2nd Lt.	O801165	Bloomington	IL
Echols, Julius P.	45-G-TE	10/16/1945	Flt. Officer	T70553	Chicago	IL
Edwards, James E., Jr.	44-J-TE	12/28/1944	Flt. Officer	T67979	Wenatchee	WA
Edwards, Jerome T.	42-J-SE	11/10/1942	2nd Lt.	O793707	Steubenville	OH
Edwards, John E.	44-G-SE	8/4/1944	2nd Lt.	O835407	Steubenville	OH
Edwards, William H.	44-G-SE	8/4/1944	Flt. Officer	T64653	Birmingham	AL
Elfalan, Jose R.	45-H-TE	11/20/1945	2nd Lt.	O843354	Prospect	KY
Ellington, Spurgeon N.	43-E-SE	5/28/1943	2nd Lt.	O804549	Winston-Salem	NC
Ellis, Carl F.	44-F-SE	6/27/1944	2nd Lt.	O835324	Chicago	IL
Ellis, Everett M.	45-I-TE	1/29/1946	2nd Lt.	O210201	Baltimore	MD
Ellis, William B.	43-G-SE	7/28/1943	2nd Lt.	O1637362	Washington	DC
Elsberry, Joseph D.	42-H-SE	9/6/1942	2nd Lt.	O792420	Langston	OK
Esters, Maurice V.	43-E-SE	5/28/1943	2nd Lt.	O804550	Webster City	IA
Ewing, James	44-F-TE	6/27/1944	Flt. Officer	T64271	Helena	AR
Exum, Herven P.	44-I-1-TE	10/16/1944	Flt. Officer	T66409	Wilson	NJ
Farley, William H.	44-B-TE	2/8/1944	2nd Lt.	O821903	Savannah	GA
Faulkner, William J.	43-D-SE	4/29/1943	2nd Lt.	O801166	Nashville	TN
Fears, Henry T.	44-I-TE	11/20/1944	Flt. Officer	T67153	Muncie	IN
Finley, Clarence C.	45-A-SE	3/11/1945	2nd Lt.	O847266	Chicago	IL

Name	Class	Date of Graduation	Grade	Serial Number	City	State
Finley, Otis	45-F-TE	9/8/1945	2nd Lt.	O843245	St. Louis	MO
Fischer, James H.	44-G-SE	8/4/1944	Flt. Officer	T64634	Stoughton	MA
Flake, Thomas M.	44-J-TE	12/28/1944	Flt. Officer	T67980	Detroit	MI
Fleming, Rutledge H., Jr.	45-A-TE	3/11/1945	Flt. Officer	T68761	Nashville	TN
Fletcher, Henry F.	43-J-SE	11/3/1943	2nd Lt.	O814140	San Antonio	TX
Ford, Harry E., Jr.	45-E-TE	8/4/1945	Flt. Officer	T70233	Detroit	MI
Foreman, Samuel J.	44-E-SE	5/23/1944	Flt. Officer	T63112	Tulsa	OK
Foreman, Walter T.	43-D-SE	4/29/1943	2nd Lt.	O801167	Washington	DC
Francis, William V.	45-D-SE	6/27/1945	Flt. Officer	T70098	Philadelphia	PA
Franklin, Earl N.	45-C-SE	5/23/1945	2nd Lt.	O842880	Joliet	IL
Franklin, George E.	44-H-SE	9/8/1944	2nd Lt.	O838028	Joliet	IL
Freeman, Eldridge E.	45-B-TE	4/15/1945	Flt. Officer	T69754	Chicago	IL
Friend, Robert J.	43-K-SE	12/5/1943	2nd Lt.	O817584	New York	NY
Fulbright, Stewart B., Jr.	43-K-TE	12/5/1943	2nd Lt.	O817599	Springfield	MO
Fuller, William A., Jr.	45-E-SE	8/4/1945	Flt. Officer	T70223	Detroit	MI
Fuller, Willie H.	42-G-SE	8/5/1942	2nd Lt.	O790934	Tarboro	NC
Funderburg, Frederick D.	43-K-SE	12/5/1943	2nd Lt.	O817585	Monticello	GA
Gaines, Thurston L., Jr.	44-G-SE	8/4/1944	Flt. Officer	T64635	Freeport	NY
Gaiter, Roger Bertram	44-B-SE	2/8/1944	2nd Lt.	O821910	Seaside Hgts.	NJ
Gallwey, James H.	46-A-SE	3/23/1946	2nd Lt.	O2078775	Oswego	NY

Name	Class	Date	Rank	Serial	City	State
Gamble, Howard C.	43-K-SE	12/5/1943	2nd Lt.	O817585	Charleston	WV
Gant, Morris E.	44-H-SE	9/8/1944	Flt. Officer	T66141	Chicago	IL
Garrett, Alfred E., Jr.	45-G-SE	10/16/1945	Flt. Officer	T70547	Fort Worth	TX
Garrison, Robert E., Jr.	44-G-SE	8/4/1944	2nd Lt.	O835408	Columbus	OH
Gash, Joseph E.	45-A-SE	3/11/1945	2nd Lt.	O841258	Denver	CO
Gaskins, Aaron C.	45-E-SE	8/4/1945	2nd Lt.	O843105	Hartford	CT
Gay, Thomas L.	44-B-SE	2/8/1944	2nd Lt.	O821911	Detroit	MI
Gibson, John A.	42-I-SE	10/9/1942	2nd Lt.	O792782	Chicago	IL
Giles, Ivie V.	45-D-SE	6/27/1945	Flt. Officer	T70090	Kansas City	KS
Gilliam, William L.	45-B-SE	4/15/1945	Flt. Officer	T69740	New York	NY
Givings, Clemenceau M.	43-E-SE	5/28/1943	2nd Lt.	O804551	Richmond	VA
Gladden, Thomas	44-I-SE	11/20/1944	2nd Lt.	O839086	Washington	DC
Glass, Robert M.	44-I-I-SE	10/16/1944	Flt. Officer	T66405	Pittsburgh	PA
Gleed, Edward C.	42-K-SE	12/13/1942	2nd Lt.	O794528	Lawrence	KS
Glenn, Joshua	44-K-SE	2/1/1945	Flt. Officer	T68705	Newark	NJ
Goins, Nathaniel W.	45-H-TE	11/20/1945	1st Lt.	O582738	St. Paul	MN
Golden, Newman C.	44-G-SE	8/4/1944	Flt. Officer	T64635	Cincinnati	OH
Goldsby, Charles S.	45-A-TE	3/11/1945	Flt. Officer	T68764	Detroit	MI
Gomer, Joseph P.	43-E-SE	5/28/1943	2nd Lt.	O804552	Iowa Falls	IA
Goodall, Ollie O., Jr.	44-K-TE	2/1/1945	Flt. Officer	T68715	Detroit	MI
Goodenough, Purnell J.	43-I-SE	10/1/1943	2nd Lt.	O814191	Birmingham	AL
Goodwin, Luther A.	44-H-TE	9/8/1944	1st Lt.	O1581140	Bakersfield	CA
Gordon, Elmer	43-C-SE	3/25/1943	2nd Lt.	O798047	Portsmouth	VA

Name	Class	Date of Graduation	Grade	Serial Number	City	State
Gordon, Joseph E.	44-B-SE	2/8/1944	2nd Lt.	O821912	Brooklyn	NY
Gordon, William M.	43-C-SE	3/25/1943	2nd Lt.	O798948	Mobile	AL
Gorham, Alfred M.	44-B-SE	2/8/1944	2nd Lt.	O821913	Waukesha	WI
Gould, Cornelius P., Jr.	44-B-SE	2/8/1944	Flt. Officer	T62306	Pittsburgh	PA
Govan, Claude B.	43-B-SE	2/16/1943	2nd Lt.	O797219	Newark	NJ
Gray, Elliott H.	45-F-SE	9/8/1945	2nd Lt.	O843236	Tuskegee Inst.	AL
Gray, George E.	43-E-SE	5/28/1943	2nd Lt.	O804553	Hemphill	WV
Gray, Leo R.	44-G-SE	8/4/1944	2nd Lt.	O835409	Roxbury	MA
Green, James L.	44-I-1-TE	10/16/1944	Flt. Officer	T66405	Philadelphia	PA
Green, Paul L.	44-G-SE	8/4/1944	2nd Lt.	O835417	Xenia	OH
Green, Smith W.	43-H-SE	8/30/1943	2nd Lt.	O811280	Los Angeles	CA
Green, William W.	43-G-SE	7/28/1943	2nd Lt.	O809240	Staunton	VA
Greenlee, George B., Jr.	43-G-SE	7/28/1943	2nd Lt.	O809241	Pittsburgh	PA
Greenwell, Jacob W.	46-A-SE	3/23/1946	2nd Lt.	O2090283	Fort Worth	TX
Greer, James W.	44-J-SE	12/28/1944	Flt. Officer	T67969	Detroit	MI
Griffin, Frank	45-I-SE	1/29/1946	Flt. Officer	T149962	Asbury Park	NJ
Griffin, Jerrold D.	45-E-TE	8/4/1945	2nd Lt.	O843112	Philadelphia	PA
Griffin, William E.	43-B-SE	2/16/1943	2nd Lt.	O797220	Birmingham	AL
Groves, Weldon K.	43-F-SE	6/30/1943	2nd Lt.	O805985	Edwardsville	KS
Guilbaud, Eberle J.	44-D-TE	4/15/1944			Port au Prince	Haiti

Name	Class	Date	Rank	Serial	City	State
Guyton, Eugene L.	44-J-SE	12/28/1944	Flt. Officer	T67970	Cleveland	OH
Haley, George J.	43-I-SE	10/1/1943	2nd Lt.	O814192	Bath	NY
Hall, Charles B.	42-F-SE	7/3/1942	2nd Lt.	O790457	Brazil	IN
Hall, James L., Jr.	44-C-SE	3/12/1944	2nd Lt.	O824848	Washington	DC
Hall, Leonard C., Jr.	45-D-SE	6/27/1945	2nd Lt.	O843004	Philadelphia	PA
Hall, Milton T.	42-K-SE	12/13/1942	2nd Lt.	O794599	Owensboro	KY
Hall, Richard W.	43-G-SE	7/28/1943	2nd Lt.	O809242	Albany	GA
Hamilton, John L.	43-E-SE	5/28/1943	2nd Lt.	O1576078	Greenwood	MS
Hancock, Victor L.	45-F-TE	9/8/1945	Flt. Officer	T70428	St. Louis	MO
Harden, Argonne F.	45-A-TE	3/11/1945	2nd Lt.	O841270	Philadelphia	PA
Harder, Richard S.	44-B-SE	2/8/1944	2nd Lt.	O821914	Brooklyn	NY
Hardy, Bennett G.	45-F-SE	9/8/1945	2nd Lt.	O2080900	Kokomo	IN
Hardy, Ferdinand A.	46-B-TE	5/14/1946	Unknown	Unknown	Unknown	
Hardy, George E.	44-H-SE	9/8/1944	2nd Lt.	O838029	Philadelphia	PA
Harmon, Arthur C.	45-G-TE	10/16/1945	2nd Lt.	O2082535	Los Angeles	CA
Harper, Samuel W.	44-A-TE	1/7/1944	2nd Lt.	O819448	Oliver Springs	TN
Harris, Alfonso L.	45-G-SE	10/16/1945	Flt. Officer	T70545	Dallas	TX
Harris, Archie H., Jr.	44-K-TE	2/1/1945	2nd Lt.	O841163	Ocean City	NJ
Harris, Bernard	44-I-TE	11/20/1944	2nd Lt.	O839095	Detroit	MI
Harris, Cassius A.	42-G-SE	8/5/1942	2nd Lt.	O790936	Philadelphia	PA
Harris, Edward	44-G-SE	8/4/1944	Flt. Officer	T64625	Pittsburgh	PA
Harris, Herbert S.	43-F-SE	6/30/1943	2nd Lt.	O806279	Philadelphia	PA
Harris, James E.	44-J-SE	12/28/1944	2nd Lt.	O840204	Xenia	OH

Name	Class	Date of Graduation	Grade	Serial Number	City	State
Harris, John S.	45-E-TE	8/4/1945	2nd Lt.	O843113	Richmond	KY
Harris, Louis K.	44-E-SE	5/23/1944	2nd Lt.	O830786	St. Louis	MO
Harris, Maceo A., Jr.	43-I-SE	10/1/1943	2nd Lt.	O814193	Boston	MA
Harris, Richard H.	43-F-SE	6/30/1943	2nd Lt.	O807096	Montgomery	AL
Harris, Stanley L.	43-K-SE	12/5/1943	2nd Lt.	O817587	St. Paul	MN
Harris, Thomas D., Jr.	45-F-SE	9/8/1945	2nd Lt.	O843233	Brooklyn	NY
Harrison, Alvin E., Jr.	45-H-TE	11/20/1945	Flt. Officer	T70447	Chicago	IL
Harrison, James E.	45-D-SE	6/27/1945	2nd Lt.	O843005	Texarkana	TX
Harrison, John L., Jr.	43-K-TE	12/5/1943	2nd Lt.	O817600	Omaha	NE
Harrison, Lonnie	45-G-TE	10/16/1945	Flt. Officer	T70543	Huston	LA
Harvey, James H., Jr.	44-I-1-SE	10/16/1944	2nd Lt.	O838153	Mountain Top	PA
Hathcock, Lloyd S.	43-K-SE	12/5/1943	2nd Lt.	O817588	Dayton	OH
Hawkins, Donald A.	44-I-TE	11/20/1944	Flt. Officer	T67154	San Bernardino	CA
Hawkins, Kenneth R.	44-A-TE	1/7/1944	2nd Lt.	O819449	San Bernardino	CA
Hawkins, Thomas L.	44-E-SE	5/23/1944	Flt. Officer	T63113	Glen Rock	NJ
Hayes, Lee A.	45-I-TE	1/29/1946	Flt. Officer	T144946	East Hampton	NY
Hayes, Reginald W.	44-C-TE	3/12/1944	2nd Lt.	O824825	Holicong	PA
Hays, George K.	44-E-SE	5/23/1944	2nd Lt.	O830787	Los Angeles	CA
Hays, Milton S.	44-D-SE	4/15/1944	2nd Lt.	O828050	Los Angeles	CA
Haywood, Vernon V.	43-D-SE	4/29/1943	2nd Lt.	O801168	Raleigh	NC

Name	Class	Date	Serial No.	Rank	City	State
Heath, Percy L., Jr.	44-K-SE	2/1/1945	O841137	2nd Lt.	Philadelphia	PA
Helm, George W.	45-C-SE	5/23/1945	O842881	2nd Lt.	Reidsville	NC
Henderson, Eugene R.	44-I-TE	11/20/1944	O839098	2nd Lt.	Jacksonville	FL
Henry, Milton R.	43-F-SE	6/30/1943	O1636030	2nd Lt.	Philadelphia	PA
Henry, Warren E.	44-H-TE	9/8/1944	O838037	2nd Lt.	Plainfield	NJ
Henry, William T.	44-K-SE	2/1/1945	T6870	Flt. Officer	New York	NY
Henson, James W.	45-B-SE	4/15/1945	O842523	2nd Lt.	Baltimore	MD
Herrington, Aaron	44-E-SE	5/23/1944	O830733	2nd Lt.	Raleigh	NC
Herron, Walter	44-J-TE	12/28/1944	O1311535	1st Lt.	Memphis	TN
Hervey, Henry P., Jr.	43-K-TE	12/5/1943	O817601	2nd Lt.	Chicago	IL
Heywood, Herbert H.	44-C-SE	3/12/1944	O824833	2nd Lt.	St. Croix	VI
Hicks, Arthur N.	45-C-SE	5/23/1945	O842882	2nd Lt.	Dayton	OH
Hicks, Frederick P.	44-B-TE	2/8/1944	O103C252	2nd Lt.	San Francisco	CA
Higginbotham, Mitchell	44-K-TE	2/1/1945	O841164	2nd Lt.	Sewickley	PA
Highbaugh, Earl B.	44-E-SE	5/23/1944	O830799	2nd Lt.	Indianapolis	IN
Highbaugh, Richard B.	43-K-TE	12/5/1943	O817605	2nd Lt.	Indianapolis	IN
Hill, Charles A., Jr.	44-F-SE	6/27/1944	O835525	2nd Lt.	Detroit	MI
Hill, Charles D.	44-B-TE	2/8/1944	O443955	2nd Lt.	Washington	DC
Hill, Louis G., Jr.	44-B-TE	2/8/1944	O1573279	1st Lt.	Indianapolis	IN
Hill, Nathaniel M.	42-I-SE	10/9/1942	O792783	2nd Lt.	Washington	DC
Hill, William E.	43-H-SE	8/30/1943	O811281	2nd Lt.	Narragansett	RI
Hill, William L.	43-K-SE	12/5/1943	T61773	Flt. Officer	Huntington	WV
Hillary, Harold A.	43-K-TE	12/5/1943	O817502	2nd Lt.	New York	NY

Name	Class	Date of Graduation	Grade	Serial Number	City	State
Hockaday, Wendell W.	44-E-SE	5/23/1944	2nd Lt.	O830781	Norfolk	VA
Hodges, Jerry T., Jr.	45-F-TE	9/8/1945	2nd Lt.	O843246	Heth	AR
Holbert, Bertrand J.	45-A-SE	3/11/1945	2nd Lt.	O841259	Dallas	TX
Holland, Henry T.	45-E-SE	8/4/1945	2nd Lt.	O2075546	Baltimore	MD
Holloman, William H., III	44-H-SE	9/8/1944	2nd Lt.	O838030	St. Louis	MO
Holloway, Lorenzo W.	45-G-SE	10/16/1945	2nd Lt.	O2082600	Detroit	MI
Holman, William D.	45-C-SE	5/23/1945	Flt. Officer	T69973	Suffolk	VA
Holsclaw, Jack D.	43-G-SE	7/28/1943	2nd Lt.	O809243	Spokane	WA
Hopson, Vernon	44-I-SE	11/20/1944	Flt. Officer	T67146	San Antonio	TX
Houston, Heber C.	43-D-SE	4/29/1943	2nd Lt.	O801170	Detroit	MI
Hubbard, Lyman L.	45-H-TE	11/20/1945	Flt. Officer	T70485	Springfield	IL
Hudson, Elbert	44-C-SE	3/12/1944	2nd Lt.	O824834	Los Angeles	CA
Hudson, Lincoln T.	44-F-SE	6/27/1944	2nd Lt.	O835326	Chicago	IL
Hudson, Perry E., Jr.	43-J-SE	11/3/1943	2nd Lt.	O814818	Atlanta	GA
Hughes, Andrew James	46-B-TE	5/14/1946	Unknown	Unknown	Unknown	
Hughes, Samuel R., Jr.	45-B-SE	4/15/1945	Flt. Officer	T69741	Los Angeles	CA
Hunter, Charles H.	44-A-TE	1/7/1944	2nd Lt.	O367472	Washington	DC
Hunter, Henry A.	44-I-1-SE	10/16/1944	2nd Lt.	O1314639	Williamsport	PA
Hunter, Marcellus L.	45-G-TE	10/16/1945	2nd Lt.	O843343	Washington	DC
Hunter, Samuel	44-J-TE	12/28/1944	2nd Lt.	O840206	Colorado Spgs.	CO

Name	Class	Date	Rank	Serial No.	City	State
Hunter, Willie S.	43-F-SE	6/30/1943	2nd Lt.	O807097	Albany	GA
Hurd, James A.	44-H-TE	9/8/1944	1st Lt.	O1030158	Leavenworth	KS
Hurd, Sylvester H., Jr.	45-H-SE	11/20/1945	Flt. Officer	T70545	Chicago	IL
Hurt, Wesley, D.	45-E-SE	8/4/1945	2nd Lt.	O843109	Philadelphia	PA
Hutchins, Freddie E.	43-D-SE	4/29/1943	2nd Lt.	O801171	Donaldsonville	GA
Hutton, Oscar D.	43-J-SE	11/3/1943	2nd Lt.	O814830	Chicago	IL
Hymes, William H.	44-K-SE	2/1/1945	2nd Lt.	O841160	Lincoln Univ.	PA
Iles, George J.	44-E-SE	5/23/1944	2nd Lt.	O830720	Quincy	IL
Irving, Wellington	43-K-SE	12/5/1943	2nd Lt.	O817559	Belzoni	MS
Jackson, Charles L.	44-D-SE	4/15/1944	Flt. Officer	T62810	Circleville	OH
Jackson, Charles S. Jr.	44-A-SE	1/7/1944	2nd Lt.	O819450	Chicago	IL
Jackson, Donald E.	45-H-TE	11/20/1945	Flt. Officer	T70482	Kansas City	KS
Jackson, Frank A., Jr.	44-I-1-SE	10/16/1944	Flt. Officer	T66407	Youngstown	OH
Jackson, Julien D., Jr.	45-G-SE	10/16/1945	Flt. Officer	T70543	Norfolk	VA
Jackson, Leonard M.	43-D-SE	4/29/1943	2nd Lt.	O801172	Fort Worth	TX
Jackson, Melvin T.	42-J-SE	11/10/1942	2nd Lt.	O793708	Warrenton	VA
Jackson, William T.	44-F-TE	6/27/1944	Flt. Officer	T64262	Chicago	IL
Jamerson, Charles F.	43-C-SE	3/25/1943	2nd Lt.	O798949	Pasadena	CA
James, Daniel Jr.	43-G-SE	7/28/1943	2nd Lt.	O809244	Pensacola	FL
James, Voris S.	44-J-TE	12/28/1944	2nd Lt.	O839099	San Antonio	TX
Jamison, Clarence C.	42-D-SE	4/29/1942	2nd Lt.	O789220	Cleveland	OH
Jamison, Donald S.	45-F-TE	9/8/1945	Flt. Officer	T140106	Wilmington	DE
Jefferson, Alexander	44-A-SE	1/7/1944	2nd Lt.	O819461	Detroit	MI

Name	Class	Date of Graduation	Grade	Serial Number	City	State
Jefferson, Lawrence B.	43-H-SE	8/30/1943	2nd Lt.	O811282	Grand Rapids	MI
Jefferson, Samuel	43-H-SE	8/30/1943	2nd Lt.	O811283	Galveston	TX
Jefferson, Thomas W.	44-E-SE	5/23/1944	Flt. Officer	T63114	Chicago	IL
Jenkins, Edward M.	45-A-SE	3/11/1945	2nd Lt.	O841267	Nutley	NJ
Jenkins, Garfield L.	44-I-SE	11/20/1944	2nd Lt.	O839087	Chicago	IL
Jenkins, Joseph E.	44-I-1-TE	10/16/1944	2nd Lt.	O1320946	Ardmore	PA
Jenkins, Silas M.	44-I-1-TE	10/16/1944	2nd Lt.	O838168	Lansing	MI
Jenkins, Stephen S., Jr.	44-H-SE	9/8/1944	2nd Lt.	O838031	Columbus	OH
Johnson, Alvin J.	44-I-SE	11/20/1944	2nd Lt.	O1169183	Chicago	IL
Johnson, Andrew Jr.	44-I-SE	11/20/1944	2nd Lt.	O839088	Greensboro	NC
Johnson, Carl E.	43-I-SE	10/1/1943	2nd Lt.	O814194	Charlottesville	VA
Johnson, Charles B.	43-I-SE	10/1/1943	2nd Lt.	O814195	Philadelphia	PA
Johnson, Charlie A.	44-I-TE	11/20/1944	Flt. Officer	T67159	Marshall	TX
Johnson, Clarence	45-D-SE	6/27/1945	2nd Lt.	O843006	Newark	NJ
Johnson, Conrad A., Jr.	44-G-SE	8/4/1944	2nd Lt.	O835411	New York	NY
Johnson, Earl C.	45-C-SE	5/23/1945	Flt. Officer	T69974	Baltimore	MD
Johnson, Langdon E.	43-E-SE	5/28/1943	2nd Lt.	O804554	Rand	WV
Johnson, Louis W.	44-I-SE	11/20/1944	2nd Lt.	O839094	San Antonio	TX
Johnson, Robert M.	44-H-SE	9/8/1944	Flt. Officer	T66142	Pittsburgh	PA
Johnson, Rupert C.	44-F-SE	6/27/1944	2nd Lt.	O835327	Los Angeles	CA

Name	Class	Date	Rank	Serial	City	State
Johnson, Theopolis W.	45-B-TE	4/15/1945	2nd Lt.	O842589	Carbon Hill	AL
Johnson, Wilbert H.	43-F-SE	6/30/1943	2nd Lt.	O807098	Los Angeles	CA
Johnston, William A., Jr.	45-D-SE	6/27/1945	Flt. Officer	T70100	Sewickley	PA
Jones, Beecher A.	44-K-SE	2/1/1945	Flt. Officer	T68706	Chillicothe	OH
Jones, Edgar L.	43-I-SE	10/1/1943	2nd Lt.	O814196	New York	NY
Jones, Frank D.	45-C-SE	5/23/1945	Flt. Officer	T69975	Hyattsville	MD
Jones, Hubert L.	43-H-SE	8/30/1943	2nd Lt.	O811284	Institute	WV
Jones, Major E.	44-D-SE	4/15/1944	2nd Lt.	O828051	Cleveland	OH
Jones, Robert Jr.	45-A-SE	3/11/1945	Flt. Officer	T68756	Jamestown	NY
Jones, William M.	45-G-SE	10/16/1945	2nd Lt.	O2082624	Columbus	OH
Jordan, Lowell H.	45-B-TE	4/15/1945	2nd Lt.	O842590	Fort Huachuca	AZ
Keel, Daniel	45-G-TE	10/16/1945	Flt. Officer	T131953	Boston	MA
Keith, Laurel E.	44-F-TE	6/27/1944	2nd Lt.	O835319	Cassopolis	MI
Kelley, Thomas A.	45-D-SE	6/27/1945	Flt. Officer	T70101	Pasadena	CA
Kelly, Earl	45-F-SE	9/8/1945	2nd Lt.	O843227	Los Angeles	CA
Kennedy, Elmore M.	43-K-TE	12/5/1943	1st Lt.	O387720	Philadelphia	PA
Kennedy, James V., Jr.	45-A-TE	3/11/1945	2nd Lt.	O841271	Chicago	IL
Kenney, Oscar A.	43-F-SE	6/30/1943	2nd Lt.	O807099	Tuskegee Inst.	AL
Kimbrough, Benny R.	44-G-SE	8/4/1944	2nd Lt.	O83542	Cincinnati	OH
King, Celestus	44-D-TE	4/15/1944	2nd Lt.	O828038	Los Angeles	CA
King, Earl E.	42-G-SE	8/5/1942	2nd Lt.	O790937	Bessemer	AL
King, Haldane	43-J-SE	11/3/1943	2nd Lt.	O814819	Jamaica	NY
Kirkpatrick, Felix J.	43-E-SE	5/28/1943	2nd Lt.	O804555	Chicago	IL

Name	Class	Date of Graduation	Grade	Serial Number	City	State
Kirksey, Leeroy	44-J-SE	12/28/1944	Flt. Officer	T67977	St. Louis	MO
Knight, Calvin M.	45-D-SE	6/27/1945	Flt. Officer	T70102	Norfolk	VA
Knight, Frederick D., Jr.	45-H-TE	11/20/1945	2nd Lt.	O843355	Columbus	OH
Knight, William H.	45-B-SE	4/15/1945	Flt. Officer	T69742	Topeka	KS
Knighten, James B.	42-E-SE	5/20/1942	2nd Lt.	O789449	Tulsa	OK
Knox, George L.	42-E-SE	5/20/1942	2nd Lt.	O789535	Indianapolis	IN
Kydd, George H. III	44-D-TE	4/15/1944	2nd Lt.	O828043	Charleston	WV
Lacy, Hezekiah	43-F-SE	6/30/1943	2nd Lt.	O807100	River Rouge	MI
Laird, Edward	43-J-SE	11/3/1943	2nd Lt.	O814831	Brighton	AL
Lanauze, Harry E.	46-A-SE	3/23/1946	2nd Lt.	O2084156	Washington	DC
Lancaster, Theodore W.	44-I-1-SE	10/16/1944	2nd Lt.	O838155	Rochester	NY
Lane, Allen G.	42-F-SE	7/3/1942	2nd Lt.	O790458	Demopolis	AL
Lane, Charles A., Jr.	44-H-SE	9/8/1944	Flt. Officer	T66143	St. Louis	MO
Lane, Earl R.	44-D-SE	4/15/1944	2nd Lt.	O828052	Wickliffe	OH
Langston, Carroll N., Jr.	43-I-SE	10/1/1943	2nd Lt.	O814197	Chicago	IL
Lanham, Jimmy	44-E-SE	5/23/1944	2nd Lt.	O830791	Philadelphia	PA
Lankford, Joshua J.	45-H-TE	11/20/1945	2nd Lt.	O2069227	San Antonio	TX
Lawrence, Erwin B.	42-F-SE	7/3/1942	2nd Lt.	O790460	Cleveland	OH
Lawrence, Robert W.	44-F-SE	6/27/1944	2nd Lt.	O1640660	Bloomfield	NJ
Lawson, Herman A.	42-I-SE	10/9/1942	2nd Lt.	O792784	Fresno	CA

Name	Class	Date	Rank	Serial No.	City	State
Lawson, Walter E.	42-G-SE	8/5/1942	2nd Lt.	O791783	Newton	VA
Leahr, John H.	43-G-SE	7/28/1943	2nd Lt.	O809245	Cincinnati	OH
Lee, Frank	44-F-TE	6/27/1944	2nd Lt.	O835320	Los Angeles	CA
Leftenant, Samuel G.	44-H-SE	9/8/1944	2nd Lt.	O838032	Amityville	NY
Leftwich, Ivey L.	43-J-SE	11/3/1943	2nd Lt.	O814832	Fairfield	AL
Leonard, Wilmore B.	42-H-SE	9/6/1942	2nd Lt.	O792421	Salisbury	MD
Leslie, William A.	45-G-TE	10/16/1945	2nd Lt.	O2082651	Boston	MA
Lester, Clarence D.	43-K-SE	12/5/1943	2nd Lt.	O817590	Chicago	IL
Lewis, Herbert Jr.	45-H-SE	11/20/1945	Flt. Officer	T70551	South Bend	IN
Lewis, Joe A.	43-F-SE	6/30/1943	2nd Lt.	O807101	Denver	CO
Lewis, William R.	43-K-SE	12/5/1943	2nd Lt.	O817591	Boston	MA
Lieteau, Albert J.	44-H-SE	9/8/1944	1st Lt.	O1014240	New Orleans	LA
Liggins, Wayne V.	43-F-SE	6/30/1943	2nd Lt.	O807102	Springfield	OH
Lindsey, Perry W.	45-G-TE	10/16/1945	2nd Lt.	O2066905	New Albany	IN
Lockett, Claybourne A.	43-G-SE	7/28/1943	2nd Lt.	O809246	Los Angeles	CA
Long, Clyde C., Jr.	45-B-SE	4/15/1945	Flt. Officer	T69751	Itasca	TX
Long, Wilbur F.	44-B-SE	2/8/1944	2nd Lt.	O821915	New Rochelle	NY
Love, Thomas W., Jr.	46-A-SE	3/23/1946	2nd Lt.	O2102098	Ardmore	PA
Lucas, Wendell M.	44-E-SE	5/23/1944	1st Lt.	O430199	Fairmont Hgts.	MD
Lyle, John H.	44-G-SE	8/4/1944	Flt. Officer	T64538	Chicago	IL
Lyle, Payton H.	44-C-TE	3/12/1944	1st Lt.	O1577497	Chicago	IL
Lynch, George A.	44-F-SE	6/27/1944	Flt. Officer	T64373	Valley Stream	NY
Lynch, Lewis J.	44-F-SE	6/27/1944	2nd Lt.	O835328	Columbus	OH

Name	Class	Date of Graduation	Grade	Serial Number	City	State
Lynn, Samuel	43-K-TE	12/5/1943	2nd Lt.	O817603	Jamaica	NY
Macon, Richard D.	44-B-SE	2/8/1944	2nd Lt.	O821916	Birmingham	AL
Manley, Edward E.	44-H-SE	9/8/1944	Flt. Officer	T66147	Los Angeles	CA
Mann, Hiram E.	44-F-SE	6/27/1944	2nd Lt.	O830329	Cleveland	OH
Manning, Albert H.	43-E-SE	5/28/1943	2nd Lt.	O804556	Hartsville	SC
Manning, Walter P.	44-D-SE	4/15/1944	2nd Lt.	O828053	Philadelphia	PA
Maples, Andrew	43-A-SE	1/14/1943	2nd Lt.	O796264	Orange	VA
Maples, Harold B.	45-E-TE	8/4/1945	Flt. Officer	T136668	Orange	VA
Marshall, Andrew D.	44-C-SE	3/12/1944	2nd Lt.	O824835	Wadesboro	NC
Martin, August J.	45-F-SE	9/8/1945	2nd Lt.	O843238	Bronx	NY
Martin, Maceo C.	46-B-SE	5/14/1946	Unknown	Unknown	Unknown	
Martin, Robert L.	44-A-SE	1/7/1944	2nd Lt.	O819462	Dubuque	IA
Masciana, Andrea P.	44-A-TE	1/7/1944	2nd Lt.	O819454	Washington	DC
Mason, James W.	43-G-SE	7/28/1943	2nd Lt.	O809247	Monroe	LA
Mason, Ralph W.	45-F-SE	9/8/1945	2nd Lt.	O843239	Detroit	MI
Mason, Theodore O.	44-I-1-TE	10/16/1944	2nd Lt.	O838167	Cadiz	OH
Mason, Vincent J.	43-J-SE	11/3/1943	2nd Lt.	O814820	Orange	NJ
Matthews, Charles R.	46-A-TE	3/23/1946	2nd Lt.	O2090286	Philadelphia	PA
Matthews, George B.	44-B-TE	2/8/1944	2nd Lt.	O821904	Los Angeles	CA
Matthews, Samuel	44-H-SE	9/8/1944	Flt. Officer	T66144	Birmingham	AL

Name	Class	Date	Rank	Serial No.	City	State
Mattison, William T.	42-I-SE	10/9/1942	2nd Lt.	O792785	Conway	AR
Maxwell, Charles C.	44-I-1-TE	10/16/1944	Flt. Officer	T66407	New York	NY
Maxwell, Robert L.	45-F-TE	9/8/1945	2nd Lt.	O843247	Bronx	NY
May, Cornelius F.	43-I-SE	10/1/1943	2nd Lt.	O814158	Indianapolis	IN
McCarroll, Rixie H.	44-C-SE	3/12/1944	2nd Lt.	O824857	Gary	IN
McClelland, Harvey L.	45-A-TE	3/11/1945	Flt. Officer	T68762	Asheville	NC
McClenic, William B., Jr.	43-H-SE	8/30/1943	2nd Lt.	O811285	Akron	OH
McClure, John	42-G-SE	8/5/1942	2nd Lt.	O791538	Kokomo	IN
McCreary, Walter L.	43-C-SE	3/25/1943	2nd Lt.	O798950	San Antonio	TX
McCrory, Felix M.	44-H-SE	9/8/1944	2nd Lt.	O838033	Yuma	AZ
McCrumby, George T.	43-A-SE	1/14/1943	2nd Lt.	O796255	Fort Worth	TX
McCullin, James L.	42-H-SE	9/6/1942	2nd Lt.	O792442	St. Louis	MO
McDaniel, Armour G.	43-A-SE	1/14/1943	2nd Lt.	O796236	Martinsville	VA
McGarrity, Thomas H.	45-I-SE	1/29/1946	2nd Lt.	O2102014	Chicago	IL
McGee, Charles E.	43-F-SE	6/30/1943	2nd Lt.	O807103	Champaign	IL
McGinnis, Faythe A.	42-F-SE	7/3/1942	2nd Lt.	O790452	Muskogee	OK
McIntyre, Clinton E.	45-E-SE	8/4/1945	2nd Lt.	O2075549	Bronx	NY
McIntyre, Herbert A.	45-F-SE	9/8/1945	2nd Lt.	O2075551	Cleveland	OH
McIver, Frederick D., Jr.	44-A-SE	1/7/1944	2nd Lt.	O819456	Philadelphia	PA
McKeethen, Lloyd B.	45-H-TE	11/20/1945	2nd Lt.	O843356	East Chicago	IL
McKenzie, Alfred U.	45-A-TE	3/11/1945	Flt. Officer	T68765	Washington	DC
McKnight, James W.	45-C-SE	5/23/1945	2nd Lt.	O842883	Washington	DC
McLaurin, Eddie A.	43-G-SE	7/28/1943	2nd Lt.	O809248	Jackson	MS

Name	Class	Date of Graduation	Grade	Serial Number	City	State
McQuillan, Douglas	44-I-TE	11/20/1944	Flt. Officer	T67155	Brooklyn	NY
McRae, Ivan J., Jr.	44-J-TE	12/28/1944	2nd Lt.	O840207	Yonkers	NY
Melton, William R., Jr.	43-G-SE	7/28/1943	2nd Lt.	O809249	Los Angeles	CA
Merriweather, Elbert N.	44-G-SE	8/4/1944	Flt. Officer	T64639	Brooklyn	NY
Merriweather, Robert O.	44-K-SE	2/1/1945	Flt. Officer	T68708	Birmingham	AL
Merton, Joseph L., Jr.	44-C-SE	3/12/1944	2nd Lt.	O824836	Chicago	IL
Miller, Charles E.	44-I-1-SE	10/16/1944	2nd Lt.	O838156	Plainfield	NJ
Miller, George R.	45-E-TE	8/4/1945	Flt. Officer	T70235	Des Moines	IA
Miller, Godfrey C.	45-H-SE	11/20/1945	2nd Lt.	O843344	Bloomington	IL
Miller, Lawrence I.	44-H-SE	9/8/1944	2nd Lt.	O838034	Los Angeles	CA
Miller, Oliver O.	43-E-SE	5/28/1943	2nd Lt.	O804557	Battle Creek	MI
Miller, Willard B.	44-G-TE	8/4/1944	Flt. Officer	T64632	Portland	OR
Millett, Joseph H.	44-I-1-SE	10/16/1944	2nd Lt.	O838157	Los Angeles	CA
Mills, Clinton B.	43-A-SE	1/14/1943	2nd Lt.	O796267	Durham	NC
Mills, Theodore H.	43-J-SE	11/3/1943	2nd Lt.	O814933	New Rochelle	NY
Mitchell, James T., Jr.	44-F-SE	6/27/1944	Flt. Officer	T64247	Gadsden	AL
Mitchell, Paul G.	42-F-SE	7/3/1942	2nd Lt.	O790461	Washington	DC
Mitchell, Vincent I.	44-D-SE	4/15/1944	Flt. Officer	T62811	Mt. Clemens	MI
Moffett, Wilbur	45-A-SE	3/11/1945	Flt. Officer	T68757	Detroit	MI
Moody, Frank H.	44-B-SE	2/8/1944	2nd Lt.	O821917	Los Angeles	CA

Name	Class	Date	Rank	Serial	City	State
Moody, Paul L.	44-D-TE	4/15/1944	2nd Lt.	O828033	Cambridge	MA
Moody, Roland W.	44-D-SE	4/15/1944	2nd Lt.	O828054	Cambridge	MA
Moore, Abe B.	46-A-TE	3/23/1946	Flt. Officer	T149985	Austin	TX
Moore, Flarzell	44-J-TE	12/28/1944	Flt. Officer	T67981	Chicago	IL
Moore, Theopolis D.	43-F-SE	6/30/1943	2nd Lt.	O807164	St. Louis	MO
Moore, Willis E.	44-I-SE	11/20/1944	2nd Lt.	O839089	Chicago	IL
Moret, Calvin G.	44-I-SE	11/20/1944	Flt. Officer	T67147	New Orleans	LA
Morgan, Dempsey W.	43-E-SE	5/28/1943	2nd Lt.	O804538	Detroit	MI
Morgan, John H.	42-H-SE	9/6/1942	2nd Lt.	O792423	Cartersville	GA
Morgan, William B.	45-F-SE	9/8/1945	Flt. Officer	T70425	Yukon	PA
Morgan, Woodrow F.	43-I-SE	10/1/1943	2nd Lt.	O814199	Omaha	NE
Morris, Harold M.	44-D-SE	4/15/1944	2nd Lt.	O828046	Seattle	WA
Morrison, Thomas J., Jr.	45-A-SE	3/11/1945	2nd Lt.	O841255	Roxbury	MA
Moseley, Sidney J.	43-D-SE	4/29/1943	2nd Lt.	O801173	Norfolk	VA
Mosley, Clifford E.	45-E-TE	8/4/1945	Flt. Officer	T136674	Boston	MA
Mosley, John W.	44-G-TE	8/4/1944	2nd Lt.	O835434	Denver	CO
Moss, Richard M.	46-B-SE	5/14/1946	Unknown	Unknown	Unknown	
Mozee, David M., Jr.	45-F-TE	9/8/1945	Flt. Officer	T70429	Chicago	IL
Mulzac, John I.	44-J-TE	12/28/1944	Flt. Officer	T67987	Brooklyn	NY
Murdic, Robert J.	44-F-SE	6/27/1944	Flt. Officer	T64275	Franklin	TN
Murphy, David J., Jr.	44-I-1-TE	10/16/1944	Flt. Officer	T66406	Whiteville	NC
Murray, Louis U.	45-C-SE	5/23/1945	Flt. Officer	T69976	Gary	IN
Myers, Charles P.	44-I-SE	10/16/1944	2nd Lt.	O838158	Indianapolis	IN

Name	Class	Date of Graduation	Grade	Serial Number	City	State
Nalle, Russell C., Jr.	44-H-TE	9/8/1944	Flt. Officer	T66150	Detroit	MI
Neblett, Nicholas S.	46-C-SE	6/28/1946	2nd Lt.	O2082632	Cincinnati	OH
Nelson, Dempsey Jr.	44-J-SE	12/28/1944	Flt. Officer	T67971	Philadelphia	PA
Nelson, John W.	45-H-TE	11/20/1945	Flt. Officer	T70559	Bronx	NY
Nelson, Lincoln W.	44-I-SE	11/20/1944	2nd Lt.	O839090	San Diego	CA
Nelson, Neal V.	43-I-SE	10/1/1943	2nd Lt.	O814200	Chicago	IL
Nelson, Robert H.	43-G-SE	7/28/1943	2nd Lt.	O809250	Pittsburgh	PA
Newman, Christopher W.	43-I-SE	10/1/1943	2nd Lt.	O814201	St. Louis	MO
Newsum, Fitzroy	43-K-TE	12/5/1943	1st Lt.	O409854	Brooklyn	NY
Nicolas, Pelissier C.	44-B-TE	2/8/1944			Port au Prince	Haiti
Nightingale, Elton H.	44-C-SE	3/12/1944	2nd Lt.	O824849	Tuskegee Inst.	AL
Noches, R. F.	44-G-TE	8/4/1944	Flt. Officer	T64626	Junction City	KS
Norton, George G., Jr.	45-B-TE	4/15/1945	Flt. Officer	T69755	St. Louis	MO
Oliphant, Clarence A.	44-E-SE	5/23/1944	2nd Lt.	O830792	Council Bluffs	IA
Oliver, Luther L.	45-A-TE	3/11/1945	2nd Lt.	O841272	Montgomery	AL
O'Neal, Walter N.	45-E-TE	8/4/1945	Flt. Officer	T70236	Cleveland	OH
O'Neil, Robert	44-A-SE	1/7/1944	2nd Lt.	O819463	Detroit	MI
Orduna, Ralph	44-E-SE	5/23/1944	2nd Lt.	O830793	Omaha	NE
Page, Maurice R.	43-G-SE	7/28/1943	2nd Lt.	O809251	Los Angeles	CA
Palmer, Augustus L.	45-F-SE	9/8/1945	2nd Lt.	O843240	Newport News	VA

Name	Class	Date	Rank	Serial No.	City	State
Palmer, Walter J.	43-F-SE	6/30/1943	2nd Lt.	O807105	New York	NY
Parker, Frederick L., Jr.	44-A-TE	1/7/1944	2nd Lt.	O1166345	Chicago	IL
Parker, George J.	45-C-SE	5/23/1945	Flt. Officer	T69977	Youngstown	OH
Parker, Melvin	44-J-SE	12/28/1944	Flt. Officer	T67972	Baltimore	MD
Parkey, Robert M.	44-I-TE	11/20/1944	Flt. Officer	T67156	Des Moines	IA
Pasquet, Alix	43-H-SE	8/30/1943				Haiti
Patton, Humphrey C., Jr.	45-B-SE	4/15/1945	Flt. Officer	T69743	Washington	DC
Patton, Thomas G.	44-B-SE	2/8/1944	2nd Lt.	O821913	South Franklin	TN
Payne, Turner W.	43-J-SE	11/3/1943	2nd Lt.	O814834	Wichita Falls	TX
Payne, Verdell L.	45-B-SE	4/15/1945	Flt. Officer	T69744	Mamaroneck	NY
Peirson, Gwynne W.	43-J-SE	11/3/1943	2nd Lt.	O814835	Oakland	CA
Pendleton, Frederick D.	44-J-SE	12/28/1944	2nd Lt.	O840205	Texarkana	TX
Penn, Starling B.	43-H-SE	8/30/1943	2nd Lt.	O811285	New York	NY
Pennington, Leland H.	44-G-SE	8/4/1944	Flt. Officer	T64646	Rochester	NY
Pennington, Robert F.	45-B-SE	4/15/1945	Flt. Officer	T69745	Little Silver	NJ
Peoples, Francis B.	44-D-SE	4/15/1944	2nd Lt.	O828055	Henderson	NC
Peoples, Henry R.	44-D-SE	4/15/1944	2nd Lt.	O828056	St. Louis	MO
Perkins, John R., Jr.	44-F-TE	6/27/1944	Flt. Officer	T64270	Seattle	WA
Perkins, Roscoe C., Jr.	45-C-SE	5/23/1945	Flt. Officer	T69978	Canonsburg	PA
Perkins, Sanford M.	44-A-SE	1/7/1944	2nd Lt.	O819464	Denver	CO
Perry, Henry B.	42-H-SE	9/6/1942	2nd Lt.	O792424	Thomasville	GA
Pillow, Robert A., Jr.	44-E-SE	5/23/1944	Flt. Officer	T63115	Nashville	TN
Pinkney, Harvey A.	43-J-SE	11/3/1943	2nd Lt.	O814821	Baltimore	MD

Name	Class	Date of Graduation	Grade	Serial Number	City	State
Pokinghorne, James R.	43-B-SE	2/16/1943	2nd Lt.	O797221	Pensacola	FL
Pollard, Henry	43-K-SE	12/5/1943	2nd Lt.	O817592	Buffalo	NY
Pompey, Maurice D.	44-G-TE	8/4/1944	Flt. Officer	T64627	South Bend	IN
Ponder, Driskell B.	43-I-SE	10/1/1943	2nd Lt.	O814202	Chicago	IL
Porter, Calvin V.	45-F-TE	9/8/1945	2nd Lt.	O2075556	Detroit	MI
Porter, John H.	44-C-SE	3/12/1944	2nd Lt.	O824839	Cleveland	OH
Porter, Robert B.	45-B-SE	4/15/1945	Flt. Officer	T69746	Los Angeles	CA
Powell, William S., Jr.	45-B-SE	4/15/1945	Flt. Officer	T69747	Eggertsville	NY
Prather, George L.	45-D-SE	6/27/1945	Flt. Officer	T70103	Atlanta	GA
Prewitt, Mexion O.	45-E-TE	8/4/1945	Flt. Officer	T70238	East Berkley	WV
Price, Charles R.	45-G-TE	10/16/1945	Flt. Officer	T70556	Garden City	KS
Price, William S., III	44-C-SE	3/12/1944	2nd Lt.	O824840	Topeka	KS
Prince, Joseph A.	45-D-SE	6/27/1945	Flt. Officer	T70104	Dayton	OH
Proctor, Norman E.	45-H-TE	11/20/1945	Flt. Officer	T70561	Oberlin	OH
Proctor, Oliver W.	45-E-TE	8/4/1945	Flt. Officer	T70239	Norfolk	VA
Prowell, John	43-B-SE	2/16/1943	2nd Lt.	O797222	Lewisburg	AL
Pruitt, Harry S.	45-A-SE	3/11/1945	Flt. Officer	T68759	Independence	KS
Pruitt, Wendell O.	42-K-SE	12/13/1942	2nd Lt.	O794600	St. Louis	MO
Pullam, Richard C.	42-K-SE	12/13/1942	2nd Lt.	O794601	Kansas City	KS
Pulliam, Glenn W.	44-I-1-TE	10/16/1944	Flt. Officer	T66410	Los Angeles	CA

Name	Class	Date	Rank	Serial	City	State
Purchase, Leon	43-H-SE	8/30/1943	2nd Lt.	O811257	New York	NY
Purnell, George B.	45-B-SE	4/15/1945	Flt. Officer	T69748	Philadelphia	PA
Purnell, Louis R.	42-F-SE	7/3/1942	2nd Lt.	O790463	Wilmington	DE
Qualles, John P.	44-J-TE	12/28/1944	Flt. Officer	T67985	Bronx	NY
Quander, Charles J., Jr.	44-G-TE	8/4/1944	Flt. Officer	T64625	Washington	DC
Radcliff, Lloyd L.	45-B-SE	4/15/1945	2nd Lt.	O842534	New Haven	CT
Ragsdale, Lincoln J.	45-H-SE	11/20/1945	2nd Lt.	O843519	Ardmore	OK
Ramsey, James C.	44-E-SE	5/23/1944	Flt. Officer	T63116	Augusta	GA
Ramsey, Pierce T.	45-F-TE	9/8/1945	Flt. Officer	T70430	Philadelphia	PA
Rapier, Gordon M.	44-C-SE	3/12/1944	2nd Lt.	O824841	Gary	IN
Rayburg, Nathaniel P.	43-J-SE	11/3/1943	Flt. Officer	T61501	Washington	DC
Rayford, Lee	42-E-SE	5/20/1942	2nd Lt.	O789437	Washington	DC
Raymond, Frank R.	45-D-SE	6/27/1945	Flt. Officer	T70112	Martinville	LA
Rayner, Ahmed A., Jr.	44-C-TE	3/12/1944	2nd Lt.	O1045199	Chicago	IL
Rector, John A.	44-H-TE	9/8/1944	1st Lt.	O545517	Pittsburgh	PA
Reed, Marsille P.	45-A-SE	3/11/1945	2nd Lt.	O841564	Tillar	AR
Reeves, Ronald W.	44-G-SE	8/4/1944	2nd Lt.	O835413	Washington	DC
Reid, Maury M., Jr.	44-G-SE	8/4/1944	Flt. Officer	T64650	New York	NY
Reynolds, Clarence E., Jr.	45-E-SE	8/4/1945	Flt. Officer	T70224	Ahoskie	NC
Rhodes, George M., Jr.	43-I-SE	10/1/1943	2nd Lt.	O814203	Brooklyn	NY
Rice, Clayo C.	45-A-SE	3/11/1945	2nd Lt.	O841250	Bridgetown	NJ
Rice, Price D.	42-I-SE	10/9/1942	2nd Lt.	O792736	Montclair	NJ
Rice, William E.	44-G-SE	8/4/1944	Flt. Officer	T64641	Swarthmore	PA

Name	Class	Date of Graduation	Grade	Serial Number	City	State
Rich, Daniel L.	44-D-SE	4/15/1944	2nd Lt.	O828057	Rutherford	NJ
Richardson, Eugene J., Jr.	45-A-SE	3/11/1945	2nd Lt.	O841261	Camden	NJ
Richardson, Virgil J.	43-F-SE	6/30/1943	2nd Lt.	O807107	Bronx	NY
Roach, Charles J.	45-F-TE	9/8/1945	Flt. Officer	T70431	Brooklyn	NY
Roach, John B.	45-E-TE	8/4/1945	Flt. Officer	T70240	Boston	MA
Robbins, Emory L., Jr.	43-J-SE	11/3/1943	2nd Lt.	O814836	Chicago	IL
Roberts, Frank E.	44-A-SE	1/7/1944	2nd Lt.	O819465	Boston	MA
Roberts, George S.	42-C-SE	3/6/1942	2nd Lt.	O441127	Fairmont	WV
Roberts, Lawrence E.	44-J-TE	12/28/1944	2nd Lt.	O840208	Vauxhall	NH
Roberts, Leon C.	42-G-SE	8/5/1942	2nd Lt.	O791539	Prichard	AL
Roberts, Leroy, Jr.	44-E-SE	5/23/1944	2nd Lt.	O830794	Toccoa	GA
Roberts, Logan	45-E-SE	8/4/1945	Flt. Officer	T70225	Philadelphia	PA
Robinson, Carroll H.	44-D-SE	4/15/1944	2nd Lt.	O828058	Atlanta	GA
Robinson, Curtis C.	43-D-SE	4/29/1943	2nd Lt.	O801174	Orangeburg	SC
Robinson, Isaiah E., Jr.	45-H-TE	11/20/1945	2nd Lt.	O843357	Birmingham	AL
Robinson, Robert C., Jr.	44-G-SE	8/4/1944	2nd Lt.	O835414	Asheville	NC
Robinson, Robert L., Jr.	45-D-SE	6/27/1945	2nd Lt.	O843007	Wilcoe	WV
Robinson, Spencer M.	45-A-SE	3/11/1945	2nd Lt.	O841262	Monroe	NJ
Robinson, Theodore W.	45-H-TE	11/20/1945	2nd Lt.	O843358	Chicago	IL
Robnett, Harris H., Jr.	44-G-TE	8/4/1944	Flt. Officer	T64629	Denver	CO

Name	Class	Date	Rank	Serial	City	State
Rodgers, Marion R.	44-B-SE	2/8/1944	2nd Lt.	O821920	Elizabeth	NJ
Rogers, Amos A.	43-K-TE	12/5/1943	Flt. Officer	T61780	Tuskegee Inst.	AL
Rogers, Cornelius G.	43-G-SE	7/28/1943	2nd Lt.	O809252	Chicago	IL
Rogers, John W.	42-G-SE	8/5/1942	2nd Lt.	O791540	Chicago	IL
Rohlsen, Henry E.	44-C-SE	3/12/1944	2nd Lt.	O574032	Christiansted	VI
Romine, Roger	43-H-SE	8/30/1943	2nd Lt.	O811238	Oakland	CA
Ross, Mac	42-C-SE	3/6/1942	2nd Lt.	O441129	Dayton	OH
Ross, Merrill Ray	45-I-SE	1/29/1946	2nd Lt.	O2102015	Pineville	KY
Ross, Washington D.	43-I-SE	10/1/1943	2nd Lt.	O814204	Ashland	KY
Rowe, Claude A.	46-C-TE	6/28/1946	2nd Lt.	O2102115	Detroit	MI
Rucker, William A.	44-A-TE	1/7/1944	2nd Lt.	O819250	Washington	PA
Russell, James C.	45-G-TE	10/16/1945	Flt. Officer	T70558	Los Angeles	CA
Samuels, Frederick H.	44-H-TE	9/8/1944	Flt. Officer	T66149	Philadelphia	PA
Sanderlin, Willis E.	45-C-SE	5/23/1945	2nd Lt.	O842884	Washington	DC
Satterwhite, Harry J.	45-E-TE	8/4/1945	2nd Lt.	O2075559	New York	NY
Saunders, Martin G.	45-E-SE	8/4/1945	2nd Lt.	O843106	Jamaica	NY
Saunders, Pearlee E.	43-C-SE	3/25/1943	2nd Lt.	O798951	Bessemer	AL
Sawyer, Harold E.	43-D-SE	4/29/1943	2nd Lt.	O801175	Columbus	OH
Scales, Norman W.	43-I-SE	10/1/1943	2nd Lt.	O814205	Austin	TX
Schell, Wyrain T.	44-F-SE	6/27/1944	Flt. Officer	T64230	Brooklyn	NY
Schwing, Herbert J.	45-A-TE	3/11/1945	2nd Lt.	O841273	New York	NY
Scott, Floyd R., Jr.	45-F-SE	9/8/1945	Flt. Officer	T70423	Asbury Park	NJ
Scott, Henry B.	43-I-SE	10/1/1943	2nd Lt.	O814206	Jersey City	NJ

Name	Class	Date of Graduation	Grade	Serial Number	City	State
Scott, Joseph P.	45-E-SE	8/4/1945	2nd Lt.	O843107	Chicago	IL
Scott, Wayman E.	45-H-TE	11/20/1945	Flt. Officer	T70561	Oberlin	OH
Selden, Wiley W.	43-F-SE	6/30/1943	2nd Lt.	O807108	Norfolk	VA
Sessions, Mansfield L.	45-C-SE	5/23/1945	2nd Lt.	O842885	Los Angeles	CA
Sheats, George H.	45-B-SE	4/15/1945	2nd Lt.	O842585	New Haven	CT
Shepherd, James H.	44-G-TE	8/4/1944	Flt. Officer	T64630	Washington	DC
Sheppard, Harry A.	43-E-SE	5/28/1943	2nd Lt.	O804559	Jamaica	NY
Sherard, Earl S., Jr.	43-J-SE	11/3/1943	2nd Lt.	O814837	Columbus	OH
Sherman, George	45-G-SE	10/16/1945	Flt. Officer	T70350	Albany	IL
Shivers, Clarence L.	44-J-SE	12/28/1944	Flt. Officer	T67973	St. Louis	MO
Shults, Lloyd R.	44-D-TE	4/15/1944	2nd Lt.	O828044	N. Plainfield	NJ
Sidat-Singh, Wilmeth W.	43-C-SE	3/25/1943	2nd Lt.	O798952	Washington	DC
Simeon, Albert B., Jr.	45-D-SE	6/27/1945	Flt. Officer	T70105	Detroit	MI
Simmons, Alphonso	43-I-SE	10/1/1943	2nd Lt.	O814207	Jacksonville	FL
Simmons, Donehue	45-I-TE	1/29/1946	Flt. Officer	T149963	Chicago	IL
Simmons, Paul C., Jr.	43-J-SE	11/3/1943	2nd Lt.	O814838	Detroit	MI
Simons, Richard A.	44-I-1-SE	10/16/1944	2nd Lt.	O838159	White Plains	NY
Simpson, Jesse H.	44-G-TE	8/4/1944	Flt. Officer	T64631	Fresno	CA
Singletary, Lloyd G.	43-C-SE	3/25/1943	2nd Lt.	O798953	Jacksonville	FL
Sloan, John S.	43-F-SE	6/30/1943	2nd Lt.	O807109	Louisville	KY

Name	Class	Date	Rank	Serial No.	City	State
Smith, Albert H.	45-A-SE	3/11/1945	Flt. Officer	T68758	Jersey City	NJ
Smith, Burl E.	45-B-SE	4/15/1945	2nd Lt.	O842586	Oakland	CA
Smith, Edward	43-G-SE	7/28/1943	2nd Lt.	O809253	Philadelphia	PA
Smith, Eugene D.	43-J-SE	11/3/1943	2nd Lt.	O814959	Cincinnati	OH
Smith, Frederick D.	45-C-TE	5/23/1945	2nd Lt.	O842877	Pasadena	CA
Smith, Graham	42-F-SE	7/3/1942	2nd Lt.	O790465	Ahoskie	NC
Smith, Harold E., Jr.	44-I-1-TE	10/16/1944	1st Lt.	O420985	Memphis	TN
Smith, Lewis C.	43-D-SE	4/29/1943	2nd Lt.	O801176	Los Angeles	CA
Smith, Luther H.	43-E-SE	5/28/1943	2nd Lt.	O804550	Des Moines	IA
Smith, Quentin P.	45-A-TE	3/11/1945	2nd Lt.	O841274	East Chicago	IL
Smith, Reginald V.	45-E-SE	8/4/1945	Flt. Officer	T70226	Ahoskie	NC
Smith, Robert C.	45-D-SE	6/27/1945	Flt. Officer	T70107	Muskogee	OK
Smith, Robert H.	43-I-SE	10/1/1943	2nd Lt.	O814208	Baltimore	MD
Smith, Thomas W.	44-J-SE	12/28/1944	Flt. Officer	T67974	Lebanon	KY
Spann, Calvin J.	44-G-SE	8/4/1944	Flt. Officer	T64642	Rutherford	NJ
Spears, Leon W.	44-F-SE	6/27/1944	Flt. Officer	T64276	Pueblo	CO
Spencer, Roy M.	43-B-SE	2/16/1943	2nd Lt.	O797223	Tallahasee	FL
Spicer, Cecil	45-H-TE	11/20/1945	2nd Lt.	O843360	Greenville	OH
Spriggs, Thurman E.	45-H-SE	11/20/1945	2nd Lt.	O843350	Des Moines	IA
Spurlin, Jerome D.	43-J-SE	11/3/1943	2nd Lt.	O814322	Chicago	IL
Squires, John W.	44-H-SE	9/8/1944	Flt. Officer	T6615	St. Louis	MO
Stanton, Charles R.	43-A-SE	1/14/1943	2nd Lt.	O796258	Portland	OR
Starks, Arnett W., Jr.	44-E-SE	5/23/1944	Flt. Officer	T63109	Los Angeles	CA

Name	Class	Date of Graduation	Grade	Serial Number	City	State
Stephenson, William W.	44-J-SE	12/28/1944	Flt. Officer	T67975	Washington	DC
Stevens, Richard G.	44-I-1-SE	10/16/1944	2nd Lt.	O838160	Washington	DC
Steward, Lowell C.	43-G-SE	7/28/1943	2nd Lt.	O809254	Los Angeles	CA
Stewart, Harry T., Jr.	44-F-SE	6/27/1944	2nd Lt.	O835330	Corona	NY
Stewart, Nathaniel C.	43-J-SE	11/3/1943	2nd Lt.	O814840	Philadelphia	PA
Stiger, Roosevelt	44-C-SE	3/12/1944	2nd Lt.	O824842	Jackson	MI
Stoudmire, Norvel	43-H-SE	8/30/1943	2nd Lt.	O811289	St. Louis	MO
Stovall, Charles L.	44-I-1-SE	10/16/1944	2nd Lt.	O838161	Wichita	KS
Streat, William A., Jr.	45-H-TE	11/20/1945	Flt. Officer	T70562	Lawrenceville	VA
Street, Thomas C.	44-G-SE	8/4/1944	2nd Lt.	O835415	Springfield	NJ
Suggs, John J.	43-E-SE	5/28/1943	2nd Lt.	O804561	Terre Haute	IN
Surcey, Wayman P.	44-I-TE	11/20/1944	Flt. Officer	T67160	Jacksonville	FL
Talton, James E.	45-F-TE	9/8/1945	Flt. Officer	T136691	Merchantville	NJ
Tate, Charles W.	43-H-SE	8/30/1943	2nd Lt.	O811290	Pittsburgh	PA
Taylor, Elmer W.	43-G-SE	7/28/1943	2nd Lt.	O809255	Pittsburgh	PA
Taylor, George A.	43-H-SE	8/30/1943	2nd Lt.	O811291	Philadelphia	PA
Taylor, James	45-B-TE	4/15/1945	Flt. Officer	T69756	Champaign	IL
Taylor, Ulysses S.	43-D-SE	4/29/1943	2nd Lt.	O801177	Kaufman	TX
Taylor, William H., Jr.	45-E-TE	8/4/1945	Flt. Officer	T70241	Inkster	MI
Temple, Alva N.	43-G-SE	7/28/1943	2nd Lt.	O809256	Carrollton	AL

Name	Class	Date	Rank	Serial No.	City	State
Terry, Kenneth E.	45-F-TE	9/8/1945	Flt. Officer	T70432	Emporia	KS
Terry, Roger C.	44-K-TE	2/1/1945	2nd Lt.	O811165	Los Angeles	CA
Theodore, Eugene G.	44-I-SE	11/20/1944	2nd Lt.	O839091	Port of Spain	Trin.
Thomas, Edward M.	43-J-SE	11/3/1943	2nd Lt.	O814841	Chicago	IL
Thomas, Walter H., Jr.	45-D-SE	6/27/1945	Flt. Officer	T70108	Redlands	CA
Thomas, William H.	43-J-SE	11/3/1943	2nd Lt.	O814842	Los Angeles	CA
Thompson, Donald N., Jr.	44-I-1-SE	10/16/1944	2nd Lt.	O838162	Philadelphia	PA
Thompson, Floyd A.	43-H-SE	8/30/1943	2nd Lt.	O811292	London	WV
Thompson, Francis R.	45-A-TE	3/11/1945	2nd Lt.	O841273	Brooklyn	NY
Thompson, James A.	45-G-SE	10/16/1945	Flt. Officer	T141246	Cleveland	OH
Thompson, Reid E.	43-K-SE	12/5/1943	2nd Lt.	O817524	New Rochelle	NY
Thorpe, Herbert C.	45-G-TE	10/16/1945	2nd Lt.	O2080935	Brooklyn	NY
Thorpe, Richard E.	44-I-1-SE	10/16/1944	2nd Lt.	O338163	Brooklyn	NY
Tindall, Thomas J.	45-C-SE	5/23/1945	Flt. Officer	T69973	East Orange	NJ
Toatley, Ephraim E., Jr.	44-K-SE	2/1/1945	2nd Lt.	O841161	Philadelphia	PA
Tompkins, William D.	43-J-SE	11/3/1943	2nd Lt.	O814823	Fall River	MA
Toney, Mitchel N.	45-E-TE	8/4/1945	Flt. Officer	T70242	Austin	TX
Toppins, Edward L.	42-H-SE	9/6/1942	2nd Lt.	C792425	San Francisco	CA
Tresville, Robert B., Jr.	42-K-SE	12/13/1942	2nd Lt.	C25761	Bay City	TX
Trott, Robert G.	45-D-SE	6/27/1945	2nd Lt.	O843008	Mt. Vernon	NY
Tucker, Paul	45-B-SE	4/15/1945	Flt. Officer	T69749	Detroit	MI
Turner, Allen H.	44-I-1-SE	10/16/1944	2nd Lt.	O838155	Flint	MI
Turner, Andrew D.	42-I-SE	10/9/1942	2nd Lt.	O792737	Washington	DC

Name	Class	Date of Graduation	Grade	Serial Number	City	State
Turner, Gordon G.	45-E-SE	8/4/1945	2nd Lt.	O2075566	Los Angeles	CA
Turner, John B.	44-F-TE	6/27/1944	2nd Lt.	O835321	Atlanta	GA
Turner, Leon L.	44-A-TE	1/7/1944	2nd Lt.	O406744	Washington	DC
Turner, Leonard F.	43-F-SE	6/30/1943	2nd Lt.	O807110	Washington	DC
Turner, Ralph L.	44-D-SE	4/15/1944	Flt. Officer	T62812	Los Angeles	CA
Twine, Saint M., Jr.	44-A-TE	1/7/1944	Flt. Officer	T61710	Los Angeles	CA
Tyler, William A., Jr.	45-C-TE	5/23/1945	2nd Lt.	O842878	Pittsburgh	PA
Valentine, Cleophus W.	45-A-TE	3/11/1945	2nd Lt.	O841276	Detroit	MI
Vaughan, Leonard O.	44-I-SE	11/20/1944	Flt. Officer	T67149	Brooklyn	NY
Velasquez, Frederick B.	44-J-TE	12/28/1944	Flt. Officer	T67982	Chicago	IL
Verwayne, Peter C.	42-K-SE	12/13/1942	2nd Lt.	O794602	New York	NY
Waddell, Reginald C., Jr.	44-I-SE	11/20/1944	Flt. Officer	T67150	Chicago	IL
Walker, Charles E.	44-A-TE	1/7/1944	2nd Lt.	O819451	Jackson	MI
Walker, Frank D.	43-F-SE	6/30/1943	2nd Lt.	O807111	Richmond	KY
Walker, James A.	43-E-SE	5/28/1943	2nd Lt.	O804562	Manning	SC
Walker, John B., Jr.	45-A-SE	3/11/1945	2nd Lt.	O841263	Canton	OH
Walker, Quitman C.	43-A-SE	1/14/1943	2nd Lt.	O796269	Indianola	MS
Walker, William C., Jr.	44-E-SE	5/23/1944	2nd Lt.	O830795	Atlantic City	NJ
Walker, William H.	42-K-SE	12/13/1942	2nd Lt.	O794603	Suffolk	VA
Walker, William H.	43-B-SE	2/16/1943	2nd Lt.	O797225	Carbondale	IL

Name	Class	Date	Rank	Serial	City	State
Wanamaker, George E.	45-C-SE	5/23/1945	Flt. Officer	T69980	Montclair	NJ
Warner, Hugh St. Clair	43-J-SE	11/3/1943	2nd Lt.	O814843	New York	NY
Warren, James W.	44-I-SE	10/16/1944	Flt. Officer	T66402	Brooklyn	NY
Warrick, Calvin T.	45-A-TE	3/11/1945	2nd Lt.	O841273	Elkton	MD
Washington, Milton	44-H-SE	9/8/1944	Flt. Officer	T66146	Willow Grove	PA
Washington, Morris J.	44-I-TE	11/20/1944	Flt. Officer	T67157	Atlantic City	NJ
Washington, Samuel L.	44-F-SE	6/27/1944	Flt. Officer	T64278	Cleveland	OH
Washington, William M.	44-I-SE	11/20/1944	2nd Lt.	O839092	Chicago	IL
Watkins, Edward W.	45-F-SE	9/8/1945	Flt. Officer	T70424	Omaha	NE
Watkins, Edward Wilson	43-I-SE	10/1/1943	2nd Lt.	O814269	Freeman	WV
Watson, Dudley M.	43-E-SE	5/28/1943	2nd Lt.	O804553	Frankfort	KY
Watson, Spann	42-F-SE	7/3/1942	2nd Lt.	O790457	Hackensack	NJ
Watts, Samuel W., Jr.	44-E-SE	5/23/1944	2nd Lt.	O830725	New York	NY
Weatherford, Richard	45-G-TE	10/16/1945	Flt. Officer	T70557	Albion	MI
Weathers, Luke J.	43-D-SE	4/29/1943	2nd Lt.	O801178	Memphis	TN
Webb, Rhohelia J.	44-F-TE	6/27/1944	2nd Lt.	O835322	Baltimore	MD
Wells, Johnson C.	43-F-SE	6/30/1943	2nd Lt.	O807112	Buffalo	NY
Wells, Wendell D.	43-K-TE	12/5/1943	2nd Lt.	O817606	Washington	DC
Westbrook, Shelby F.	44-B-SE	2/8/1944	2nd Lt.	O821921	Toledo	OH
Westmoreland, Julius C.	45-F-SE	9/8/1945	2nd Lt.	O843241	Washington	DC
Westmoreland, Walter D.	43-G-SE	7/28/1943	2nd Lt.	O809257	Atlanta	GA
Wheeler, Jimmie D.	44-D-SE	4/15/1944	2nd Lt.	O828359	Detroit	MI
Wheeler, William M.	44-C-SE	3/12/1944	2nd Lt.	O824543	Detroit	MI

Name	Class	Date of Graduation	Grade	Serial Number	City	State
White, Charles L.	44-C-SE	3/12/1944	2nd Lt.	O824844	St. Louis	MO
White, Cohen M.	44-B-SE	2/8/1944	2nd Lt.	O821922	Detroit	MI
White, Ferrier H.	44-I-1-SE	10/16/1944	2nd Lt.	O1824829	Oberlin	OH
White, Harold L.	44-G-SE	8/4/1944	2nd Lt.	O835416	Detroit	MI
White, Harry W.	45-C-SE	5/23/1945	Flt. Officer	T69981	Baltimore	MD
White, Haydel J.	44-K-TE	2/1/1945	Flt. Officer	T68712	New Orleans	LA
White, Hugh J.	44-F-SE	6/27/1944	2nd Lt.	O835331	St. Louis	MO
White, Joseph C.	44-G-SE	8/4/1944	Flt. Officer	T64643	Chattanooga	TN
White, Marvin C.	45-E-SE	8/4/1945	Flt. Officer	T70227	Wichita	KS
White, Raymond M.	44-I-TE	11/20/1944	Flt. Officer	T67158	Bronx	NY
White, Sherman W.	42-E-SE	5/20/1942	2nd Lt.	O789431	Montgomery	AL
White, Vertner J., Jr.	45-F-TE	9/8/1945	2nd Lt.	O843248	Cleveland	OH
Whitehead, John L., Jr.	44-H-SE	9/8/1944	2nd Lt.	O838035	Lawrenceville	VA
Whiten, Joseph	43-K-TE	12/5/1943	2nd Lt.	O817604	New York	NY
Whiteside, Albert	45-E-TE	8/4/1945	Flt. Officer	T70243	San Antonio	TX
Whitney, Yenwith K.	44-F-SE	6/27/1944	Flt. Officer	T64279	New York	NY
Whittaker, Peter H.	44-C-SE	3/12/1944	2nd Lt.	O824845	Detroit	MI
Whyte, James W., Jr.	44-I-TE	11/20/1944	2nd Lt.	O839096	New Haven	CT
Wiggins, Leonard W.	45-E-SE	8/4/1945	Flt. Officer	T70228	Detroit	MI
Wiggins, Robert H.	43-G-SE	7/28/1943	2nd Lt.	O809259	New York	NY

Name	Class	Date	Rank	Serial	City	State
Wilburn, Arthur J.	44-A-SE	1/7/1944	2nd Lt.	O819466	Asheville	NC
Wiley, James T.	42-F-SE	7/3/1942	2nd Lt.	O790469	Pittsburgh	PA
Wilhite, Emmet J.	45-D-SE	6/27/1945	2nd Lt.	O843000	Los Angeles	CA
Wilkerson, Oscar L., Jr.	45-F-TE	9/8/1945	2nd Lt.	O843240	Chicago Hgts.	IL
Wilkerson, William G.	43-F-SE	6/30/1943	2nd Lt.	O807113	Camden	NJ
Wilkins, Laurence D.	43-E-SE	5/28/1943	2nd Lt.	O804564	Los Angeles	CA
Wilkins, Ralph D.	44-I-SE	11/20/1944	2nd Lt.	O839093	Washington	DC
Willette, Leonard R.	44-B-SE	2/8/1944	Flt. Officer	T62308	Belleville	NJ
Williams, Andrew B., Jr.	45-H-TE	11/20/1945	Flt. Officer	T70563	Los Angeles	CA
Williams, Charles I.	43-D-SE	4/29/1943	2nd Lt.	O801173	Lima	OH
Williams, Charles T.	44-C-SE	3/12/1944	2nd Lt.	O824845	Los Angeles	CA
Williams, Clarence	44-A-TE	1/7/1944	Flt. Officer	T61749	Fairfield	AL
Williams, Craig H.	43-E-SE	5/28/1943	2nd Lt.	O804565	Chicago	IL
Williams, Edward J.	43-K-SE	12/5/1943	Flt. Officer	T61777	Columbus	GA
Williams, Eugene W.	45-E-SE	8/4/1945	2nd Lt.	O843108	Roanoke	VA
Williams, Herbert	44-A-TE	1/7/1944	2nd Lt.	O819452	Los Angeles	CA
Williams, James L.	45-F-SE	9/8/1945	Flt. Officer	T70423	Philadelphia	PA
Williams, James R.	45-G-TE	10/16/1945	2nd Lt.	O2068906	Bryn Mawr	PA
Williams, Joseph H.	44-I-TE	11/20/1944	2nd Lt.	O839097	Chicago	IL
Williams, Kenneth I.	44-B-SE	2/8/1944	2nd Lt.	O821923	Los Angeles	CA
Williams, LeRoi S.	43-G-SE	7/28/1943	2nd Lt.	O809250	Roanoke	VA
Williams, Leslie A.	43-J-SE	11/3/1943	2nd Lt.	O814324	San Mateo	CA
Williams, Raymond L.	45-D-SE	6/27/1945	Flt. Officer	T70109	Jersey City	NJ

Name	Class	Date of Graduation	Grade	Serial Number	City	State
Williams, Robert E., Jr.	44-G-SE	8/4/1944	Flt. Officer	T64644	Chicago	IL
Williams, Robert W.	44-E-SE	5/23/1944	2nd Lt.	O830797	Ottumwa	IA
Williams, Romeo M.	42-K-SE	12/13/1942	2nd Lt.	O794604	Marshall	TX
Williams, Thomas E.	45-F-SE	9/8/1945	2nd Lt.	O843242	Philadelphia	PA
Williams, Vincent E.	44-D-SE	4/15/1944	Flt. Officer	T62813	Los Angeles	CA
Williams, William F.	43-F-SE	6/30/1943	2nd Lt.	O807114	Cleveland	OH
Williams, William L., Jr.	44-J-TE	12/28/1944	Flt. Officer	T67983	New London	OH
Williams, Yancey	44-J-SE	12/28/1944	1st Lt.	O423693	Tulsa	OK
Williamson, Willie A.	44-J-SE	12/28/1944	Flt. Officer	T67976	Detroit	MI
Wilson, Bertram W., Jr.	44-E-SE	5/23/1944	2nd Lt.	O830798	Brooklyn	NY
Wilson, Charles E.	44-C-TE	3/12/1944	Flt. Officer	T62057	Chicago	IL
Wilson, James A.	44-D-SE	4/15/1944	2nd Lt.	O828060	Marion	IN
Wilson, LeRoy J.	45-F-TE	9/8/1945	2nd Lt.	O843250	Independence	KS
Wilson, Myron	44-D-SE	4/15/1944	Flt. Officer	T62808	Danville	IL
Wilson, Theodore A.	43-F-SE	6/30/1943	2nd Lt.	O807115	Roanoke	VA
Winslow, Eugene	44-A-TE	1/7/1944	2nd Lt.	O819453	Chicago	IL
Winslow, Robert W.	45-B-SE	4/15/1945	2nd Lt.	O842587	East St. Louis	IL
Winston, Charles H., Jr.	45-B-SE	4/15/1945	Flt. Officer	T69750	Seattle	WA
Winston, Harry P.	45-A-SE	3/11/1945	Flt. Officer	T68760	Franklin	VA
Wise, Henry A.	44-B-SE	2/8/1944	2nd Lt.	O821924	Cheriton	VA

Name	Class	Date	Rank	Serial	City	State
Wofford, Kenneth O.	45-C-SE	5/23/1945	2nd Lt.	O842888	Springfield	MO
Woods, Carl J.	44-D-SE	4/15/1944	Flt. Officer	T62814	Mars	PA
Woods, Carrol S.	43-H-SE	8/30/1943	2nd Lt.	O811294	Valdosta	GA
Woods, Isaac R.	45-E-SE	8/4/1945	Flt. Officer	T70229	Tulsa	OK
Woods, Willard L.	43-H-SE	8/30/1943	2nd Lt.	O811295	Memphis	TN
Wooten, Howard A.	44-J-TE	12/28/1944	Flt. Officer	T67985	Lovelady	TX
Wright, Frank N.	44-F-SE	6/27/1944	2nd Lt.	O835332	Elmsford	NY
Wright, Hiram	44-E-SE	5/23/1944	Flt. Officer	T63117	Los Angeles	CA
Wright, James W., Jr.	44-F-SE	6/27/1944	2nd Lt.	O835338	Pittsburgh	PA
Wright, Kenneth M.	44-E-SE	5/23/1944	2nd Lt.	O1031458	Sheridan	WY
Wright, Sandy W.	45-F-SE	9/8/1945	Flt. Officer	T70426	Berkeley	CA
Wyatt, Beryl	43-G-SE	7/28/1943	2nd Lt.	O809265	Independence	KS
Wynn, Nasby Jr.	44-J-TE	12/28/1944	Flt. Officer	T67984	Mt. Vernon	NY
Yates, Phillip C.	45-D-SE	6/27/1945	Flt. Officer	T70110	Washington	DC
York, Oscar H.	44-I-TE	11/20/1944	2nd Lt.	O469633	Los Angeles	CA
Young, Albert L.	44-C-SE	3/12/1944	2nd Lt.	O824847	Memphis	TN
Young, Benjamin Jr.	45-C-SE	5/23/1945	2nd Lt.	O842887	Philadelphia	PA
Young, Eddie Lee	46-B-SE	5/14/1946	Unknown	Unknown	Unknown	
Young, Lee W.	45-D-SE	6/27/1945	Flt. Officer	T70111	Litchfield Park	AZ
Young, William W.	45-F-SE	9/8/1945	Flt. Officer	O843243	Oberlin	OH

Notes

Chapter One

1. *Chicago Defender*, April 1, 1943.
2. Memo G-1 [Personnel Section] for Chief of Staff, April 26, 1937.
3. Reynold D. Pruitt to Unknown Addressee, March 3, 1941. Library of Congress, Washington, D.C.
4. Howard Williams to Franklin D. Roosevelt, September 16, 1940. Library of Congress, Washington, D.C.
5. S. Elmo Johnson to the NAACP, General Office, March 16, 1941. Library of Congress, Washington, D.C.
6. Dudley M. Archer to NAACP, March 21, 1941. Library of Congress, Washington, D.C.
7. V. L. Burge, Lieutenant Colonel, Air Corps, Acting Corps Area Air Officer to Zannie T. Overstreet Jr., July 1, 1940. Library of Congress, Washington, D.C.
8. Major General E. S. Adams, Adjutant General, War Department to Howard Williams, October 1, 1940. Library of Congress, Washington, D.C.
9. *Chicago Defender*, August 3, 1940.
10. *Chicago Defender*, November 9, 1940.

Chapter Three

1. File RG18 (Army Air Forces Project Files: Air Fields 1939-1942). National Archives, College Park, Maryland.
2. *Chicago Defender*, April 19, 1941.
3. Brigadier General W. R. Weaver to Major General George H. Brett, Office of the Chief of the Air Corps, Washington, D.C., April 24, 1941. National Archives, College Park, Maryland.

4. George H. Brett, Major General, U.S. Army Acting Chief of Air Corps to Brigadier General W. R. Weaver, April 26, 1941. National Archives, College Park, Maryland.
5. William Varner to John H. Bankhead and Lister Hill, Senators, April 23, 1941. National Archives, College Park, Maryland.
6. Transcript of telephonic conversation between George H. Brett, Major General, U.S. Army, Acting Chief of Air Corps and secretary to Senator Lister Hill, April 28, 1941. National Archives, College Park, Maryland.

Chapter Four

1. Proceedings of the Faculty Board of the Tuskegee Army Flying School, June 1942. National Archives, College Park, Maryland.
2. C. Alfred Anderson to Major General H. H. Arnold, January 5, 1942. National Archives, College Park, Maryland.
3. Major General H. H. Arnold to C. Alfred Anderson, January 22, 1942. National Archives, College Park, Maryland.
4. Captain Noel F. Parrish to General H. H. Arnold, December 3, 1941. National Archives, College Park, Maryland.

Chapter Five

1. Special Inspection, Air Corps Advanced Flying School, Tuskegee, Alabama, May 6, 1942. National Archives, College Park, Maryland.
2. Personal letter to Colonel Frederick v. H. Kimble from Colonel P. L. Sadler, 21 September 1942, p. 44, History of Tuskegee Army Air Field, 1943-February 1944, 289.283 (Iris #00179150), USAF Collection, AFHRA, Maxwell AFB, Alabama.
3. *Chicago Defender*, November 28, 1942.
4. *Pittsburgh Courier*, January 2, 1943.
5. Under Secretary of War Robert Patterson to Wilbur La Roe Jr., chairman of the committee on civic affairs of the Washington Federation of Churches, April 8, 1943. National Archives, College Park, Maryland.
6. *Pittsburgh Courier*, March 6, 1943.

Chapter Seven

1. *Pittsburgh Courier*, April 24, 1943.

Chapter Thirteen

1. *The Training of Negro Combat Units by the First Air Force*, Volume I, 420.04C (IRIS #00199006), 136, USAF Collection, AFHRA, Maxwell AFB, Alabama.

2. Testimony of Colonel Robert R. Selway Jr., AC, Commanding 477th Bombardment Group, Freeman Field, Seymour, Indiana, taken at Freeman Field, April 16, 1945, by Lieutenant Colonel Smith W. Brookhart Jr. National Archives, College Park, Maryland.

3. Osur, *Blacks in the Army Air Forces During World War II: The Problem of Race Relations*, Washington, D.C.: Office of Air Force History, 1977, 98.

4. *The Training of Negro Combat Units by the First Air Force*, Volume I, 420.04C (IRIS #00199006), 38-40, USAF Collection, AFHRA, Maxwell AFB, Alabama.

Chapter Fourteen

1. Communication from members of the 118th Army Air Force Base Unit to the Inspector General, War Department, Washington, D.C. WDSIG 291.2, Freeman Field, Seymour, Indiana, 6 April 1945. National Archives, College Park, Maryland.

2. Testimony of Colonel Robert R. Selway Jr., AC, Commanding 477th Bombardment Group, Freeman Field, April 16, 1945, by Lt. Colonel Smith W. Brookhart Jr. National Archives, College Park, Maryland.

3. *The Training of Negro Combat Units by the First Air Force*, Volume I, 420.04C (IRIS #00199006), 217, USAF Collection, AFHRA, Maxwell AFB, Alabama.

4. Osur, *Blacks in the Army Air Forces During World War II: The Problems of Race Relations*, 92.

5. Osur, *Blacks in the Army Air Forces During World War II: The Problems of Race Relations*, 93.

6. Osur, *Blacks in the Army Air Forces During World War II: The Problems of Race Relations*, 93.

7. Memorandum for the Secretary of War by John J. McCloy, Assistant Secretary of War, June 1945. National Archives, College Park, Maryland.

Bibliography

Books

Applegate, Katherine. *The Story of Two American Generals, Benjamin O. Davis, Jr. and Colin L. Powell.* New York, New York: Dell Publishing, 1992.

Bowers, Peter M. *Curtiss Aircraft 1907-1947.* London: Putnam, 1979.

Davis, Benjamin O., Jr. *Benjamin O. Davis, Jr., American.* Washington, D.C. Smithsonian Press, 1991.

Dryden, Charles. *A-Train: The Autobiography of a Tuskegee Airman.* Birmingham, Alabama: The University of Alabama Press, 1997.

Fletcher, Marvin E. *America's First Black General, Benjamin O. Davis, Sr. 1880-1970.* Lawrence, Kansas: University Press of Kansas, 1989.

Francis, Charles E. *The Tuskegee Airmen: The Men Who Changed a Nation.* Boston, Massachusetts: Branden Publishing Company, 1988.

Gropman, Alan L. *The Air Force Integrates, 1945-1964.* Washington, D. C. Office of Air Force History, 1978.

Hardesty, Von and Pisano, Dominick. *Black Wings.* Washington, D.C.: Smithsonian Press, 1984.

Harris, Jacqueline L. *The Tuskegee Airmen, Black Heroes of World War II.* Parsippany, New Jersey: Dillon Press, 1996.

Hastie, William H. *On Clipped Wings; The Story of Jim Crow in the Army Air Corps.* New York, New York: National Association for the Advancement of Colored People, 1943.

Homan, Lynn M. and Reilly, Thomas. *Images of America: The Tuskegee Airmen.* Charleston, South Carolina: Arcadia Publishing, 1998.

Jakeman, Robert J. *The Divided Skies: Establishing Segregated Flight Training at Tuskegee, Alabama, 1934-1942.* Birmingham, Alabama: The University of Alabama Press, 1992.

Lee, Ulysses. *United States Army in World War Two: The Employment of Negro Troops.* Washington, D.C.: Office of the Chief of Military History, U.S. Army, 1966.

McGovern, James R. *Black Eagle: General Daniel "Chappie" James, Jr.* Birmingham, Alabama: The University of Alabama Press, 1985.

McKissack, Patricia and McKissack, Fredrick. *Red-Tail Angels.* New York, New York: Walker Publishing Company, Inc., 1995.

Osur, Allan M. *Blacks in the Army Air Forces During World War II: The Problem of Race Relations.* Washington, D.C.: Office of Air Force History, 1977.

Palmer, Walter J. A. *Flying with Eagles.* Indianapolis, Indiana: Nova Graphics, Inc., 1993.

Powell, William J. *Black Wings.* Los Angeles, California: Ivan Deach, Jr., 1934.

Rich, Doris. *Queen Bess, Daredevil Aviator.* Washington, D.C.: Smithsonian Institution Press, 1993.

Sadler, Stanley. *Segregated Skies: All-black Combat Squadrons of WWII.* Washington, D.C.: Smithsonian Institution Press, 1992.

Scott, Lawrence P. and Womack, William M. Sr. *Double V: The Civil Rights Struggle of the Tuskegee Airmen.* Ann Arbor, Michigan: Michigan State University Press, 1994.

Smith, Charlene McGee. *Tuskegee Airman: The Biography of Charles E. McGee.* Boston, Massachusetts: Brandon Publishing Company, 1999.

Washington, George L. *The History of Military and Civilian Pilot Training of Negroes at Tuskegee, Alabama, 1939-1945.* Washington, D.C.: George L. Washington, 1972.

Articles

Butler, Wanda. "Dreams of Flight." *Southern Living,* (October 1996): 104-106.

"Pioneer Aviator Bessie Coleman Dies in Jacksonville Aircraft Mishap." *Florida Aviation Historical Society News,* (May 1995): 5.

Glines, C. V. "Red Tail Fighters." *The Retired Officer Magazine,* (September 1992): 26-30.

The *Lantern,* Lockbourne Air Force Base, Volume 1, Number 43, (May 27 1943).

Purnell, Louis R. "The Flight of the Bumblebee." *Air & Space Magazine,* (October/November 1989).

Periodicals and Newspapers

Air Service News

Time, 1943.

Afro-American

The Call

The Crisis

Chicago Daily News

Chicago Defender

Chicago Sunday Tribune

Columbus Evening Dispatch

Florida Times Union

The Houston Informer

Houston Post-Dispatch

Jacksonville Journal

New York Times

The Norfolk Journal and Guide

Pittsburgh Courier

St. Petersburg Times

The Savannah Tribune

Tampa Tribune

Personal Interviews and Photographs

Rayfield Anderson

Lee A. Archer

Charles P. Bailey

LeRoy Battle

Henry C. L. Bohler

Arthur L. Carter

Jack Chin

Woodrow W. Crockett

Arque B. Dickerson

Alvin Downing

Bernice "Bunny" Downing

Roscoe Draper

Jean R. Esquerre

Edwina Westmoreland Ford

Harry E. Ford

Charles R. Foxx

Harold L. Gaulden

Pompey L. Hawkins Sr.

Charles A. Hill Jr.

Mary Morgan Hill

William H. Holloman III

William F. Holton

James A. Hurd

Alexander Jefferson

Theopolis W. Johnson

Elmer Jones

Haldane King

Theophila Lee

Wesley McClure

Walter L. McCreary

Faye J. McDaniel

Charles E. McGee

Richard D. Macon

Hiram E. Mann

Kathadaza Mann

Frankie Minnis

Walter J. Palmer

Florence Parrish-St. John, Ph.D.

Frances Patterson

Peggy Peterman

William Phears, Ph.D.

Louis R. Purnell

Maury M. Reid Jr.

Sherman Rose

Raymond Sanderlin

Fenton B. Sands

Robert Saunders

Harry A. Sheppard

Harry T. Stewart Jr.

John J. Suggs

Andrew Turner Jr.

Spann Watson

Yenwith K. Whitney, Ph.D.   James E. Wright

Donald Williams   Nasby Wynn

Miscellaneous

Air Force Historical Research Agency, Maxwell AFB, Alabama.

Charles P. Bailey Distinguished Flying Cross Citation, May 29, 1945.

Chicago Race Commission Report, *Chicago Daily News*, October 5, 1922.

Bessie Coleman to R. E. Norman, February 23, 1926, Lilly Library, Indiana University-Bloomington, Indiana.

Fédération Aéronautique Internationale License, June 15, 1921.

Godman Field Yearbook, 1945.

Tuskegee Army Flying School and AAF 66th FTD Yearbook, 1942.

The National Archives, College Park, Maryland.

The Smithsonian Institution, National Air and Space Museum.

Tape-Recorded Interview with Matilde Moisant, Columbia University Oral History Collection.

Tuskegee Airmen, Inc., Air Force Association Building, 1501 Lee Highway, Suite 130, Arlington, Virginia 22208.

Index